# TOOLS FOR SUCCESS Soft Skills for the Construction Industry

**Second Edition**

*Special thanks to original author, Steven A. Rigolosi,*
*and contributing editor, Michael L. Stilley,*
*Manager of Training and Development,*
*S&B Engineers and Constructors, Ltd.*

Upper Saddle River, New Jersey
Columbus, Ohio

**National Center for Construction Education and Research**

*President:* Don Whyte
*Director of Curriculum Revision and Development:* Daniele Dixon
*Tools for Success Project Manager:* Daniele Dixon
*Production Manager:* Debie Ness
*Quality Assurance Coordinator:* Jessica Martin
*Editor:* Bethany Harvey
*Desktop Publishers:* Laura Parker

NCCER would like to acknowledge the contract service provider for this curriculum:
EEI Communications, Alexandria, Virginia.

10 9 8 7 6 5
ISBN 0-13-109194-8

# Foreword

We live in a time when the prevailing mood often seems to be one of intense conflict. In politics, in public discourse, in newspapers and magazines, on television, radio, and the Internet, everyone seems to be writing, talking, or shouting, with few people listening.

Yet effective listening is at the core of every successful human relationship at home and at work. How can you be a better listener? The answer is simple. You can brush up on your soft skills—the skills that will enhance your technical skills and make you a more valuable employee.

If you have anything to do with other people, personally or professionally, you will be faced each day with decisions that require some proficiency in the soft skills. This book can help. You will learn how to speak and listen effectively, teach others, become an effective team player, resolve problems and conflicts, and succeed in a diverse and ever-changing workforce.

Before you begin to learn and practice your soft skills, though, you must first understand your own values. As a future construction professional, one of your values should be a passionate belief in the worthiness of the work that you do. This belief is the cornerstone of success in the construction industry.

But you must not only believe in the work you do. You must also love it. It must excite and energize you. The construction industry is certainly a career that has excitement built in. At the end of a project, you can walk away from something that you helped build. Years from now, your children and grandchildren are likely to walk past that same project.

With strong values and a passionate commitment to your work, you will rapidly become a construction professional. You will be a person who realizes not only the value of the final product, but also the importance of the teamwork needed to achieve it. Teamwork is what the soft skills are all about.

This book was developed to give you the fundamental tools necessary to ensure your success in the construction industry. Certainly being a skilled craftsperson is very important. But in today's competitive workplace, the soft skills have become equally important. In fact, many successful construction company owners say that they have no trouble finding qualified craftspeople. They find it much harder to hire those who are good team players.

Combined with craft and safety training, this soft skills training will complete your blueprint for a very successful career in construction. Your future is what you make of it. Good luck in your construction career!

*—Michael L. Stilley, Manager of Training and Development,*
*S&B Engineers and Constructors, Ltd.*

# Introduction

As the work world becomes more competitive, workers are increasingly discovering that they need more than technical skills to be successful. They also need skills in handling human relations, the so-called soft skills. Among these skills are teamwork, conflict management, communication skills, and critical thinking. Unfortunately, the soft skills are often ignored in training programs designed for craft workers. Yet the soft skills are directly related to increased efficiency and productivity and, perhaps most important, safety.

*Tools for Success: Soft Skills for the Construction Industry* is the first text of its kind. Unlike other human relations texts, which are designed for people working in corporate settings, this book is designed specifically for people who have chosen a career in construction. To that end, the examples and activities focus on the types of situations typically encountered on a construction site. Construction professionals have reviewed the text to ensure that it retains its real-world emphasis throughout. This second edition has been revised and expanded to incorporate feedback and reaction to the first edition from professionals in training and construction. It has been updated to reflect changes in the makeup of the construction workforce as well as the laws concerned with workplace behaviors. In addition, a new, instructor's handbook (available from the National Center for Construction Education and Research) has been developed to help instructors and trainers use the materials effectively.

The text is organized into 12 modules rather than chapters. This design provides flexibility to instructors and trainers who can present the material in the order that best suits their needs. Following is an overview of each module:

- *Module 1, First Impressions: Starting Your New Job* discusses the importance of having a positive attitude, describes characteristics construction companies seek, reviews workplace culture, and stresses punctuality and attendance. The emphasis is on personal responsibility and professionalism.
- *Module 2, Building a Strong Relationship with Your Supervisor* includes guidelines for understanding the supervisor's role and tips for developing a positive and professional relationship with the boss. The emphasis is on the supervisor as manager and mentor.
- *Module 3, Teamwork: Getting Along with Your Co-Workers* introduces the importance of teamwork on the construction site and offers tips for becoming an effective team member. The emphasis is on personal responsibility and treating others with respect.
- *Module 4, Diversity in the Workplace* offers an overview of workplace diversity and provides strategies for learning to work successfully in a diverse workplace. The emphasis is on focusing on the positive aspects of a diverse workforce.
- *Module 5, Communication Skills I: Listening and Speaking* offers tips on becoming a better listener and speaker. The emphasis is on listening to worksite instructions, asking appropriate questions, and giving clear instructions and directions.

- *Module 6, Communication Skills II: Reading and Writing* includes instructions for reading common workplace documents, tips for filling out employment forms, and guidelines for writing construction industry correspondence. The emphasis is on developing strategies for reading and understanding workplace materials, and writing clearly and accurately.
- *Module 7, Managing Stress on the Job* includes tips for avoiding and coping with stress and managing time wisely. The emphasis is on learning how to recognize stress and developing strategies to manage stress in positive ways.
- *Module 8, Thinking Critically and Solving Problems* includes tips for questioning and analyzing information. The emphasis is on learning strategies for breaking down complex problems into manageable units.
- *Module 9, Resolving Conflict* includes a step-by-step process for dealing with conflict and difficult co-workers. The emphasis is on learning strategies for handling workplace problems professionally.
- *Module 10, Giving and Receiving Criticism* emphasizes the importance of constructive criticism as a learning tool. The emphasis is on learning how to give constructive criticism and deal with receiving both negative and constructive criticism.
- *Module 11, Sexual Harassment* presents the legal definition of sexual harassment and includes guidelines for preventing and dealing with sexual harassment in the workplace. The emphasis is on learning to treat members of the opposite sex with dignity and respect.
- *Module 12, Drug and Alcohol Abuse on the Job* explores the problems and effects of drugs and alcohol in the construction industry. The emphasis is on personal responsibility and professionalism.

Each module is organized using the same format and features. Features include the following:

- *Self-Assessment,* a tool designed to help trainees develop self-awareness (Some modules include an *Awareness Questionnaire* designed to help trainees learn more about the topic covered.)
- *Dos and Don'ts,* practical examples of on-the-job situations with suggestions for ways to deal effectively with each
- *On-the-Job Quiz,* which tests recall of the material and encourages discussion about actual work-related problems and issues
- *Individual and Group Activities,* which give trainees the opportunity to practice the skills learned in each module

## A Note for Trainees

In a time when many jobs are moving overseas or being replaced by computers, the demand for construction workers is higher than ever. According to the Bureau of Labor Statistics the construction industry is one of the largest industries in the United States, with over 6 million wage and salary jobs and 1.6 million self-employed workers. It is estimated that this industry must attract and train nearly 200,000 new workers each year to meet the country's building needs. This huge demand means that construction apprentices can expect to earn good money very early in their careers. When they graduate and become skilled workers, most will be earning salaries in the $30,000 to $40,000 range, depending on location and skill. Best of all, construction is one of the few industries in the United States where an individual can realistically begin at an entry-level position and someday own his or her own company.

Construction workers are some of the best-trained and most highly skilled people in the country. They are usually experts in one area, such as carpentry, plumbing, masonry, or electrical work, and they must master the technical skills in their chosen area. But to be an effective employee in today's construction workforce, they must also master the so-called soft skills. They must be able to work effectively as part of a team and that means learning how to deal with workplace conflicts and problems in a professional manner. This book is designed to help you develop and sharpen the so-called soft skills. After completing this training you will know how to do the following:

- Develop and maintain a good work attitude
- Build a positive professional working relationship with your supervisor
- Work effectively in teams and manage workplace conflicts
- Get along with co-workers from cultures and backgrounds that are different from yours
- Listen to, understand, and carry out spoken instructions and give clear spoken instructions to others
- Read, analyze, and understand forms and documents related to your job and write clear instructions, memos, emails, and other workplace documents
- Recognize harmful stress and develop healthy ways of dealing with it
- Resolve problems and workplace conflicts professionally and positively
- Analyze workplace problems, break them down into manageable steps, and develop workable solutions
- Work effectively with difficult people or in difficult situations
- Give and receive constructive criticism
- Deal effectively and professionally with sexual harassment
- Deal effectively with drug and alcohol abuse

By the time you finish this training you may feel that learning the soft skills is as challenging as learning the technical skills. However, in time and with a little practice you will soon master these skills, and you will be a much more valuable and effective employee as a result.

## Acknowledgments

This curriculum was revised as a result of the farsightedness and leadership of the following sponsors:

Associated Builders and Contractors, Inc.
Associated General Contractors
Calvert Cliffs Nuclear Power Plant
Constellation Power Source Generation
Guilford Technical Community College
Hensel Phelps Construction Company, Inc.
Holder Engineering Services
Manatee Technical Institute
Monroe #1 Board of Cooperative Education
North Carolina Department of Public Instruction
NE Florida Builders Association
Tabacon Systems, Inc./Beam Up, Inc.
Winter Construction

This curriculum would not exist were it not for the dedication and unselfish energy of those volunteers who served on the Authoring Team. A sincere thanks is extended to the following:

John Ambrosia
Joe Beyer
Richard W. Carr
Fred Day
Jim Evans
Doug Garcia
Charlie Haas
Chuck Hogg
R. P. Hughes
Connell Linson
Bruce Miller
Steven Miller
Denise Peek

# Table of Contents

# Part One

# Essential Workplace Skills

# First Impressions: Starting Your New Job

## Self-Assessment

### How ready are you for your first construction job?

Are you ready for a job in the construction industry? Take this quiz to find out. Rate yourself honestly on each of the following questions.

| | Always | Sometimes | Rarely |
|---|---|---|---|
| 1. When I say I'll get something done, I do it. | ❑ | ❑ | ❑ |
| 2. I respect the work my company does. | ❑ | ❑ | ❑ |
| 3. I believe in putting in a day's work for a day's pay. | ❑ | ❑ | ❑ |
| 4. I don't repeat information that's been told to me in confidence. | ❑ | ❑ | ❑ |
| 5. I'm willing to help out, even when I don't like a task. | ❑ | ❑ | ❑ |
| 6. I'm willing to learn new things. | ❑ | ❑ | ❑ |
| 7. I like working in a variety of environments. | ❑ | ❑ | ❑ |
| 8. I take pride in my work. | ❑ | ❑ | ❑ |
| 9. I accept responsibility for my mistakes. | ❑ | ❑ | ❑ |
| 10. I'm positive in my approach to my job. | ❑ | ❑ | ❑ |
| 11. I'm open minded and willing to listen to new ideas. | ❑ | ❑ | ❑ |
| 12. I keep up with new technology in construction. | ❑ | ❑ | ❑ |
| 13. I'm a hard worker. | ❑ | ❑ | ❑ |

***Scoring:*** Count the number of times you checked "Always," "Sometimes," and "Rarely." Enter the total for each of these terms in the spaces provided. Multiply each total by the factors shown, and then add up your total score. For example, multiply the total number of times you checked "Always" by 3.

| | | | |
|---|---|---|---|
| Number of "Always" | ________ | × 3 = | ________ |
| Number of "Sometimes" | ________ | × 2 = | ________ |
| Number of "Rarely" | ________ | × 1 = | ________ |
| TOTAL | | | ________ |

***Assessment:***

33–39 points: You have what it takes to be an excellent and valued member of a construction team. This module will help you make the most of your new job.

27–32 points: You are aware of several important traits that a worker should have, but you will benefit from following the advice in this module.

13–26 points: You may have developed some negative work habits. This module will help you get on track so that you can make the most of your construction career.

## Introduction

Imagine that you want to hire someone to work on your car or your house. How do you choose the best person for the job?

The answer is simple. First you make sure the mechanic, plumber, or electrician knows how to do the job correctly. Second, and equally important, you make sure that you hire a professional. A professional is mature and businesslike, and treats customers with respect. A professional shows up for work on time, takes pride in the work, and has technical expertise. A professional is someone you can talk to and discuss ideas with.

When you find workers with these qualities, you are glad to hire them and to recommend them to your friends. Just as you look for certain qualities in people you hire, your potential employer will look for certain qualities in you. As you start your construction career, how can you make sure that you always present yourself as a competent and qualified professional? In this module, you will learn what employers are looking for, and you will also learn how to become a worker employers are eager to hire.

## What are employers looking for?

When you are just starting out, you may not have all of the skills and experience required. However, if you have the basic skills and are willing to learn and to work hard, you have a better chance of landing a good job. Your chances of getting and keeping that job increase when you demonstrate your ability to work as a professional. Professional workers have the following qualities:

**Dependable.** Dependable workers can be trusted to get the job done correctly and promptly. Dependable people show up for work every day and on time. When dependable workers say they'll do something, they follow through.

**Work-oriented.** Employers are looking for workers with a strong work ethic. That is, they like to hire and promote people who believe in giving a day's work for a day's pay. People with a strong work ethic enjoy working, and they derive satisfaction from doing a good job. Their work is important to them, and they believe that they can contribute to any project they're working on.

**Organized.** The best workers keep their tools and work areas clean, neat, and organized. They have a plan for what they have to accomplish each day, and they approach their jobs in an organized fashion. Being organized and prepared is more than just a matter of looking good. These qualities also help keep workers safe. For example, organized workers don't leave their tools lying around where they might fall on co-workers or into machinery. They don't leave debris in the work area and are careful to properly store or dispose of flammable materials.

**Technically qualified.** People who are technically qualified know how to operate machinery and equipment safely. They know which tools and techniques get the job done. They always are looking to expand their technical knowledge. To do so, they keep up with advances in the industry, including computers and other technology.

**Flexible.** Companies like to hire workers who are willing to pitch in and help. The best workers are willing to learn new tasks, try new ideas, and keep up with the changing times.

**Honest.** Honest workers value honesty in others and are honest themselves. They call in sick only when they're really ill. They take care of their employer's property and tools and leave those items at the work site when the job is completed. They leave work early only when they have made arrangements with their supervisor to do so. If they are struggling with a problem, they seek guidance from a supervisor and actively work on ways to solve it.

**Prepared.** Employers judge craftworkers by how they maintain their tools. The best workers know what tools they are responsible for, and they keep those tools in good working order. Professional workers know that maintaining their tools is essential for safety. They check their tools for frayed cords, dull edges, missing or jammed parts, or anything that might cause an accident. Prepared workers also know how to follow manufacturers' guidelines for using, maintaining, and repairing tools.

**Respectful of the rules.** Professionals know that construction sites are full of tools and materials that can cause injuries or even death if used improperly. They always wear the right safety gear and follow all safety rules. Professionals also know that their raises and promotions depend on how well their company performs, so they follow company rules designed to keep the project on time and on budget.

**Respectful of the company.** Professionals recognize that they represent their company even when they are not on the work site. They are careful about what they say when they talk about their company. Being respectful of the company also means taking care of company equipment and using work time only for company-related projects.

**Well-groomed and appropriately dressed.** Companies are more likely to hire a skilled person who is clean and well-groomed than one who is not. Employers feel that workers who take pride in their appearance will also take pride in their work. On the work site, sloppiness is a safety hazard. For example, long, messy hair can get caught in machinery and untied shoelaces can cause falls. Many companies require employees to wear special equipment for certain jobs. Keeping that equipment clean, in good repair, and ready to go is an important part of dressing appropriately on the job.

**Note**

The special safety equipment that workers wear is called personal protective equipment. This equipment includes hard hats, gloves, safety goggles, appropriate footwear, face shields, respirators, ear protection, and fall protection.

## Two keys to success: Attendance and punctuality

To make a profit and stay in business, construction companies operate under tight schedules. These schedules are built around workers. When a worker is late or doesn't show up, immediate and expensive adjustments become necessary.

When supervisors talk about the most common problems they face on the job, they always point to two: lateness and absenteeism. Here are some suggestions to help you achieve an excellent record of attendance and punctuality.

**1. Think about what would happen if all workers were late or frequently absent.** Having empathy means that you can put yourself in another person's place and understand that person's feelings. It is one of the most important workplace skills you can develop. Put yourself in your supervisor's place. How could you get the job done on budget and on time if workers were always late or just didn't show up? Would you worry about your workers' safety if there weren't enough people around to do the job properly?

**2. Think about your co-workers.** It is also important to have empathy for your co-workers. When you are late or absent, they will have to pick up the slack. It's not fair to them if you are always late or call in sick when you are not actually ill. Good attendance and being on time are very important factors in workplace safety. Employees who have to work longer hours or do more tasks to cover for a late or absent worker might get tired sooner, and that can lead to accidents.

**3. Understand when it is OK to call in sick.** Call in sick only when you are really ill or have a family emergency. All companies have rules that tell their employees how to use sick leave. You must learn and follow your company's sick-leave policy.

**4. Notify your supervisor as soon as possible if you must be late or must call in sick.** Call your supervisor as soon as you know that you'll be late or absent. It is best to call as close as possible to the start of your shift. Make the call yourself. Don't ask someone else to do it for you.

**5. Keep your supervisor posted if you have to be out for more than a day.** Remember the empathy rule. Your absence affects scheduling and work assignments, so let your boss know when you'll be back on the job. Also, if you know that you must be absent for a non-illness reason, such as jury duty, let your boss know as far in advance as possible.

**6. Give yourself enough time to get to work.** Pay attention to weather, roadwork, and traffic conditions that can affect your commute. Allow yourself more time when these conditions cause traffic delays. Find different routes to get to work when your usual route is blocked. Think about how good you'll look if you show up a few minutes early!

**7. Go to your supervisor immediately when you are late.** Don't try to sneak onto the job site hoping that nobody notices. Report to your boss, apologize for being late, and offer an explanation. Take responsibility for your actions.

**8. Remember, being on time means more than showing up for work on time.** It also means using only the allotted amount of time for your meals or breaks. It also means working until the end of your scheduled shift. If you must leave early for a good reason, talk to your supervisor in advance.

**9. Get enough rest.** In most construction jobs, you will start your workday very early; therefore, you should not stay up late on work nights. When you get enough rest, you'll be alert and able to do your job to the best of your abilities.

## A good attitude: The right start

During your schooling and training, you will learn many technical skills. You will fine-tune these skills on the job site working with skilled craftworkers. Technical skill is very important to your success in the construction industry, but your attitude is almost as important. In fact, one construction professional remarked that success on the job is only 60 percent technical skill and 40 percent attitude. Think about it. Who would you rather work with? Someone who complains all the time, does not do a good job, and does not treat you with respect? Or someone who is upbeat, enjoys working, and treats you with courtesy and respect? Most employers would rather hire the upbeat employee. That is because workers with a good attitude are the most productive workers and influence everyone with their positive outlook. How can you keep your attitude positive? It's not hard to do if you keep a few things in mind:

**1. Be upbeat.** Nobody likes to be around someone who is gloomy, cranky, or mean. Smile. Look on the bright side of things. You have a job that challenges you both physically and mentally. You have a job that rewards hard work and skill. The construction industry offers you plenty of opportunities to succeed. You've got lots of things to feel good about, so feel good!

**2. Take pride in your work and in your tools.** No matter what you do on the construction site, whether you're a trainee or a master craftworker, take pride in the skills you've worked so hard to develop. Let your pride show in every task you do. Keeping your tools clean and in good working order is a sign of this pride. Don't let pride slip into arrogance, though. Remember that it is always possible to learn new things.

**3. Cooperate.** Be willing to lend a hand to somebody who needs it. If you're given a task that you don't like doing, think instead about the valuable experience you'll gain. Look at every task as an opportunity to learn something. Whenever your supervisor asks you to do a task, do it without complaining. (Note that there may be times when you are justified in complaining. Tips for discussing complaints fairly and professionally with your supervisor are covered in Module 2.)

**4. Take initiative.** You'll get more satisfaction from your job and convey a positive attitude if you think of and share new ideas. Can you improve a process or help the company save money? Let your supervisor know. When you report to the job site, start working on time—don't wait for someone to tell you what to do. Finish up what you were working on yesterday and then move on to the next task. Take charge of your job.

**5. Accept responsibility.** It's great to take credit for a job well done, but you must also accept responsibility for your mistakes. Don't try to blame someone else for mistakes you make. You must never try to cover up a mistake. Doing so could hide a problem that might result in workers being injured or killed. Instead, explain what happened calmly and clearly and without becoming defensive. Then work to correct the problem and help get the project back on track.

**6. Have a sense of humor.** Having a sense of humor does not mean you should become the workplace clown or tell off-color jokes. In fact, many people consider those types of jokes to be sexual harassment. Of course, you can share appropriate jokes with your co-workers and supervisors. People with a sense of humor don't take themselves too seriously. They manage to stay positive no matter what, so being around them makes the workday enjoyable.

**7. Listen and keep an open mind.** Imagine this. You come up with an idea that you think is good and your boss or co-worker immediately says, "Don't waste your time! That will never work!" You want people to listen to you with an open mind, so return the favor. When you are willing to listen, others will talk to you, and you may learn something new and interesting. (For tips on listening skills, see Module 5.)

**8. Be customer-centered.** You may not think you have customers, but you do. Everyone who is immediately affected by your work is, in fact, your customer. Therefore, the company's client, the owner of the company, your supervisor, and even your co-workers are all your customers. Think about how the work you do affects others and deliver your best effort. Keep in mind that you're a representative of your company, even when you're not at work. Don't do or say anything that would embarrass your supervisor or the company.

**9. Regard your job as a learning experience.** In construction, the new hires often end up doing what nobody else wants to do—for example, sweeping up the job site, cleaning machinery, putting tools away, and loading or unloading materials. Sweeping the floor probably was not what you had in mind when you applied for the job, but everyone has to start somewhere. Keep in mind that many of the workers around you started the same way. Do all of your assigned tasks with a positive attitude and do them well. Your supervisor will see that you have a good work ethic, and soon other new hires will be doing those tasks!

## Workplace culture

What is a workplace culture? A simple definition is, "It's the way we do things around here." A workplace culture develops as a result of the day-to-day actions of owners, supervisors, and co-workers. You usually won't find it defined in company manuals. For example, in one workplace, everyone uses titles, such as Mr., Ms., or Dr. In another workplace, everyone uses first names. In some places, workers go out together every Friday, while in others, they go their separate ways at the end of the workweek. A company's culture is reflected in its values, its goals, and its climate or atmosphere. When deciding where you will work, consider how a company's culture will affect you.

**Values.** What does the company value? Does it value initiative and action in its employees, or does it prefer workers who follow orders? Is the company committed to hiring the best workers regardless of race, color, sex, religion, national origin, age, or disability? Does it contribute to the community? Answers to these questions tell you a lot about the company's values.

**Goals.** Every company has goals and a way of meeting them. For example, one company may focus on giving customers the most economical price. Another company may focus on high-end, high-priced custom work. Both companies need workers with different types of skills to help them meet their goals. Knowing a company's goals can help you in your career. The cost-conscious company will welcome ideas that improve efficiency but probably will reject ideas that increase costs. The custom builder also wants efficiency but generally is more interested in ideas that make it stand out from the competition. If you work for this type of company, you probably would not suggest replacing a porcelain bathtub with a plastic shower stall, for example.

**Climate.** What is the company's general atmosphere? Is it one of friendship, where people go out together on Friday nights, or do the workers go their separate ways at the end of the week? Have supervisors been promoted from inside the company, or do they tend to get hired from the outside? Is management very strict, or are supervisors open and flexible? The answers to all these questions will help you determine what's expected of you.

### A Word of Advice

When in doubt, it's always better to be too formal than too informal. Use titles such as Mr. or Ms., especially when speaking to owners, supervisors, or anyone older than you. In today's workplace, almost everyone is on a first-name basis, but it never hurts to show a little respect. Let others tell you when it's OK to use first names.

## Tips for succeeding in your new job

If you have a positive attitude, you are well on your way to succeeding in the construction industry. When you start a new job, you will go through a period when you feel like you don't know anything at all. The following tips will help get you off to a good start:

**1. Take notes when appropriate.** At the start of a new job, you will have a lot of information thrown at you. You can't really be expected to remember everything, but you have to make your best effort. Take notes when you receive instructions or learn procedures. It's not always practical to take notes, so if you don't fully understand something, ask. Don't be shy about it. Your supervisor will see that you are serious about doing your job safely and well.

**2. Make a positive first impression, but don't show off.** An important part of your job happiness involves having good relationships with your co-workers. We'll talk about getting along with your co-workers in Module 3, but, for now, remember that you have to walk a fine line. On the one hand, you want your supervisor to know you're working hard. On the other hand, you don't want your co-workers to think you're showing off or "kissing up" to the boss. Ask questions, but don't overdo it.

**3. Learn how to fit in.** When you start a new job, you won't know how you should behave at first, and you won't find out by reading an employee manual. Instead, use your eyes and ears and pay attention to what others say and how they act. It's a good idea to listen more than you talk. In no time, you will learn how to fit in.

## On-the-Job Quiz

Here's a quick quiz that asks you to apply what you've learned in this module.

**1.** You've overheard the company owner telling your supervisor to hire only people who have a strong work ethic. The owner means that only people who _____ should be hired.
   a. are technically qualified
   b. believe in giving a day's work for a day's pay
   c. are from different ethnic groups
   d. pass a loyalty test

**2.** Most bosses say that _____ are two of the most common problems management has with workers.
   a. alcoholism and depression
   b. absenteeism and lateness
   c. poor skills and language barriers
   d. laziness and gossip

**3.** You get a job in highway construction, and your supervisor says that you must wear an orange vest to be visible to drivers. You think this is a stupid rule. What is your BEST course of action?
   a. See if other workers are wearing their vests to decide whether you really have to wear one too.
   b. Recognize the reason for the rule and wear your vest.
   c. Tell your supervisor that, legally, no one can tell you what to wear.
   d. Wear the vest, but explain to your supervisor why you don't agree with the rule.

**4.** Because of a situation beyond your control, you'll be 15 minutes late for work today. You should _____.
   a. start working as soon as you arrive and hope nobody noticed you were late
   b. call your supervisor as soon as you know you'll be late, explain the situation, and apologize
   c. ask a friend to punch in for you, and then work an extra 15 minutes to make up for the time
   d. ask somebody else to call your boss to explain that you're on your way and will be there soon

5. You've made a serious mistake that will cost $1,500 to fix. Because you're very friendly with your co-workers, they agree to share the responsibility to take some of the heat off you. You should _____.
   a. accept their offer, because co-workers should stick together through thick and thin
   b. try to cover up the problem, so that nobody will get in trouble
   c. thank your co-workers, but take full responsibility for your mistake
   d. accept responsibility, but defend yourself because the mistake was not entirely your fault
6. Your boss tells you that you have to please many customers in your job. Which of the following would *not* be considered your customers?
   a. Your co-workers
   b. Your supervisor
   c. The owner of the company
   d. The company's bankers
7. You are the supervisor on a kitchen renovation job that you've estimated should be done by Friday, when the homeowners want to have a dinner party. Unavoidable delays crop up, and it looks like the job won't be finished until the following week. Which of the following is your best course of action?
   a. Ask the homeowners to postpone their dinner party until the work is done.
   b. Cut corners and rush the workers so you can get the job done earlier and the homeowners can have their party.
   c. Hire extra people so you can finish by Friday. You won't have to ask the homeowners, but make sure you increase your bill.
   d. Clean up the area and make the kitchen as functional as possible before you leave on Friday night so the homeowners can have their party.
8. You're a trainee carpenter who is working hard to become a master carpenter. One day, your boss asks for volunteers to help the masonry crew, which is shorthanded. What is your best course of action?
   a. Volunteer to help out and learn as much as you can about masonry.
   b. Volunteer to help out if your boss treats your work with the masons as overtime.
   c. Explain to your boss that your skill is in carpentry and that working in other areas will hold you back.
   d. Welcome the opportunity as a mini-vacation from your real job and help out with simple tasks like unloading supplies.

**9.** In school you learned that it is best to use formal titles when speaking to bosses. Shortly after starting your first job, however, you notice that everyone calls your supervisor T.J. Is it OK for you to call your supervisor T.J. as well?
   a. No, because new hires should always use formal titles in the workplace.
   b. No, because you will not impress your new boss by being informal and you might upset your co-workers.
   c. Yes, because addressing bosses informally seems to be part of the company's culture.
   d. Yes, because it is now considered old-fashioned to be formal in the workplace.

**10.** It is more important to impress your supervisor than it is to get along with your co-workers.
   a. True
   b. False

# Individual Activities

## Activity 1: Making the Right Impression

Read the following case study, then answer the questions that follow.

### *Case Study: New on the Job*

You have landed your first construction job with a company that builds warehouses, silos, and other storage facilities for the agriculture industry. You are so excited to start work the next day that you can't sleep. When your alarm buzzes, you hit the snooze button a couple of times, then grab a quick shower, brush your teeth, and comb your hair. A glance at your watch shows you are running only about 10 minutes late.

At the job site, your supervisor introduces you to the owner of the company. You shake hands, say how happy you are to have this job, and promise to give 110 percent. You say that this job is a dream come true and talk about how you always played with tools as a kid. The owner smiles and starts to move away, but you keep talking for a few more minutes.

Your supervisor hands you a broom and tells you to sweep the floor. You take the broom, roll your eyes, and sigh in disappointment and disgust. You did not apply for the job to sweep the floor! As you sweep, you notice several tools lying on the floor against the wall, so you put them back where they belong. You also notice that the broom handle feels a little loose, so you tighten it. When the trash bin is full you move it out to the trash collection area.

You've been asked to finish the job in one hour, but you are a fast, neat worker and finish 15 minutes early. Because you missed breakfast, you relax with a candy bar for 15 minutes. Then you report to your supervisor, who introduces you to an older worker who will train you on a new piece of equipment.

Your trainer is grumpy. You feel uneasy, so you don't much pay attention during the training. Luckily, it's soon lunchtime and you can escape this grouch for awhile. At lunch you buy soft drinks for four other new workers to celebrate getting hired. You have such a good time talking to them that you lose track of time. Though you are only a few minutes late getting back from lunch, you sense that your trainer is annoyed. After you make several mistakes on the new equipment, you get a lecture about being on time and paying attention. Part of you feels the trainer is being unfair, but you want to do well, so you apologize for being late, then promise to try harder and pay better attention.

List at least four things you did right.

1. ______________________________
2. ______________________________
3. ______________________________
4. ______________________________

List at least four mistakes you made.

1. ______________________________
2. ______________________________
3. ______________________________
4. ______________________________

Think about what you could do differently to make your second day better than your first.

## Activity 2: Projecting a Good Attitude

The following Rate Your Work Attitude chart lists some behaviors that convey a negative attitude. Evaluate yourself honestly to determine whether you exhibit any of these behaviors. For each "Sometimes" or "Often" you check, come up with an action plan for improving your behavior. A sample problem and action plan have been provided for you following the chart.

| | Never | Rarely | Sometimes | Often |
|---|---|---|---|---|
| 1. I show up late for work. | ❑ | ❑ | ❑ | ❑ |
| 2. I complain about my workload. | ❑ | ❑ | ❑ | ❑ |
| 3. I am moody and unpredictable. | ❑ | ❑ | ❑ | ❑ |
| 4. I am sarcastic. | ❑ | ❑ | ❑ | ❑ |
| 5. I act superior to my co-workers. | ❑ | ❑ | ❑ | ❑ |
| 6. I shift the blame for my mistakes. | ❑ | ❑ | ❑ | ❑ |
| 7. I think I work harder than everyone else. | ❑ | ❑ | ❑ | ❑ |
| 8. I don't accept criticism gracefully. | ❑ | ❑ | ❑ | ❑ |
| 9. I have a short temper. | ❑ | ❑ | ❑ | ❑ |
| 10. I use obscene language at work. | ❑ | ❑ | ❑ | ❑ |
| 11. I don't finish my work on time. | ❑ | ❑ | ❑ | ❑ |
| 12. I don't accept new ideas. | ❑ | ❑ | ❑ | ❑ |
| 13. I drink alcohol at work. | ❑ | ❑ | ❑ | ❑ |
| 14. I show up for work dirty or unkempt. | ❑ | ❑ | ❑ | ❑ |
| 15. I treat others badly because of their race. | ❑ | ❑ | ❑ | ❑ |
| 16. I treat others badly because of their sex. | ❑ | ❑ | ❑ | ❑ |

*(continued)*

| | Never | Rarely | Sometimes | Often |
|---|---|---|---|---|
| 17. I treat others badly because of their religion. | ❑ | ❑ | ❑ | ❑ |
| 18. I treat others badly because they are from a different country than I am. | ❑ | ❑ | ❑ | ❑ |
| 19. I treat others badly because of their age. | ❑ | ❑ | ❑ | ❑ |
| 20. I treat others badly because they are disabled. | ❑ | ❑ | ❑ | ❑ |
| 21. I look down on people who know less than I do about construction. | ❑ | ❑ | ❑ | ❑ |
| 22. I don't clean up my work area when I finish working. | ❑ | ❑ | ❑ | ❑ |
| 23. I disregard safety rules. | ❑ | ❑ | ❑ | ❑ |
| 24. I say, "That's not my job." | ❑ | ❑ | ❑ | ❑ |
| 25. I sneak out of work early. | ❑ | ❑ | ❑ | ❑ |
| 26. I am argumentative or contrary. | ❑ | ❑ | ❑ | ❑ |
| 27. I talk when I should keep quiet. | ❑ | ❑ | ❑ | ❑ |

## Action Plan for Improvement

**Sample Problem:** *Showing up late for work.*

**Sample Action Plan:**

1. Go to sleep half an hour earlier and wake up half an hour earlier.
2. Buy a reliable alarm clock.
3. Check the news for traffic or weather conditions that could delay your commute.
4. Don't drink alcohol during the week.
5. Ask a co-worker to help you get to work on time.

Problem: ____________________

Action Plan: ____________________

____________________

Problem: ____________________

Action Plan: ____________________

____________________

Problem: ____________________

Action Plan: ____________________

____________________

## Group Activities

### Activity 3: Surveying the Company Culture

This activity will help you better understand your company's culture—its values, goals, and climate. It may also give you ideas for dealing with situations that you are not sure how to handle. On a separate sheet of paper, write down answers to the questions on the Workplace Culture Questionnaire. Base your answers on the company you work for. Then break into groups of three or four to discuss the similarities and differences among companies.

**Team Members**

1. ______________________ 2. ______________________

3. ______________________ 4. ______________________

### *Workplace Culture Questionnaire*

1. What are some of the behavior standards or practices in your workplace? What does the company value?
2. What are your company's *goals,* and how does it attempt to meet those goals?
3. What is the climate or atmosphere like? Is it easygoing or strict, friendly or unfriendly, serious or humorous?
4. Name one behavior that is acceptable in your workplace.
5. Name one behavior that is unacceptable in your workplace.
6. How did you learn which behaviors are acceptable and which are unacceptable?
7. Do you often hear remarks beginning "You can't," "You shouldn't," or "Don't"?
8. Do you often hear remarks beginning "Let's try," "What do you think about," or "I have an idea"?
9. Does your company employ people regardless of race, color, sex, religion, national origin, age, or disability? Is everyone treated equally?
10. Write down any workplace culture situations that you're not sure how to handle. You will discuss these with your teammates and get some ideas that may help you.

## Activity 4: Examining the Effects of a Negative Attitude

Throughout this module, we've talked about the importance of a good attitude. The benefits of a good attitude include faster promotions, better relationships with supervisors and co-workers, and more personal happiness. It is equally important to realize the effects of a negative attitude.

In this activity, you will examine the effects of a negative attitude. To complete the chart, work in groups of three and assign roles as follows:

**Team Members**

1. ______________________________ plays the part of a worker with a negative attitude.
2. ______________________________ plays the part of a co-worker.
3. ______________________________ plays the part of a supervisor.

***How Workers with Negative Attitudes Affect Themselves, Co-Workers, and Supervisors***

(The first row has been completed to get you started.)

| Problem | Effect on Worker with a Negative Attitude | Effect on Co-Workers | Effect on Supervisor |
|---|---|---|---|
| 1. Often argues with co-workers about unimportant matters | • Scares off co-workers<br>• Has no friends on the job<br>• Will probably lose this job | • Diminishes team spirit<br>• Makes it hard to communicate, which could lead to mistakes<br>• Makes the job less desirable | • Wastes time being the referee<br>• Draws attention away from more important problems<br>• Causes problems with higher management |
| 2. Often is late or absent | | | |
| 3. Uses obscene language | | | |
| 4. Takes credit for others' work | | | |

*(continued)*

| Problem | Effect on Worker with a Negative Attitude | Effect on Co-Workers | Effect on Supervisor |
|---|---|---|---|
| 5. Gossips or spreads rumors | | | |
| 6. Is lazy, does not pull weight | | | |
| 7. Has a "good enough" attitude instead of a "quality" attitude | | | |

## Activity 5: Examining the Effects of Absenteeism and Tardiness

In this activity, you will work in groups of four to examine the effects of absenteeism and tardiness. Imagine that you and your team are assigned to a difficult welding project. The work area is located on a busy downtown street with many people walking past. Your boss has allotted four hours to get the job done. All four of you must be at the job site on time, for the full four hours, to get the job done on time and on budget. Assign the following roles and then answer the discussion questions.

**Team Members**

1. ______________________ plays the part of the worker in charge of getting the work area ready. You must put up safety barriers and keep passersby a safe distance from the welders.
2. ______________________ and ______________________ play the part of the welders. The job cannot be completed on time without both of you.
3. ______________________ plays the part of the worker responsible for responding to emergencies. You must stand by with a fire extinguisher.

## Discussion Questions

1. Suppose one of the crew doesn't show up for work. What is likely to happen? Will the job get done on time? How can the existing team rearrange itself to get the work done?
2. Now suppose that two of the workers on the team do not show up. Can the job get done? If so, how? If not, why not?
3. When workers don't show up or show up late, how is safety affected?
4. What will happen if one worker leaves early? What if two workers leave early?

# Building a Strong Relationship with Your Supervisor

## Self-Assessment

### What Does Your Boss Think of You?

Do you know what your boss thinks of you? Use this self-assessment quiz to find out. For each situation, choose the option that best describes your most likely response. Be sure to choose your most likely response, not what you think you should respond. In the third column, write the number that corresponds to that response.

| Situation | What Would You Do? | Your Most Likely Response |
|---|---|---|
| Your boss does something you don't approve of. | 1. Complain to several other co-workers about it.<br>2. Tell my boss that I disapprove.<br>3. Talk about it with one or two co-workers I consider friends, but otherwise keep a low profile. | |
| Your friend works for another construction company and tells you about its great benefits package. | 1. Tell all my co-workers about the other company's benefits package.<br>2. Tell my boss about the benefits the other company is giving its workers as soon as I report to work.<br>3. Wait till the boss is free, and then ask to discuss the other company's benefits package. | |
| You've heard a rumor that one of the supervisors is going to be fired and replaced by someone much younger. | 1. Tell your co-workers right away before someone else tells them.<br>2. Wait until mealtime or a break, then tell your co-workers.<br>3. Keep the rumor to yourself, because you don't know if it's true or not. | |
| Your boss assigns you to work with someone you don't like. | 1. Refuse to work with that person as soon as your boss makes the assignment.<br>2. Wait until the next day, explain the situation to your boss, and ask for another assignment.<br>3. Accept the decision as final and try to make the best of the situation, figuring your boss has a good reason for the assignment. | |
| You've been invited to the company picnic with your family. You work with these people all week, and you don't want to spend your weekend with them, too. | 1. Skip the picnic without telling anyone, and hope no one will notice you're not there.<br>2. Say you can't attend because you have other plans you can't break (even if that isn't true).<br>3. Go to the picnic and try to make the best of it. | |

*(continued)*

| Situation | What Would You Do? | Your Most Likely Response |
|---|---|---|
| Your boss gives you specific directions for completing a task, but you think you know a better way to do it. | 1. Tell your boss you want to do the task your way, which is better.<br>2. Say nothing, but do it your way. It doesn't matter how you do a task as long as it gets done.<br>3. Ask if your boss would be willing to listen to your suggestions for doing the task differently. | |
| A co-worker complains that the new supervisor is hard to get along with. | 1. Sympathize, because there is no such thing as a good boss.<br>2. Tell your co-worker to make the best of it, because managers come and go.<br>3. Offer your co-worker tips for getting along better with the supervisor. | |
| A problem has come up on the job, but it's not urgent. Your boss is busy with the owner, who is visiting the site for the day. | 1. Interrupt your boss right away before someone else reports the problem.<br>2. Use your cell phone so you can avoid reporting the problem face-to-face.<br>3. Wait until the owner is gone, and then report the problem. | |

***Scoring:*** Add up all the numbers in the third column to determine your final score: ___________

***Assessment:***

22–24 points: Your boss is likely to think of you as dedicated, loyal, dependable, and trustworthy. This module will help you maintain the positive impression you've already made.

17–21 points: Your boss probably thinks well of you, though you occasionally do things that are annoying. This module will help you correct the mistakes you've been making and help you emphasize your positive qualities.

8–16 points: Your boss may see you as someone who isn't very dedicated to the job. This module will help you build a much better relationship with your boss.

## Introduction

At this time, you're probably working as a trainee or craft professional, or you're taking classes to prepare for your career. As a new construction worker, you're already one step ahead of many other people, because construction pays better than many of the unskilled trades. An added bonus is that most construction jobs offer many opportunities for training on an ongoing basis.

As you continue to gain new skills and experience, you may want a job that gives you more responsibility and higher pay. To earn more money, you may decide to become a supervisor. Becoming a supervisor has many benefits, and the job is excellent training if you want to start your own business some day.

For now, though, you must focus on your current job. No matter where you work, a large part of your success depends on how well you get along with your supervisor. In this module, you'll read about what a supervisor's job entails, and then learn some ways to build a positive relationship with your boss. Along the way, you'll also gain some perspective on the stresses and pressures that supervisors face.

## The supervisor's job

Your boss can be your best mentor and help you in your training and in pursuing your career. Ask your boss for advice on how you can do a better job and what additional training you may need. Let's take a look at your supervisor's job.

Supervisors are responsible for all the parts of a project and making sure that all the pieces come together. They must ensure that all of the team members do their jobs well. They are responsible for delivering a quality job on time and on budget. Supervisors must coordinate all of the tasks on a project and ensure that employees are working together in the way that makes the most sense. Therefore, supervisors must take a broad view of every issue and base their decisions on what is best for the project overall. You might say that a supervisor is like a juggler who must keep lots of different balls in the air at the same time.

In contrast, you have a much more focused job. You work on specific tasks, and you do what your boss asks you to do. By doing your tasks in a professional manner, you can help to make your supervisor's job easier. A supervisor who can rely on you to work as a professional has more time to deal with the many other responsibilities that come with the job. In general, supervisors are responsible for the following:

**1. Productivity and quality.** Supervisors make sure that quality work gets done on time. They ensure that workers are using the most efficient tools, equipment, and procedures. They're always watching to make sure that workers aren't wasting time or supplies, and they're always looking for ways to do the job better or more efficiently. The smallest mistake, or the slightest decrease in productivity, may have ripple effects that can cost the company thousands of dollars.

**2. Coordination.** Supervisors make sure that a project runs smoothly. They must schedule workers and tasks so that the different trades don't get in each other's way. Supervisors must also ensure that workers don't have a lot of down time; it's too expensive to have workers waiting around to work because supplies have not been delivered or because of scheduling delays. Supervisors also must answer to their own bosses and follow their directions.

**3. Cost control.** Construction is a profit-oriented industry. To be profitable, a job must come in at or under the budgeted costs. To this end, supervisors make sure that no money is wasted, that contractors don't overbill, and that suppliers don't overcharge. Because time is money, supervisors also watch to make sure that workers are reporting to work on time, taking a reasonable amount of time for meals and breaks, and putting in a full day's work.

**4. Safety.** While safety is everyone's responsibility, supervisors are in charge of ensuring the safety of every work site. Both state and federal laws govern workplace safety. Companies that do not follow workplace safety laws risk losing workers to injury or even death and can expect to pay thousands of dollars in fines. Therefore, construction companies take safety very seriously and expect their supervisors to oversee this important task.

**5. Leadership.** Supervisors are team leaders who motivate workers and make them feel like an important part of the work crew. They are teachers and coaches and even, when necessary, counselors for employees struggling with problems at work or at home.

## Tips for getting along with your supervisor

Most supervisors are confident and have strong personalities. They must have these qualities to deal with their bosses, workers, suppliers, inspectors, and clients. They must also deal confidently with the pressures that come with being in charge. Even the most easygoing supervisors could never be described as pushovers.

In addition, most supervisors have both technical and management skills. Their years of experience add up to knowledge you should respect. Chances are your supervisor has done your job or one very like it at some point. You might know something your supervisor does not, but when you are just starting out, it's not likely.

Most supervisors respect your efforts and have a lot of sympathy for the challenges you face. They have been in your shoes. You might find it a little more difficult to put yourself in your supervisor's shoes, but you must try. Respect is the key. You may not actually like some of your bosses, but you can respect the job they are trying to do. Keep in mind that when you make an effort to respect and get along with your bosses, you will have more job satisfaction and find it easier to get pay raises and promotions.

How can you put your best foot forward with your boss? Here are some suggestions and things to keep in mind:

**1. Remember that your boss is not the enemy.** Your boss is not an evil creature who spends most of the day thinking up ways to make your life difficult. Supervisors greatly appreciate and trust reliable workers and reward those who perform to the best of their ability. It is also their job to keep workers in line. You may think it's personal when your boss chews you out, but in most cases it's not. If you imagine that your boss has it in for you personally, you will probably not have a very good working relationship. Take a moment and think about your attitude toward your boss. You would like your boss to be honest, fair, open-minded, and even-tempered. Are you?

**2. Respect the boss/worker relationship.** Although it's true that your boss is not your enemy, it is also true that your boss is required to maintain a professional relationship with you and your co-workers. The reason for this is simple, if you think about it. Would you be willing to give orders to your friends? Could you still be friends with someone you have to reprimand for doing a bad job? Probably not. There has to be some distance between bosses and workers. Most bosses and workers appreciate this fact. They know that everything works more smoothly when bosses and workers are friendly but maintain a professional working relationship. The boss/worker relationship is best defined as a business relationship based on mutual needs. Your boss needs your skills and talents, and you need a salary and benefits. If you meet your boss or your boss's supervisor outside of work, you should be cordial and professional, just as you are at work.

Keep in mind that your boss has bosses, too. Supervisors must account to their bosses not only for their own actions, but also for your actions and the actions of your co-workers.

**3. Offer solutions, not complaints.** Your boss has authority over you in the workplace. When your boss tells you to do something, you must do it without argument and without complaint. Grumbling just uses up energy that you could use in another way. For example, suppose your boss tells you to do a task one way and you have figured out a better way to do it. Instead of saying, "I don't want to do this your way," you should say, "I figured out a way to do this that will save time. Can I show you?" Bosses appreciate workers who offer solutions, not complaints. However, you don't have to think up new ideas to get along with your boss. Most bosses would say that doing your job well and accepting assignments without argument is just fine. A little cooperation goes a long way.

Note that no one expects you to follow orders blindly and without thinking. There might be times when you will have a justifiable reason for not following instructions. In such cases, you must state your reasons calmly and respectfully.

**4. Be flexible.** Although you are learning to be a specialist in one of the construction trades, your supervisor will appreciate your willingness to help out in other areas. Be flexible. If your boss asks you to help out in another area, work at a different site, or work different hours, treat the request as a learning opportunity. Remember, the more experience you get under your belt, the sooner you can become a supervisor yourself. Even if becoming a supervisor is not in your plans, it never hurts to learn something new.

**5. Communicate wisely.** Supervisors are very busy people. They are willing to answer questions and give guidance. However, like most busy people, they don't want to be constantly interrupted or embarrassed. If you must speak with your boss, choose your time wisely. Is your boss having a bad day? If so, this might not be the best time to ask for time off, for a raise, or for help with a personal problem.

You will do yourself a favor by simply arranging to talk at a time that is best for your supervisor. Is the owner on site for a visit? If so, this is probably not a good time to interrupt your boss. What if the problem can't wait? In this case, you would interrupt politely and calmly and ask your boss to step aside for a few moments. It is important not to do or say anything in front of the owner—or anyone—that might embarrass your boss.

**6. Follow the chain of authority.** It is usually not a good idea to go to your supervisor's boss with problems. Doing so will make your supervisor look incompetent and will probably result in resentment toward you. If you can, you should try to work out problems you may have with co-workers on your own. If you can't, give your boss a fair chance to resolve the problem. As a general rule, you should follow the chain of authority. That means that you must report directly to your boss who then reports to his or her boss, and so on. When trying to solve a problem, a good rule of thumb is to go over your supervisor's head only as a last resort.

**7. Deal with your mistakes.** Everyone makes mistakes. You must work carefully to avoid mistakes, but when you do make one, admit it, take responsibility, and work to make corrections and limit damage. Don't make the even bigger mistake of trying to cover up, hoping that the boss will never find out. When you take responsibility, your boss may get angry at you for making a mistake in the first place, but he or she will also respect your honesty, integrity, and willingness to make things right.

Note that covering up some types of mistakes could create a safety problem for you, your co-workers, or the people who will one day live in the house or work in the building you helped construct.

**8. Respect your boss around co-workers.** It's tempting to complain to your co-workers about the boss, especially after a hard day. However, co-workers will probably repeat what you say, and if your complaints get back to your boss, you could be in for some trouble. You may not approve of everything your supervisor does, but it is best to keep your opinions to yourself. As a good rule of thumb, don't talk behind another person's back. If you won't state your problem to that person directly, it is best to say nothing to anyone else.

**9. Empathize, empathize, empathize.** As you learned in Module 1, empathy is one of the most important communication skills you can learn. Therefore, you should try to put yourself in your supervisor's shoes. That can be difficult, especially when your supervisor is chewing you out! Keep in mind that you see your job mainly in terms of how it affects you. Your boss, however, must look at you in terms of how you affect the overall job. If you are late, waste materials, or do a poor job, it is your supervisor's duty to reprimand you and get you back on track.

Try not to second-guess your supervisor's authority. Say that you find what you think might be an error in some work done by a co-worker, and you are not sure what to do about it. You might think that you should just correct the mistake without talking to your supervisor, but your best course of action is to bring the matter to your supervisor's attention.

## A word on nonverbal communication and body language

You may say all the right things to your boss, but your body language can send a different message entirely. "Right away, boss," does not sound respectful when you roll your eyes or shake your head in disgust. Research has shown that more than 90 percent of all communication is nonverbal (see *Table 2–1*). That means you are communicating even when you haven't said a single word. Following are some tips to help you use the right body language when communicating with your boss:

- **Stand up straight.** Slouching makes you look like you are not listening or are bored with what you hear.
- **Avoid crossing your arms.** When you cross your arms, you send several negative signals: "I am not listening," or "I do not like you," or "I do not agree with anything you say."
- **Maintain eye contact.** Look at your supervisor when communicating. When you look at the floor or off to the side, you appear to be dishonest. When you roll your eyes or look at the ceiling, you appear to be bored, impatient, or disrespectful.
- **Avoid frowning or clenching your fists.** When you do this, you send a clear signal that you are angry and defensive.

**Table 2-1. Interpreting Body Language**

| Body Language | Interpretation |
|---|---|
| Standing with hands on hips | Readiness, aggression |
| Arms crossed on chest | Defensiveness |
| Rubbing hands | Anticipation |
| Tapping feet or drumming fingers, pen, or pencil | Impatience |
| Patting or playing with hair | Lack of self-confidence or insecurity |
| Tilted head, leaning forward | Interest |
| Stroking chin | Thoughtfulness, deciding |
| Biting nails | Insecurity, nervousness |
| Rubbing eyes | Doubt, disbelief |
| Sitting with hands clasped behind head, legs crossed | Confidence, superiority |
| Brisk, erect walk | Self-confidence |
| Turning your back to another person | Dismissal |
| Looking out of the corner of your eyes | Disdain, scorn |

Source: *Your Executive Image.* Victoria A. Seitz. Holbrook, MA: Adams Media Corporation.

## Workplace politics

The term *workplace politics* describes the behavior of employees who attempt to influence events in the workplace. Workplace politics can be fairly complicated and often frustrating. However, there are two simple things you can do to avoid problems with workplace politics: avoid doing or saying anything that will make your boss look bad with upper management, and behave professionally at all times.

Here are some suggestions to help you achieve these goals:

**1. Deal with troublemakers.** A worker with a bad attitude is like a virus—one person can infect everyone else. Most people would like to avoid these troublemakers, but it's not always possible. If one of your co-workers has a bad attitude, try the following tips to keep that bad attitude from infecting you:

- Lead by example. Stay upbeat and let your positive attitude influence negative workers.
- Do not become a sounding board. Negative people need an audience. Don't provide one.
- Encourage positive action. For example, point out that there is work to do and provide a good example by getting on with the work yourself.
- Do not get pulled into causing trouble yourself. Misery does love company. Don't provide it.

**2. Don't be a pest.** You are not the only worker who must deal with the pressures that come with work and a personal life. Others will be sympathetic to your problems at first, but if you become known as a whiner, they will soon avoid you. Here are some tips to help you avoid becoming a pest:

- Keep your problems in perspective. Everyone has ups and downs. They are part of life.
- Take positive action. If you don't like the job you have, get training for the job you want. Ask your supervisor for guidance.
- Be patient. The job that you don't like now may be a stepping-stone to better things. When you show your boss that you can handle any job well, you will find it easier to get raises and promotions.

**3. Don't step on people.** If you do not respect your supervisors or if you take advantage of them, they will soon lose respect for you. In fact, once you get a reputation for being someone who steps on others, most people will lose respect for you. Here are a couple of tips to keep that from happening:

- Be considerate. Don't take advantage of your supervisor's good nature by slacking off on the job.
- Be thoughtful. Keep your supervisor informed regarding your availability. Don't leave a supervisor hanging and wondering where you are.
- Be professional. Avoid goofing off or playing practical jokes on others. What may seem like harmless fun could cause a problem for your supervisor.

## On-the-Job Quiz

Here's a quick quiz that asks you to apply what you've learned in this module.

**1.** Your supervisor, whom you respect and admire, is moving to another state to take a new job. A few weeks later you meet your new supervisor, who is coming from a rival construction company. You should assume that _____.
   a. your new supervisor will know next to nothing about the way your company works and you will have to baby-sit
   b. you will never have the good relationship with the new supervisor that you had with your old one
   c. your new supervisor is skilled and capable, but probably a bit nervous about starting with a new crew and company, and you should be as helpful as possible
   d. your new supervisor knows nothing about your skills, and now you will never get ahead

**2.** You've just started a new job, and you like your supervisor, who seems easygoing and laid back. After a couple weeks of working hard, you start to slack off. You should assume that your supervisor _____.
   a. will probably just casually mention the workplace rules and give you a friendly reminder
   b. is a pushover and probably won't notice a little slacking off here and there
   c. will tell you in clear language to straighten up and follow the workplace rules
   d. is cool and probably feels that as long as the job gets done eventually, a little slacking off is OK

**3.** It's a quiet Friday afternoon. Everyone is in a pretty good mood because on Wednesday your crew finished up a huge job on time and on budget. You have a week's vacation coming, and you want to take a trip in two weeks. Is now a good time to ask your boss for time off?
   a. No, because two weeks is not enough notice.
   b. No, because you should make these types of requests on Monday when the human resources office can handle it.
   c. Yes, because you have the right to take a vacation whenever you want.
   d. Yes, because your boss can more easily spare you now that the pressure of the big job is over.

**4.** You've been on the job a couple of weeks and always hear your co-workers bad-mouthing the supervisor. You want to get in good with your co-workers, but you also want to get ahead. You should _____.
   a. join in the bad-mouthing sessions so that your co-workers will bond with you
   b. avoid bad-mouthing the boss until you have been on the job longer
   c. avoid bad-mouthing the boss and focus on treating your supervisor with respect
   d. lecture your co-workers about their bad behavior, then tell on them to your boss

**5.** You hear your boss bawling out a co-worker who left tools out in the rain overnight. You look at the situation from your supervisor's point of view and decide that _____.
   a. there's just no excuse for yelling at a worker
   b. your boss should have given the worker a warning instead of a lecture
   c. your co-worker didn't know it was going to rain, so it was an accident that your boss should overlook
   d. tools are expensive, and they shouldn't be left out overnight, rain or no rain, so your boss was justified in reprimanding your co-worker

**6.** You're reading a blueprint, and it's not making any sense to you. There seems to be a serious mistake in it, but because you're not that experienced, you're not sure. You should _____.
   a. assume that the person who drafted the blueprint knows more than you do, and follow it exactly
   b. ask your supervisor to look at the blueprint and give you advice on what to do
   c. trust your own judgment, ignore the blueprint, and complete the work your way to show that you have initiative
   d. ask a co-worker to look at the blueprint and give you advice on what to do

**7.** You're feeling pretty annoyed. Your co-worker is supposed to relieve you at 4:00 P.M. Yesterday you were not able to leave until 4:03, and today it was 4:04 before you could punch out. You're not getting paid overtime, and you resent having to wait. You should _____.
   a. complain to your supervisor right away
   b. be patient for a day or so, but if the problem continues, explain to your co-worker that you need to leave at 4:00 each day
   c. complain to your supervisor's boss
   d. tell your boss that you are willing to wait till your co-worker shows up, but you expect to be paid overtime for any time worked after 4:00

**8.** You are out shopping with your family and bump into your supervisor's boss, who is also out shopping with family. You should introduce your family and _____.

a. mention how much you enjoy your job and working for your supervisor, and then be on your way
b. seize this opportunity to suggest things you think your supervisor could be doing better
c. seize this opportunity to get in with upper management by talking shop and passing on some recent gossip
d. leave as soon as possible because you don't want one of your co-workers or your own supervisor to see you schmoozing with upper management

**9.** You're talking to your supervisor about having trouble getting the permits needed to start a job. However, your supervisor keeps glancing out the door and tapping a pencil on a desk piled with papers. Based on the nonverbal cues you're receiving, you should _____.

a. speak more slowly
b. offer to come back later to talk about the problem
c. state that you are busy too, and all you need is a few minutes
d. close the door so your boss will stop looking at whatever the distraction is

**10.** Your first week on the job, a more experienced worker tells you to go get a skyhook and not to come back until you find one. You are told to ask around because there is sure to be one on site. Several hours later you realize that there's no such thing as a skyhook, and the senior workers were playing a little joke on you. Now, a couple of new trainees are starting. You have a few ideas for pranks that will make them look just as silly as you did. You should _____.

a. play the pranks, because it's all in good fun
b. play the pranks, because hazing is an acceptable workplace custom that every new worker has to put up with
c. ask your boss if it's OK to have some fun with the new workers, and if you get the go-ahead, play the pranks
d. not play the pranks, because it's not right to step on co-workers, and your pranks can cause a problem for your supervisor

# Individual Activities

## Activity 1: Managing Difficult Situations with Your Supervisor

In this module, we emphasized the importance of following orders without complaint. Yet, sometimes you will have to manage your boss in the same way that your boss manages you, especially when you have to resolve conflicts.

When conflicts come up, there are good ways to make your case and there are bad ways. Following are several techniques that you can use to present your case fairly and politely to your boss. Match each situation in the left column with the best conflict-resolution technique in the right column.

| Situation | Resolution Technique |
|---|---|
| _____ 1. The company has a pressing deadline, and your boss asks you to put in 20 hours of overtime over the weekend. This means that you'll miss your kids' baseball game and a family outing. You don't want to work the overtime, but you want to help your boss out. So you offer to work overtime in exchange for two days off when the project is complete. | a. Reasoning: Use simple facts and data to support your case. Don't get hot under the collar or lose your temper. Be calm and reasonable to best present your side of the story or to get information you need. |
| _____ 2. Your supervisor has strong opinions about the specific way a wiring job should be done. You are an expert electrician and think you know a cheaper and easier way to do it. You say, "Boss, if I could suggest an easier and cheaper way to get this job done, would you be willing to give it a try?" | b. Bargaining: Trade one thing for another. When two people exchange favors, both parties win. |
| _____ 3. Your boss has given you some instructions that you don't think make any sense. You realize that your boss is busy and hasn't had time to really think the instructions through. You calmly and patiently ask questions so that you can get all the information you need to do the job correctly. | c. Courtesy and a bit of flattery: Accept criticism gracefully. Recognize that your boss has skills and experience that you do not. Compliment your supervisor's techniques and methods and express a willingness to learn. |
| _____ 4. You and your team members would like the boss to order a new piece of equipment. However, the equipment is expensive, and your boss is reluctant to order it. The team makes a list of ways that the equipment would help them be more productive. | d. Experience and expertise: If you have a lot of experience or expertise in a certain area, you'll be able to explain your situation from the perspective of an expert. Just be sure you do so in a professional and courteous manner. |
| _____ 5. Your boss is critical of your work. Instead of getting upset at the criticism, you ask what you can to do to improve your performance, then work to improve. You also express admiration for your supervisor's skill and experience. | e. Team backup: Get your co-workers to help you present your case or make a good suggestion. Never gang up on the supervisor. Rather, present your case as a group solution to a pressing problem. |

## Activity 2: Responding to Your Boss

In this activity, you will figure out the best way to respond to something your boss says to you. Write down what you should say and not what you want to say. Note that at the work site, you won't always have a chance to think through what you should say. If your boss upsets you, you will probably say the first thing that comes into your head, so remember this exercise. When you are back on the job and your boss says something that makes you angry, try counting to five before responding.

1. **Your boss:** "How many times do I have to tell you to clean up your work area before you go to eat? Are you deaf or something?"

   **You:** ________________________________________

   ________________________________________

2. **Your boss:** "Hey, while you're out, would you mind getting me a sandwich and some coffee?"

   **You:** ________________________________________

   ________________________________________

3. **Your boss:** "I need someone to take a ride to the supplier to pick up a bunch of things we need. Any volunteers?"

   **You:** ________________________________________

   ________________________________________

4. **Your boss:** "This is the fifth day in a row you've been late. Go home and think about whether you still want this job. We'll talk about it on Monday."

   **You:** ________________________________________

   ________________________________________

5. **Your boss:** "All right, everyone, the owner of the company is going to show up some time this week, probably when we least expect it. I need all of you to be on your best behavior. That means no joking around and no long breaks!"

   **You:** ________________________________________

   ________________________________________

6. **Your boss:** "I'm always amazed at the quality of your work. Good job."

   **You:** ________________________________________

   ________________________________________

## Group Activities

### Activity 3: Role-Playing Exercise: Understanding Body Language and Tone of Voice

This activity requires five people (one supervisor and four workers). Those assigned to play the roles will read the script out loud, then everyone will discuss the questions that follow. Role-players should follow the acting cues written in parentheses.

**Team Members**

Supervisor: ______________________ (fill in name of classmate)

Workers: J.R., T.K., Conner, and Lee

**Supervisor:** *(For each conversation, look each worker in the eye, stand up straight, and speak in a firm, but calm tone of voice. Keep your arms at your sides and don't frown.)* "I know we all work hard around here, but I'm not sure that all of you are doing your share. J.R., did you help T.K. move that come-along like I asked you to?"

**J.R.:** *(Sigh, roll your eyes, slouch, and use a sarcastic tone.)* "Yeah. I did it just like you said to, boss."

**Supervisor:** "T.K., you are taking too long for your meal breaks. What's going on?"

**T.K.:** *(Grin a little sheepishly, but stand up straight and look the boss in the eye.)* "Sorry, boss. I'm studying for a course I'm taking in CAD design. I'll try to keep better track of my time."

**Supervisor:** "Conner, you weren't here on time this morning. Did I see you sneaking in late?"

**Conner:** *(First look down at the floor and sigh, but then straighten up and look the boss in the eye.)* "Well...yes. I got stuck in traffic. I'm sorry. I should have told you this morning. I'll try to leave home earlier so I won't be late again."

**Supervisor:** "What about you, Lee? I thought I saw you sneaking out half an hour early yesterday."

**Lee:** *(Make a face, cross your arms, and look at the wall behind the boss. Speak in an angry tone of voice.)* "No—that wasn't me. I was here until 5:00. Reagan can vouch for me—we were finishing up some drywalling."

### Discussion Questions

1. Was the supervisor too rough on the workers?
2. Did the supervisor focus on the personal characteristics of each worker or on work-related problems?
3. Which worker or workers responded in an appropriate way?
4. Which worker or workers responded inappropriately? What made these responses inappropriate? Was it only the words they used?
5. Based on body language alone, what can you assume about each worker? Can you tell who might be avoiding the truth? Can you tell who is avoiding responsibility?
6. If you were the boss, which of these workers would you most want to have on your team? Which of them would you least like to have on your team?

## Activity 4: Analyzing Your Supervisor

Using a separate sheet of paper, complete the Supervisor Worksheet. Then, working in groups of three or four, discuss each question with your team members.

**Team Members**

| | |
|---|---|
| 1. ____________________ | 2. ____________________ |
| 3. ____________________ | 4. ____________________ |

## Supervisor Worksheet

1. How long has your supervisor worked for the company?

2. What is your supervisor's background?

3. What things do workers do that most annoy your supervisor?

4. What five words best describe your supervisor?

5. Do your co-workers like your supervisor? Do they respect your supervisor?

6. Describe your supervisor's management style (easygoing, strict, perfectionist, etc.).

7. How does your supervisor express anger?

8. Does your supervisor have a sense of humor?

9. Do you feel comfortable asking your supervisor questions or for advice?

10. You know what you think of your supervisor. What do you think your supervisor thinks of you?

## Team Discussion Questions

When you discuss your answers to this worksheet with your team members, keep the following questions in mind:

1. Do our bosses have similar styles?
2. Do our bosses tend to get annoyed by the same things?
3. Do our bosses come from similar backgrounds?
4. Do our bosses communicate with their workers in similar ways?
5. What advice can we give one another on how to get along better with our bosses?

# Teamwork: Getting Along with Your Co-Workers

## Self-Assessment

### Are You a Team Player?

Do people enjoy working with you? Will you work effectively on a construction crew? Take this self-assessment quiz to find out. Be sure to answer all the questions honestly.

| | Good | Fair | Weak |
|---|---|---|---|
| 1. How good am I at accepting that someone else might be more skilled than I am in a particular area? | ❑ | ❑ | ❑ |
| 2. What are my chances of maintaining a positive attitude when I have to work with other people, instead of alone? | ❑ | ❑ | ❑ |
| 3. What are my chances of quickly resolving a conflict with my co-workers or supervisors? | ❑ | ❑ | ❑ |
| 4. How good am I at cooperating when I know my cooperation will benefit others more than me? | ❑ | ❑ | ❑ |
| 5. What is my level of patience when I am working with people who are slower than I am? | ❑ | ❑ | ❑ |
| 6. How receptive am I to a goal set for me by others? | ❑ | ❑ | ❑ |
| 7. How well do I work with people who belong to ethnic groups other than mine? | ❑ | ❑ | ❑ |
| 8. How understanding am I of people with a different opinion or point of view? | ❑ | ❑ | ❑ |
| 9. How comfortable am I with counting on other people to get their jobs done? | ❑ | ❑ | ❑ |
| 10. How successful am I at keeping my ego from affecting my relationships with co-workers? | ❑ | ❑ | ❑ |

Source: Adapted from *Your Attitude Is Showing.* Elwood M. Chapman. Upper Saddle River, NJ: Prentice Hall, 1999, pp. 85–93.

***Scoring:*** A response of "good" is worth 3 points, "fair" is worth 2 points, and "weak" is worth 1 point. Count the number of times you gave each response and multiply that number by its point value. Then add up your total score.

| | | | |
|---|---|---|---|
| Good | ________ | × 3 = | ________ |
| Fair | ________ | × 2 = | ________ |
| Weak | ________ | × 1 = | ________ |
| TOTAL | | | ________ |

***Assessment:***

27–30 points: You will make a good team player, and you'll get along well with your co-workers. This module will give you a refresher course in what you already know.

22–26 points: You can become a good team player by following the advice offered in this module. You'll also learn some techniques for getting along better with your co-workers.

10–21 points: You could use some additional training on teamwork. This module will give you that training. It will also offer some advice on how to build stronger relationships with your co-workers.

## Introduction

Like many other industries today, the construction industry relies on teamwork. Very few construction projects can be completed by one person. Workers with many different skills—architects, engineers, designers, plumbers, electricians, carpenters, welders, and sheet metal mechanics, to name just a few—must work together to get the job done. All of these people must be able to accomplish their tasks safely and well in a high-pressure industry. This is why teamwork is so important. Teamwork is much more than simply working alongside other people. In successful teams, all the workers actively contribute. Teams don't benefit from loners or people who think they're above it all. Think about team sports like hockey, soccer, and basketball, where players help each other to score points. Those individual players aren't playing for themselves. They know that winning the point for the team is more important than getting glory for themselves. They also know that being part of a successful team often leads to personal success.

In Module 2, we offered some suggestions on how to build a good relationship with your supervisor. In this module, we outline several ways to develop good working relations with your co-workers. As you work through this module, keep this golden rule in mind: *The best way to have good relationships with your co-workers is to be a team player.* There's nothing like being on the winning team!

## Becoming a team player

As you begin your construction career, you'll be part of a team almost from the beginning. Sometimes your team will consist of dozens of people with different skills. For example, when a team of plumbers wants to bury water lines, they need the help of a team of backhoe operators and a team of laborers. Sometimes you'll be part of a team of two. For example, an electrician who is pulling a wire needs a co-worker to feed wire into the conduit.

How can you become a valuable team member? Remember the following pointers:

**1. Team members respect one another.** You should respect your co-workers at all times, regardless of their level of skill or education. Showing disrespect is just about the worst insult you can give another person. How can you show respect for others?

- Allow others to state their ideas or viewpoints without interruption.
- Don't do anything to make a co-worker look foolish in front of others.
- Don't allow differences to affect the way you treat other people.
- Don't make negative comments about others because of their race, color, sex, religion, national origin, age, or disability. (We discuss how to get along in a culturally diverse work setting in more detail in Module 4.)
- Remember the empathy rule. How would you feel if someone treated you with disrespect?

**2. Team members help one another.** Don't ever say, "That's not my job." If you are on a team, helping out is part of your job. Although every member of a construction team has a specific job to do, a good team member is willing to lend a helping hand. Remember the empathy rule. Someday you'll find yourself in a situation where you need help. Will you want people turning their backs on you?

**3. Team members don't cause problems—they look for solutions.** Sometimes it's easy to let disagreements arise. People can lock horns over big and small issues. Dedicated team members don't let their differences drive them apart. Rather, they work together to find solutions to their problems. Try to work with your team members to solve problems. Say that you must work with someone who speaks English as a second language. Yes, communication will be more difficult, but if both of you make an effort, you can find a way to communicate and get the job done. We'll discuss some problem-solving methods in Module 8.

**4. Team members support one another.** In addition to working together, team members often rely on one another for emotional support. Sometimes a co-worker has a rough day on the job or has personal problems at home. Good team players make allowances for their co-workers from time to time. This doesn't mean that you should let others take advantage of you. It simply means that you should be aware of people's emotional needs. Sometimes co-workers just need a sympathetic friend to talk to.

**5. Team members are committed to a project.** Good team members keep their eyes on the ultimate goal, whether they are building a shopping center, wiring a new office building, or reroofing a warehouse. All of their actions are geared toward accomplishing that goal together. When faced with questions or problems on the job, you should ask yourself: "Is this good for the project? Will it benefit both me and my co-workers?" If a decision will benefit only you, but not your co-workers or the project, it might not be the best decision you can make.

## Tips for getting along with your co-workers

Very few people can live and work on their own. To feel happy and have a sense of purpose, we all need to interact with other people. An old saying goes, "To have a friend, you have to be a friend." A similar saying is true on the job: "To have good co-workers, you have to be a good co-worker." How can you be a good co-worker? The following list of "dos and don'ts" can help.

### DOs

**1. Realize that everyone works hard, not just you.** When you are busy on the job—and who isn't?—it's tempting to think that you're working harder than everyone else. Most of the time, this isn't true. Remember that your co-workers are as dedicated as you are and that you all play an important role in completing the project.

**2. When appropriate, praise your co-workers.** Everyone likes to get a compliment for a job well done. Tell your co-workers when you're impressed by their work. A compliment costs nothing, and it spreads goodwill. Saying nice things is an easy way to convey a positive attitude.

**3. Share the credit and take responsibility for mistakes.** Nobody likes a credit hog. Be willing to share the credit you receive, and your co-workers' respect for you will grow. Similarly, take responsibility for mistakes you make. Don't expect your teammates to cover for you.

**4. Recognize the contributions of others.** Understand that different people bring different talents and skills to the job. There will always be workers who are more skilled than you and workers who are less skilled than you. Learn from those who can teach you, and be patient with those who aren't at your level of ability.

**5. Meet your deadlines.** Always remember that there are workers who cannot start their tasks until you have finished yours. Complete your work on time. Meeting your deadlines means more than getting along well with co-workers. Construction schedules are tied to budgets, and work delays can cost your company thousands of dollars.

### A Special Tip: Keep Your Problems at Home!

You can't prevent your personal problems from affecting how you feel. However, you must try to keep your personal problems from affecting co-workers. None of your co-workers will appreciate it if you have a fight at home and then take out your bad feelings on them.

If you are unable to park your personal problems at the door, try discussing them at mealtimes or during breaks with co-workers you trust. It may also help to discuss your problems with your supervisor. **Remember:** You are partly responsible for the mood, safety, and success of your team. When you learn to manage your personal problems, you also boost your performance as a valued team member.

### Caution

Sometimes you must report the conduct of another worker. You must do this when you are fairly certain that your supervisor is not aware of a worker who is doing something illegal or something that would endanger you or your co-workers.

## DON'Ts

**1. Don't brag or act like a know-it-all.** This behavior will annoy your co-workers. Braggarts and know-it-alls are usually the least popular people on the construction site. Who wants to listen to people who brag about their new cars, how much money they have, or how wonderful they are? Would you want these types of people on your team? (We discuss strategies for dealing with braggarts, know-it-alls, and other types of difficult people in Module 9.)

**2. Don't gossip about your co-workers.** People are entitled to their privacy, and gossip often spreads false rumors. Gossiping about co-workers makes you look petty, and it can hurt feelings and damage relationships.

**3. Don't put other people down.** Don't pick on co-workers—don't insult their appearance, their intelligence, or anything else. Putting others down hurts the whole team, and it also hurts you.

**4. Don't shirk your responsibilities.** The work has to get done, and when you shirk your responsibilities, your co-workers will have to pick up your slack. Don't expect to be part of the team if you don't do your part. How would you feel about a co-worker you always have to cover for?

**5. Don't be a stool pigeon.** Even when workers agree that a co-worker is causing problems, they don't like tattletales. If a co-worker is slacking off, don't worry. Your supervisor is probably well aware of the problem and will deal with it. You don't have to.

## Teaching others

At some point in your career, you'll be asked to teach others what you know. Maybe you will have to explain a safety procedure or demonstrate how to operate a piece of equipment.

Training others on the job provides an excellent opportunity to build good relationships. Most people appreciate and respect a good teacher—especially if that teacher is well-informed, patient, and understanding.

How can you become a teacher others will admire and respect? Follow a few simple guidelines:

**1. Feel honored.** If you're asked to teach someone, you should feel very proud. Clearly, your supervisor thinks that you have the skills and ability to teach your job to others. The confidence and trust that others have placed in you should inspire you to be the best teacher you can be.

**2. Be patient.** It is hard to be patient when you're teaching someone who doesn't quite get it. Consider that you might be speaking too quickly or expecting too much too soon. Sometimes you may have to show how to do a task more than once. Remember how a good teacher helped you learn something, and try to apply those same skills to help another. If you're feeling frustrated, take a short break.

**3. Teach by example.** The best way to teach something is to show how it's done and then ask the person you are training to show you or another co-worker while you observe. There are several advantages to teaching by example:

- You can watch to see if the trainee is doing the job properly.
- The trainee gets practice in doing the job and in teaching another worker.
- All of you will learn to understand each other better and work better together as a team.

**4. Offer encouragement.** Show co-workers your approval by saying things like "Good job!" or "You've got it!" Workers sometimes don't have confidence in their abilities, especially when they're trying to do something they've never done before. So offer encouragement as you go along.

**5. Don't be afraid to give constructive advice.** To train others well, you have to point out their mistakes. There's a good way and a not-so-good way to do that. For example, you could say, "That is not the safest way to operate that machine. Let me show you how to protect your fingers." Avoid saying things like "No, no, that's all wrong" or "Can't you do anything right?"

**6. Be aware that everyone learns differently.** There are at least four different learning styles. A learning style is simply the way that someone prefers to learn. Although people learn using all four styles, many people tend to prefer one style over another. Consider the different ways you can learn how to do something. Which of the following ways is easiest for you?

- **Visual.** You prefer looking at a diagram or a drawing to understand how something works. In fact, you often draw pictures when explaining things.
- **Descriptive.** You prefer words to pictures. Written, step-by-step instructions are best for you, so you can refer back to them as you learn.
- **Auditory.** You prefer to hear explanations and write them down in your own words. You may also have a good memory for spoken instructions.
- **Tactile.** You are a hands-on learner. You learn best when you actually get a chance to operate equipment or use tools.

Be flexible enough to change your teaching style to better suit a co-worker's learning style. For example, if words are not working, try drawing a picture instead.

## On-the-Job Quiz

Here's a quick quiz that asks you to apply what you've learned in this module.

**1.** Car troubles are making a co-worker, who lives just around the corner from you, late for work. To be a good team member, you should _____.

a. remind your co-worker that there's no excuse for being late to work
b. tell your supervisor to cut your co-worker some slack
c. get yourself transferred to another team so your co-worker's tardiness doesn't affect your productivity
d. volunteer to give your co-worker a ride until the car gets fixed

**2.** Your company hires an excellent craftworker for your team who speaks only a few words and phrases in English. To be a good team member, you should _____.

a. complain to the manager, because everyone who works on the team should speak good English
b. avoid the new worker, because the language barrier will make you less productive
c. figure that you both speak "construction," and if you learn a little of your co-worker's language you can have a basic conversation
d. ask to be switched to another team where everyone speaks English

3. A co-worker is having a week filled with problems: a fight at home, a car accident, and a very sick dog that may die. These problems are affecting your teammate's concentration. You should _____.
   a. be sympathetic and offer to do the harder parts of the job until things get better
   b. deliver a stern lecture about the importance of paying attention
   c. tell your co-worker to keep personal problems away from work
   d. tell your co-worker to go home and come back only when the problems are resolved

4. You come to work 15 minutes early each day, never stretch your mealtimes or breaks, and are usually the last one of your team to leave at the end of the shift. Your best course of action is to _____.
   a. tell your supervisor that you are the only member of the team who works hard and should get more pay than everyone else
   b. tell your team members that you are working harder than they are and you resent their laziness
   c. recognize that everyone works hard, not just you, and that it's not fair to resent other team members for your work habits
   d. start a competition with you as the judge and a nice prize going to the team member who works harder than you do

5. Your company presents you with the Best Carpenter of the Year award at an annual breakfast meeting. The company owner asks you to say a few words. You should _____.
   a. say thanks and go straight back to your seat
   b. thank your team members for helping you achieve your success
   c. act like the award is not a big deal, because you don't want your team members to think that you're superior to them
   d. give a short speech describing how your work has made the company better

6. The electricians are scheduled to begin hanging light fixtures on Monday. They can't begin their job until you've finished yours, but you're running behind, and it's already Friday. You don't think you can finish by the end of the day. You should _____.
   a. do nothing because it's the supervisor's job to worry about schedules
   b. talk to the electricians and say you're very sorry about the delay
   c. ask your supervisor if you can work some overtime to ready the area for the electricians
   d. cut a few corners, if necessary, to finish up everything by Friday, and ask the electricians to deal with any problems

7. A family argument keeps you up late. You wake up tired and annoyed. You should _____.
   a. call in sick, because you know you'll never be able to concentrate on your job
   b. report to work around noon, when you know you'll be in a better mood
   c. get to work on time, yell at a couple of the new workers, and slam a few doors to blow off steam and reduce stress
   d. get to work on time and put last night's fight behind you so you can concentrate on work

8. One of your teammates often comes back from breaks and meals later than everyone else. You should _____.
   a. tell each of your teammates to speak to your co-worker about the problem
   b. figure that your supervisor will notice the problem and take steps to correct it
   c. write an anonymous note to your supervisor describing the problem and how it is upsetting the team
   d. get your teammates to give that worker the cold shoulder

9. Your supervisor asks you to show a new trainee how to remove and replace a broken tile in a shower stall. The trainee can't seem to figure out what to do. You should _____.
   a. do the job for the trainee, because this will save time and is less frustrating for both of you
   b. demonstrate everything slowly, step by step, and more than once if necessary
   c. tell the trainee to concentrate and stop asking so many questions
   d. tell the trainee to consider working in another area

10. You are having trouble training a co-worker to operate a drill press. You spent some of your free time last night hand-printing a chart with all the steps clearly written down and even color-coded, but your co-worker keeps making mistakes. What is your best course of action?
    a. Ask your supervisor to find someone else for the training because your co-worker just won't learn from you.
    b. Figure that maybe your co-worker is a hands-on learner and try just demonstrating how the drill press works.
    c. Complain to your co-worker that you spent your free time making this great chart and you can't understand what the problem is.
    d. Suggest that your co-worker take some courses to learn how to read better.

# Individual Activities

## Activity 1: How Do Your Co-Workers See You?

The following chart lists behaviors that make people unpopular with their co-workers. Rate yourself honestly. For each "Often" or "Sometimes" you check, come up with an action plan for improving your behavior. A sample action plan has been provided for you following the chart.

| | Often | Sometimes | Rarely | Never |
|---|---|---|---|---|
| 1. I am a loner. | ☐ | ☐ | ☐ | ☐ |
| 2. I take myself too seriously. | ☐ | ☐ | ☐ | ☐ |
| 3. I am uptight. | ☐ | ☐ | ☐ | ☐ |
| 4. I want to be the best at everything. | ☐ | ☐ | ☐ | ☐ |
| 5. I hold grudges. | ☐ | ☐ | ☐ | ☐ |
| 6. I show up late for work. | ☐ | ☐ | ☐ | ☐ |
| 7. I am inconsiderate. | ☐ | ☐ | ☐ | ☐ |
| 8. I take longer than allowed for meals or breaks. | ☐ | ☐ | ☐ | ☐ |
| 9. I like to gossip. | ☐ | ☐ | ☐ | ☐ |
| 10. I stick my nose into other people's business. | ☐ | ☐ | ☐ | ☐ |
| 11. I report on co-workers' behavior to my supervisor. | ☐ | ☐ | ☐ | ☐ |
| 12. I say or do things that make co-workers tense or unhappy. | ☐ | ☐ | ☐ | ☐ |
| 13. I bad-mouth the company or the boss. | ☐ | ☐ | ☐ | ☐ |
| 14. I can't take a joke. | ☐ | ☐ | ☐ | ☐ |
| 15. I take credit for others' work. | ☐ | ☐ | ☐ | ☐ |
| 16. I brag about my talents and skills. | ☐ | ☐ | ☐ | ☐ |
| 17. I am sarcastic. | ☐ | ☐ | ☐ | ☐ |
| 18. I refuse to listen to the ideas of others. | ☐ | ☐ | ☐ | ☐ |
| 19. I look down on people of other cultures or races. | ☐ | ☐ | ☐ | ☐ |
| 20. I am not willing to pitch in and help. | ☐ | ☐ | ☐ | ☐ |
| 21. I horse around when others are trying to work. | ☐ | ☐ | ☐ | ☐ |
| 22. I think I work harder than everyone else. | ☐ | ☐ | ☐ | ☐ |
| 23. I am stingy with compliments. | ☐ | ☐ | ☐ | ☐ |
| 24. I have a chip on my shoulder. | ☐ | ☐ | ☐ | ☐ |
| 25. I complain about my job, my co-workers, and my boss. | ☐ | ☐ | ☐ | ☐ |
| 26. I manipulate people. | ☐ | ☐ | ☐ | ☐ |
| 27. I look down on others because of their sex or age. | ☐ | ☐ | ☐ | ☐ |

## Action Plan for Improvement

### *Example*

**Sample Problem:** *Gossiping about others*

**Sample Action Plan:**

1. Walk away when people start gossiping or bad-mouthing others.
2. Don't repeat gossip I hear.
3. Keep my nose out of other people's business.
4. Focus on my own work, not on what other people are doing.

Problem: ______________________________

Action Plan: ______________________________

______________________________

Problem: ______________________________

Action Plan: ______________________________

______________________________

Problem: ______________________________

Action Plan: ______________________________

______________________________

## Activity 2: Role-Playing Exercise: Examining On-the-Job Behavior

In this activity, you will rate three workers on the basis of what they tell you about themselves. Three class members will read the following scripts. Based on what they say, rate them as co-workers using the following scale:

1 = I would really enjoy working with this person.

2 = This person would be OK to work with.

3 = I don't think I'd like working with this person.

4 = Working with this person would be terrible.

When all the scripts have been read, discuss what you liked and did not like about these co-workers. Then, as a class, or working in groups of three or four, come up with an action plan for improvement for each worker.

**Co-worker #1:** ______________________________

My co-workers say that I'm friendly and generous. I always introduce myself to the new workers and invite them to have lunch. Sort of breaks the ice, right? Me and some of the other workers, well, we kinda tease the new kids, you know? It's all in good fun. Nothing serious. Today, I shared my snack with one of the new trainees who didn't have one. That poor kid! First day on the job and car trouble! It's a long way to payday when you're new, so I offered to fix the car—no charge! I do like to talk a lot, but what the hey! Life's too short not to enjoy it. My boss says my talking interferes with my co-workers' ability to concentrate. I guess that's true. Sometimes my co-workers roll their eyes and put their hands over their ears when they see me coming!

Rating: ______________________________

Could this person be a better co-worker? If so, how?______________

______________________________

______________________________

______________________________

**Co-worker #2:** ______________________________

I work really hard. Most of the crew is on the job at 6:00 A.M., but I usually get in earlier and stay late. I don't put in for overtime either. My boss says I'm really good at my job. I've overheard some of my co-workers say that I'm impatient. Well, I'm only impatient with people who don't do their jobs right. I don't talk much with the other workers, but I'm pretty close with the boss. The boss likes to get my advice. I don't believe in beating around the bush and always say exactly what I mean. I don't care for gossip—I guess that's why I don't talk much with the other workers. They gossip a lot and just waste a lot of time. I've got lots of experience, and I don't hold with these youngsters calling me by my first name. They can show me some respect, just like *I* used to show respect to people who were older than me.

Rating: ______________________________

Could this person be a better co-worker? If so, how?______________

______________________________

______________________________

______________________________

**Co-worker #3: ______________________________________________**

I've been with the company for about 10 years. My co-workers say that I have a great sense of humor, and I'm friendly with everyone. I do gossip. I'll admit it. But so does everyone! Two of my co-workers got really mad at me today. Said I smiled in their faces and then stabbed them in the back by gossiping! Well, how would they know unless they gossip too? Enough of that. I like my job a lot. The best part is when I get to train new workers. My boss says I'm a natural-born teacher. I don't really enjoy teaching people who take forever to get it—know what I mean? It's more fun to teach people who catch on fast. But I'll stick with anyone I train, even if it takes twice as long. Some people can't help it if they're dumber than other people.

Rating: ______________________________________________

Could this person be a better co-worker? If so, how?________________

______________________________________________________________

______________________________________________________________

______________________________________________________________

## Group Activities

### Activity 3: Role-Playing Exercise: Teaching Effectively

This activity requires two people: a trainer and a trainee. Those assigned to play the roles will read the script out loud, and everyone will discuss the questions that follow. Role-players should follow the acting cues written in parentheses.

Trainer: ____________________________

Trainee: ____________________________

**Trainer:** We have to waterproof the interior wall of this foundation today. Do you know how to do waterproofing?

**Trainee:** Nope.

**Trainer:** OK, the first step is removing the paint from the wall. Then we have to clean it. That's the easy part.

**Trainee:** OK, I'm with you.

**Trainer:** Next, you have to open up the can of waterproof coating, but put on your safety gloves and goggles first. Before you can do the whole wall, you have to test the coating on a small part to make sure it's gonna work. Got it?

**Trainee:** *(Stare off into the distance, and don't answer.)*

**Trainer:** *(Sigh in disgust and frown.)* Yo! Are you gonna listen to me or what? Or do you want to do this yourself? You mess it up, it's gonna be your responsibility to fix it!

**Trainee:** *(Look annoyed.)* Sorry, I got distracted.

**Trainer:** *(Frown.)* Fine. Don't let it happen again, all right? I don't like having to teach you this stuff, and you're not making it any easier on me. Now put a little bit of the coating on the wall, working it into the concrete in a circular motion. Then smooth it out. Let it cure for a couple of hours, but check it out every half hour or so and mist it. Got it?

**Trainee:** Yeah—check every half hour and mist it. Gotcha.

**Trainer:** After it's done curing, use a ball peen hammer to try shearing the coating off the wall. If it shears off cleanly, that's not good. Clean the wall again and then do the test again. If the coating doesn't stick the second time, that means we have to waterproof the outside wall first.

**Trainee:** OK…if it doesn't work the second time, should I try it a third time?

**Trainer:** *(Sigh in disgust.)* No—if it doesn't work the second time, it's probably not gonna work the third time either. You'll have to waterproof the exterior wall.

**Trainee:** OK, but what if it does stick the second time?

**Trainer:** Then the wall's fine—mix enough of the coating to do the whole wall, but just do one section at a time. Let it cure, then do a second coat.

**Trainee:** All right, I got it. First I clean the wall, then I mix up a little bit and do the test.

**Trainer:** Don't forget the safety goggles!

**Trainee:** *(Frown.)* Yeah, yeah, I heard you the first time. If it sticks, cool—I do the whole thing. If not, try the test again. If it sticks, do the whole wall. If not, we have to waterproof the exterior wall.

**Trainer:** Right. Now I hope you do it right because I don't want to have to go over this again.

**Trainee:** Don't worry, I will.

### *Discussion Questions*

1. What things did the trainer do well?
2. What could the trainer have done better?
3. What do you think of the trainer's attitude?
4. What did the trainee do well?
5. What could the trainee have done better?
6. What do you think of the trainee's attitude?

## Activity 4: Getting to Know Your Co-Workers

Choose another member of the class, and pretend that the two of you are co-workers. Then conduct an interview to complete the following worksheet. Your goal is to learn more about your co-worker. Write down the interview answers on a separate sheet of paper. When you have completed the interview, consider these questions:

1. What surprised me about this interview?
2. What interesting things did I learn about my classmate or co-worker?

### *Co-Worker Interview Worksheet*

1. What is your full name?
2. Where were you born and raised? Where do you live now?
3. What is your specialty in construction? Why did you choose that specialty?
4. What are your hobbies and interests?
5. Do you see someone on a regular basis? Are you married? Do you have any children?
6. What accomplishments in your life are you most proud of?
7. What part of your job gives you the most satisfaction?
8. What causes you the most frustration on the job?
9. What kinds of people do you like working with? What kinds of people don't you like working with?
10. What five words would you use to describe yourself?
11. Do you think your co-workers like working with you? How do you think other people would describe you?
12. What are your hopes and dreams for the future?

When you are back on the job, try using these questions and this interviewing technique to learn more about someone you actually work with.

## Activity 5: Team Design Project

### *Materials Required*

- Three pieces of cardboard
- Markers of various colors

This activity will let you practice working toward a common goal with others. Work in teams of three. Your team is responsible for designing three letters—A, B, and C. Work with your team to decide the size, color, shape, and style of the letters. You must come up with a common design, because the letters will be used to make a sign. To successfully complete this task, you will all have to agree on several things:

- What style of letter will the team choose?
- Who will draw the letters? Each of us? One of us?
- What color should the letters be? Can there be more than one color?
- How will we resolve any disputes?

When you finish this activity discuss these questions:

1. What was the hardest part of the exercise?
2. What was the easiest part?
3. What did you learn about your co-workers' working styles?
4. What did you learn about your co-workers' learning styles?

## Activity 6: Building a Work Crew

This activity will give you practice in choosing a crew that you think will work well together. You won't often get a chance to do this in the real world. However, this exercise will help you understand how different personalities can affect the success of a crew and the outcome of a project.

Form teams of three or four, and write team members' names below. Read the construction project and decide which workers you want to work on it. When considering who will work on the project, you must consider not only skills, but also personality traits that may affect a worker's ability to work with others.

**Team Members**

1.____________________ 2.____________________

3.____________________ 4.____________________

**Construction project:** Your company is building a new terminal for a regional airport. The building owner has asked the architect to change the plans to add baby-changing stations to five men's restrooms. The new plans call for the addition of a drop-in sink and a cabinet to hold the sink and supplies. There is an electrical conduit where the sink drain must go. In addition, the cabinet requires a special countertop to ensure that babies don't accidentally roll off the counter. Two new walls—a full wall and a knee wall—must be constructed and finished for each station. This change could throw the schedule off, but with a good work crew, you feel confident that the project can be completed on time. Based on the work that must be done, you must choose five team members—one from each trade—from among the following workers:

**Carpenters**
**Pete:** A good, experienced carpenter. Pete is a loner who is often difficult to talk to and work with.
**Janice:** An outstanding carpenter, known for her fine work. Lately, Janice has been getting in late and leaving early.
**Chanelle:** A good carpenter with about four months' experience. Chanelle works fast, always wants to learn something new, and enjoys her job.

**Plumbers**

**Mike:** An outstanding plumber. Mike has a big ego and often makes co-workers feel stupid, especially those who don't know as much about plumbing as he does.

**Ahmed:** A good plumber. Ahmed has some carpentry skills as well and helped out the carpenters when their team was short a member last week.

**Jorge:** A good plumber who just became a journeyman. Jorge speaks English as a second language and has a few problems here and there with some words and phrases.

**Electricians**

**K.C.:** A good electrician who works quickly and neatly. K.C. has problems working with people from different ethnic backgrounds.

**Zack:** A good electrician who is also quick. Zack likes to tell jokes about everything, including women and minorities.

**Jenna:** A trainee who has just become a journeyman. Jenna is known for her ability to get people to work together as a team but sometimes has trouble meeting deadlines.

**Painters**

**Kwanlee:** A skilled, quick, and neat painter. Kwanlee tends to gossip about co-workers and spread rumors.

**P.J.:** A skilled painter. P.J. loves coming to work and others enjoy his upbeat personality. P.J. sometimes leaves a messy work area behind.

**Goran:** A skilled and neat painter. Goran does not like to be rushed and prefers to work quietly and alone but is cordial to co-workers.

**Cabinetmakers**

**Nadia:** An able craftworker. Nadia is quick witted and funny and tends to interrupt co-workers and finish their sentences for them.

**C.C.:** Fast, neat, and thorough. C.C. has a chip on her shoulder and feels that she works harder than everyone else and should be paid more.

**Ben:** A great craftworker with 20 years of experience. Ben is cordial and polite with co-workers but believes that women don't belong in construction.

**Workers Selected**

1. ______________________ 4. ______________________

2. ______________________ 5. ______________________

3. ______________________

### Discussion Questions

1. What do you think happens to productivity when workers won't work together as a team?
2. What ideas do you have for helping individuals work together as a team?

# Diversity in the Workplace

## Self-Assessment

### How comfortable are you with workplace diversity?

How comfortable do you feel when working with people who are different from you? Take this self-assessment quiz to find out. Choose your level of agreement with each statement. Be sure you answer the questions truthfully.

| | Strongly Agree | Sometimes Agree | Don't Agree |
|---|---|---|---|
| 1. I prefer to work with people who are from the same culture or background as me. | ☐ | ☐ | ☐ |
| 2. I think it's OK to use slang words to refer to people from ethnic groups that are different from mine. | ☐ | ☐ | ☐ |
| 3. I resent it when I have to work with people who look different from me. | ☐ | ☐ | ☐ |
| 4. I am most comfortable when working with people in the same age group as mine. | ☐ | ☐ | ☐ |
| 5. I get angry when people speak a language different from mine on the job. | ☐ | ☐ | ☐ |
| 6. I think that women workers do not belong on the construction site. | ☐ | ☐ | ☐ |
| 7. I think that promotions should go to the "true Americans" before they go to immigrants. | ☐ | ☐ | ☐ |
| 8. I would find it difficult to work for a supervisor who is from a culture that is different from mine. | ☐ | ☐ | ☐ |
| 9. I think that people who share a common culture or background all think and act the same way. | ☐ | ☐ | ☐ |
| 10. I think that life would be a lot easier if everyone believed in the same values and acted in the same way. | ☐ | ☐ | ☐ |

***Scoring:*** Give yourself 1 point for each "Strongly Agree" you checked, 2 points for each "Sometimes Agree," and 3 points for each "Don't Agree." Enter the total for each in the spaces provided. Multiply each by the factors shown, and then add up your total score.

| | | | |
|---|---|---|---|
| Strongly Agree | ________ | × 1 = | ________ |
| Sometimes Agree | ________ | × 2 = | ________ |
| Don't Agree | ________ | × 3 = | ________ |
| TOTAL | | | ________ |

***Assessment:***

25–30 points: You are quite comfortable working with people from a variety of backgrounds. This module will teach you even more about diversity in the workplace.

18–24 points: You can get along with different types of people, but you may harbor some resentment against them. This module will help you become a better team player.

10–17 points: You have difficulties working with people who are different from you. This module will help you better understand diversity in the workplace.

## Introduction

The Bureau of Labor Statistics (a bureau of the U.S. Department of Labor) collects information about the U.S. workforce. According to its report titled *Working in the 21st Century,* the workforce is changing. Before 1980, the largest segment of the overall U.S. workforce was composed of white men. In the 21st century, Asians and Hispanics will make up the fastest growing part of the labor force. In addition, before 1980, relatively few women, especially women with young children, worked outside the home. Today, in approximately 63 percent of American families, both parents work, and about 75 percent of all single mothers are in the labor force. America's workforce is also getting older. The median age of workers increased from 34 in 1978 to 38 in 1998 and is expected to continue increasing.

Of the 116 million workers in the United States, just over 6 million, or 5.1 percent, are employed in the construction industry. The construction industry is the second-largest employer in the nation; only the U.S. government, which includes the armed forces, employs more people.

White men currently make up the largest percentage of workers in the construction industry. However, in many parts of the country, Hispanic men are being hired for construction jobs in greater numbers, and in some areas they make up the largest percentage of the local construction workforce. Although they remain in the minority, women are also entering the construction field. In fact, you will find people of every age, race, sexual orientation, color, gender, ability, and ethnic background in construction jobs. Learning to work with people who don't share your background is essential to your success in the construction industry. In this module, we'll talk about workplace diversity, and we'll show how you can succeed in a diverse workplace.

## What is diversity?

The word *diversity* is used often today, but what does it mean? Diversity refers to the many different, or diverse, kinds of people on a job site. People can be different from one another in many ways. Here are just a few examples: gender, race, nationality, religion, and age.

For many years, America was called a "melting pot." It was assumed that immigrants would leave their cultures behind. Today, though, it is widely recognized that people bring their cultures with them wherever they go, including the workplace. The result is a rich, new, and interesting mixture that some people refer to as a "cultural mosaic" or a "tossed salad" to which each culture contributes while remaining distinct.

Diversity enriches our lives, bringing a wealth of perspectives and experiences to our friendships and the workplace. However, diversity can also cause tension. Negative influences such as stereotyping, prejudice, and discrimination can prevent you from building good relationships with people who are different from you.

## Working with diversity

Throughout this book, we've talked about the importance of respecting your company, supervisors, and co-workers. That means respecting everyone, not just those who are like you. Let respect be your guide, and you will receive respect in return. Here are some further tips for making the most of diversity:

**1. Remember that everyone can contribute to the team.** Consider these questions:

- Who can solve a problem more quickly: a younger worker or an older worker?
- Who should your company hire: a worker who speaks only English or a worker who speaks two or more languages?
- Who can get supplies moved more efficiently: a worker with a disability or one without a disability? a trainee or a master craftworker?
- Who is a more patient worker: a man or a woman?
- Who should be promoted first: someone who was born in America or someone who has immigrated to this country? an older worker or a younger worker?
- Who will do the best job: whites? African-Americans? Asians? Hispanics? men? women? gay or lesbian workers? straight workers?

There is no right answer to these questions, just as people are not right or wrong because of the way they look or sound. Learn to appreciate others for their individual talents and abilities, and try not to prejudge them.

**2. Be aware of cultural differences, and make allowances for them.** For example, respect the different ways that people worship and celebrate holidays. Be aware that some religions require believers to act in certain ways at certain times. You may think that some of these requirements are odd, but you must respect them just as you want others to respect your religious practices.

In addition, people from different cultures may approach a similar problem in entirely different ways. For example, people from Asia tend to solve problems as a group, with each member having input, while Americans tend to favor the "rugged individual" approach. There usually is no best way to solve a problem, so be open to new ideas.

**3. Never make fun of those who are different from you.** This is a simple rule of life, but it's amazing how many people don't follow it. Remember the empathy rule. Think about how you would feel if someone made fun of you, your family, your religion, or your way of speaking.

**4. Look for common ground.** We all know people with whom we have nothing in common. On the job, you'll undoubtedly work with some people who don't share your background, beliefs, or culture. However, you are all working on the same project and have similar goals. Those goals include doing quality work, finishing the job on time, and earning a good living for yourselves and your families. Focus on what you have in common, and it will be much easier to accept differences.

**5. Think before you speak or act.** In a diverse workforce, you will work with people who are different from you in many ways. Although it's easy to focus on how we are all different, it's better to think about ways in which we are the same. All workers want similar things. They want to be

- Treated as individuals and not as a member of a group with only one way of thinking and acting
- Valued for their skills, talents, and experience
- Treated with respect
- Accepted as members of the team

Above all else, always remember to view others as individuals. Never let any idea you have about a group affect your perception of an individual. During your career, you will encounter people from a wide variety of backgrounds. You may even work on a project in another country. It is to your benefit to learn how to adapt to other cultures, or even (if your job requires it) learn another language.

## Potential problems to watch for

When working with others, you should be on guard against three pitfalls that could damage your working relationships. These pitfalls are stereotyping, prejudice, and discrimination.

### Stereotyping

A stereotype is an unfair, untrue, and often negative description of a group. Consider these two statements: "Athletes are all muscle and no brain," and "All construction workers are uneducated." If you stop and think, you can see that these statements are mean-spirited, unfair, and simply not true.

Stereotyping is especially cruel because it hides the qualities and skills of individuals. To avoid stereotyping others, ask yourself the following questions:

- **Am I being fair?** Put yourself in the other person's shoes. How would you feel if others ignored your individuality and made general assumptions about you because of your race, color, sex, sexual orientation, religion, national origin, age, or disability?
- **Is this stereotype based on something that happened to me in the past?** At some point in the past, you may have had a negative experience with someone from a certain racial or ethnic group. Does this mean that you should harbor negative feelings about *everyone* in that group? Of course not.
- **Where did I learn this stereotype?** Think back and try to figure out how the stereotype developed. Did family members or friends convey it to you? If so, why do those people feel as they do? Did they have a negative experience that they passed on to you?

## Prejudice

Prejudice occurs when people prejudge others without knowing anything about them as individuals. In fact, prejudice leads to stereotyping. The two most common kinds of prejudice are racism (prejudice based on race) and ageism (prejudice based on age). Some of the worst tragedies of humankind, such as slavery in the United States, the Holocaust in Nazi-occupied Europe, and the murder of many Kurdish people in the Middle East, have their roots in prejudice.

Prejudice can lead people to make all kinds of mistakes, from turning down an offer of friendship to actively harassing people who are different. Actions based on prejudice can interfere with your job performance. Don't ever refuse to work with people because you feel prejudiced against them. Rather, take the time to get to know them as individuals. Ask them about their friends, their families, their hopes and dreams. You'll quickly find out that you have much more in common than you think.

## Discrimination

Discrimination occurs when workers are denied opportunities, raises, or promotions because of their race, color, sex, sexual orientation, religion, national origin, age, or disability. Discrimination is illegal, and a number of federal and state laws prohibit employers from discriminating. Like stereotyping and prejudice, discrimination is mean-spirited and unfair. All workers are entitled to equal treatment in the workplace. To avoid discriminating against others, make sure you treat everyone equally, and always remember the empathy rule. How would you feel if you were discriminated against?

### *On-the-Job Quiz*

Here's a quick quiz that asks you to apply what you've learned in this module.

1. One of your co-workers must leave early one day to celebrate Passover and has asked for your help to finish a task. (Passover requires Jews to stop work by sundown so that they may worship in the traditional way.) What is your best course of action?
   a. Give your co-worker a hand and help finish the work.
   b. Complain to your supervisor that your co-worker is trying to cheat the company out of time.
   c. Convert to Judaism, so that you can leave early too.
   d. Explain that while you respect your co-worker's religion, you don't share the belief and can't help finish the work.

2. You are working with a Muslim whose religion, Islam, requires Muslims to kneel and pray five times a day. You've just started a new project that will last two weeks. What is your best course of action?
   a. Tell your co-worker that the job site is no place for prayer.
   b. Say that you respect the religion, but in America people don't stop working to pray.
   c. Say nothing at all—just count the days until the two weeks are up.
   d. Work out a schedule so that when it's time to pray, you are not doing any task that requires both of you.
3. You've just started a new job, and you're surprised to find that your team members include an Asian-American man, a young Hispanic woman, and an older man. What is your best course of action?
   a. Assume the role of team leader and tell your co-workers how they should do their jobs.
   b. Do your work and have as little to do with your co-workers as possible.
   c. Tell your boss that you'd rather work with people of your own age and background and that you would like to be transferred to another team as soon as possible.
   d. Tell your co-workers a little bit about yourself, get to know them as individuals, and try to learn things you share in common.
4. A female electrician has just joined your team. When you meet her, what is your best course of action?
   a. Hug her and say, "Welcome aboard, sweetie."
   b. Shake her hand and welcome her to the job.
   c. Say that the work is very hard and you don't think she will like doing it or last very long at the job.
   d. Tell her to make a muscle, squeeze it, and say approvingly that she seems strong enough to do the job.
5. One of your co-workers has been with the company for 15 years. The younger workers make a lot of jokes about older people. They often use terms such as "geezer" and "old-timer." They say that their attitude and remarks are all in good fun. If asked to comment on this behavior, you should say, _____
   a. "As long as the older worker is OK with it, it's totally fine."
   b. "It's mean-spirited and disrespectful to treat older workers this way."
   c. "On a construction site, you have to know how to take a joke."
   d. "No one really cares about this 'touchy-feely' stuff, especially the older workers."

**6.** Your supervisor has recently hired a Hispanic worker to help out around the job site. At present, your new co-worker speaks only a little English. You should assume that your co-worker _____.
   a. is probably in the United States to collect welfare
   b. is probably in the United States illegally
   c. has probably come to the United States to seek a better life
   d. is taking a job away from a "real American"

**7.** A worker with a prosthetic (artificial) arm and hand is assigned to your team. You have never been around anyone with this type of disability before. What is your best course of action?
   a. Show pity for your co-worker, but assume that you will have to do extra work.
   b. Tell your co-worker how sorry you are and say that you will try to do things to make the job easier.
   c. Ask your co-worker to tell you how the disability happened and to explain how the prosthetic device works.
   d. Get to know your co-worker as an individual and make accommodations for the disability as needed.

**8.** A co-worker doesn't understand the meaning of the word *stereotype*, so you provide a few examples. What is *not* an example of stereotyping?
   a. All workers want to earn a good salary to support themselves and their families.
   b. All male construction workers are beer drinkers.
   c. All female workers are too emotional to do construction work.
   d. People with backgrounds different from mine are troublemakers.

**9.** You have a good friend at work who often makes racist remarks and tells jokes about others from different backgrounds. What is your best course of action?
   a. Laugh at the jokes, if they're funny.
   b. Ask where this prejudice comes from, and explain why you believe that prejudice and stereotypes are unfair.
   c. Say that these jokes are OK outside of work but not on the job.
   d. Keep quiet and don't say anything.

**10.** If you are a supervisor and you _____, your company could be fined for discrimination.
   a. reprimand an African-American worker for coming in late several times in one week
   b. reprimand an Asian-American worker who is not wearing safety gear
   c. refuse to promote a female worker because you think women don't belong in construction
   d. provide a special tool so that a disabled worker can perform assigned tasks

## Individual Activities

### Activity 1: Expanding Your Awareness of Cultural Diversity

Cultural differences can cause problems ranging from simple misunderstandings to hate crimes. To expand your cultural awareness, see how many of the following questions you can answer correctly. Don't look for the answers in this module—they're not here! This quiz will help you increase your multicultural knowledge, so don't feel upset if you get a low score. Instead, look on this activity as a learning experience.

**1.** According to statistics compiled by the FBI, the greatest growth in hate crimes in recent years is against _____.
a. Asian-Americans, gays, and lesbians
b. Blacks, Arabs, and Jews
c. Women, Latinos, and Muslims

**2.** The Bureau of Labor Statistics projects that by the end of the year 2010, approximately _________ of the U.S. workforce will be composed of women and minorities.
a. 30 percent
b. 50 percent
c. 80 percent

**3.** The National Association of Women in Construction was founded by a small group of women construction workers in _____.
a. 1983
b. 1963
c. 1953

**4.** Older people are making up a larger percentage of the U.S. workforce. The median age of the workforce in 1970 was 27. (Median means middle, so half of the workers are younger and half are older than the median age.) What do you think the median age of the workforce will be in 2008?
a. 41
b. 35
c. 30

**5.** Many women get paid less than men for doing the same job. As of 2002, for every $1 earned by a man, a woman in a similar job earned _____.
a. 95 cents
b. 88 cents
c. 76 cents

6. When disabled people are asked what problem they face most often in the workplace, what do you think they say?
   a. Being asked too often about their disability.
   b. Being resented by others who think that disabled people receive special treatment.
   c. Being asked to perform tasks that are beyond their abilities.
7. After English, the most commonly spoken language in the United States is _____.
   a. French
   b. Spanish
   c. Japanese
8. According to the U.S. Census for the year 2000, Asians made up _____ of the total population of the United States.
   a. 18 percent
   b. 12 percent
   c. 4 percent
9. The 1992 U.S. Census reported that there were ________disabled workers in the construction trades.
   a. about half a million
   b. about one million
   c. fewer than 500,000
10. In 2002, _____ of women working in construction were working as subcontractors.
    a. 43 percent
    b. 28 percent
    c. 18 percent

## Activity 2: Examining Differences in Communication Styles Between Men and Women

Recent research has shown that men and women tend to communicate very differently. Because women and men are working together more often in construction jobs, it pays to be aware of these differences.

Some of the differences in communication styles between men and women are listed in the chart titled Communication Styles. For each style, mark "M" if you think this style is more typical of men or "W" if you think it is more typical of women. In the third column, offer some tips for how the opposite sex can better work with each communication style. We completed the first entry as an example.

**Communication Styles**

| M or W? | Communication Style | Tips for the Opposite Sex |
|---|---|---|
| M | 1. These people communicate mostly for information. They're not usually into talking about their feelings or their emotional needs. | Women should not take it personally if men don't want to discuss their feelings or if men want to discuss only business on the job site. |
| | 2. These people often like to base their relationships on shared personal experiences and feelings. | |
| | 3. These people like to talk quite a bit—for them, it's the "glue" that holds relationships together. | |
| | 4. These people tend to base their friendships and relationships around activities, such as going places together or playing sports. | |
| | 5. These people are more often loners and have fewer close friendships. | |
| | 6. These people prefer to avoid confrontation. They would rather build consensus or give in than fight or argue. | |
| | 7. These people can be aggressive and often enjoy confrontation or competition. They can even become friendly with the people they feel most competitive with. | |
| | 8. These people tend to make more direct eye contact and to sit closer to other people. | |
| | 9. When these people talk about their problems, they prefer that someone listen to them instead of offering solutions. | |
| | 10. When these people talk about problems, their main goal is to find a solution. They're not really looking for emotional or moral support. | |

The information in this table is based on the work of Deborah Tannen. For more information, read her books *You Just Don't Understand* (New York: Ballentine, 1990) and *Talking from 9 to 5* (New York: Morrow, 1994).

# Group Activities

## Activity 3: Empathizing with Differences

One of the best ways to understand other people is to put yourself in their place. For this activity, you will work in groups of three or four. Have each member of your team read the questions; then discuss them. Your goal is to think about a time when you felt different from other people—a time when you felt you didn't fit in. For example, maybe you went to a restaurant where everybody was dressed up, and you were wearing jeans and a T-shirt. Or you were the only man in a room full of women. Or you were the only white person in a group of black people. Or you went to a party where you were the only person without a date.

**Team Members**

1. ______________________ 2. ______________________

3. ______________________ 4. ______________________

### *Discussion Questions*

1. Describe the situation. Who was there? When did it occur? What exactly happened?
2. How did the other people treat you? Did they make you feel different, either by looking at you strangely or making a comment? Or did they try to include you and make you feel comfortable?
3. How did you feel at the time? How did you behave? Do you think you handled the situation well? If not, what would you do differently if you found yourself in the same situation again?
4. Did the situation help you understand yourself better?
5. How can you learn from your experience? How can this experience help you work better with people from different age groups and other cultures or backgrounds?

## Activity 4: Understanding Diversity in Yourself and Others

This activity will help you take a closer look at yourself and learn something about another person. The goal is to help you see diversity in yourself and others. Following are two Diversity Questionnaires. Fill out the first one for yourself. Then interview a classmate to complete the second Diversity Questionnaire. (Your instructor may want you to take a questionnaire to the job site to interview a co-worker. If so, record your in-class interview on a separate sheet of paper so that you'll have a blank interview form to use at work.)

After interviewing your classmate or co-worker, ask yourself the following questions: Did any of the answers surprise you? What have you learned from this activity? Has this activity changed the way you think about the person?

### *Diversity Questionnaire: Your Personal Diversity*

Answer these questions yourself. You do not have to answer any questions you do not feel comfortable answering.

1. What is your name?

   ______________________________

   List any languages you speak in addition to English.

   ______________________________

2. What are your ethnic backgrounds?

   ______________________________

3. Do you think others hold stereotypes of people from your background?

   ______________________________

   If so, what are they? Do you think these stereotypes are true?

   ______________________________

   ______________________________

4. What is your religious background?

   ______________________________

5. Name something that people might be surprised to know about you.

   ______________________________

6. List one or two misconceptions that other people hold about you.

   ______________________________

7. List three words that accurately describe you.

   ______________________________

8. Complete the following sentences:
   a. If I could visit any place on earth, I'd visit
   b. If I could do anything I wanted for a career, I would be a(n)
   c. The quality I value most in another person is
   d. The person who has influenced me the most is
   e. Something that makes me really mad is
   f. If I could excel in any one sport, I'd choose
   g. I'm better than most people at
   h. I think my co-workers would describe me as
9. Have you ever experienced prejudice from other people? If so, describe the situation. How did you react?
10. Do you think you ever have the tendency to be prejudiced? If so, against whom?

    Why do you hold this prejudice? What steps can you take to eliminate it?

## Diversity Questionnaire: Your Classmate or Teammate

Interview your classmate or teammate and record answers to these questions. Skip any questions your interviewee does not feel comfortable answering.

1. What is your name?

   List any languages you speak in addition to English.

2. What are your ethnic backgrounds?

3. Do you think others hold stereotypes of people from your background?

   If so, what are they? Do you think these stereotypes are true?

4. What is your religious background?

5. Name something that people might be surprised to know about you.

6. List one or two misconceptions that other people hold about you.

7. List three words that accurately describe you.

8. Complete the following sentences:

   a. If I could visit any place on earth, I'd visit

   b. If I could do anything I wanted for a career, I would be a(n)

   c. The quality I value most in another person is

   d. The person who has influenced me the most is

e. Something that makes me really mad is

f. If I could excel in any one sport, I'd choose

g. I'm better than most people at

h. I think my co-workers would describe me as

9. Have you ever experienced prejudice from other people? If so, describe the situation. How did you react?

10. Do you think you ever have the tendency to be prejudiced? If so, against whom?

Why do you hold this prejudice? What steps can you take to eliminate it?

Describe three positive things about your classmate or teammate.

## Activity 5: What Makes Us Different from One Another?

You have learned a lot about diversity in this module. In this exercise, you will list all the things that make other people different from you. We have provided one difference for you. When you have finished making your list, work in groups of three or four to discuss the following questions.

**Team Members**

1. ______________________ 2. ______________________
3. ______________________ 4. ______________________

***How Others Are Different from Me***

1. Gender
2. ______________________
3. ______________________
4. ______________________
5. ______________________
6. ______________________
7. ______________________
8. ______________________
9. ______________________
10. ______________________

### Discussion Questions

1. As I move along in my career in construction, what might I learn from those who are different from me?
2. How do the differences I have listed affect someone's ability to learn the construction trade and be a good team member?

## Activity 6: Standing in Another's Shoes

Throughout this module, you have been asked to imagine what it is like to stand in another person's shoes. In this activity, you will do just that, along with some other activities that will show you what it is like to deal with the world as disabled workers must.

### *Materials Required*

- Large bandanna
- An empty box and several boxes of paper clips, pencils, pens, erasers, and buttons
- A timer or watch that can easily measure one minute
- Masking tape
- Cotton balls or earplugs
- Chalk and chalkboard or markers and flipchart

Each of the following activities will show you what it is like to work with a disability. After trying the activities, discuss the questions that follow with your classmates.

1. Have a classmate fasten the bandanna across your eyes and put an empty box and a mix of paper clips, pencils, pens, erasers, and buttons on the table or desk in front of you. You have one minute to sort the items into piles and place only the paper clips and buttons in the box.
2. Have a classmate use masking tape to tape the fingers of one of your hands, including your thumb, together. If you are right-handed, have your right hand taped; if you are left-handed, have your left hand taped. Now, using only your taped-up hand, try to pick up one paper clip or button at a time and place it in a box. Then, using your untaped hand, write the following information on the board or flipchart:
   - Your name
   - Your address
   - Your construction specialty
3. Stuff cotton balls into your ears, or use earplugs. Have a classmate give you directions. Your classmate should speak in a low tone of voice or mumble while turning away from you several times.
4. Pour a few handfuls of buttons into your shoes. Walk around the room several times.

### Discussion Questions

1. What does it feel like to be blind or have diminished hearing?
2. How did you feel when you could not use your hand?
3. How did you feel when you could not walk easily without pain?
4. Did you want your classmates to feel sorry for you?
5. Did you feel that, with a little help, you could still perform your job well?
6. Do you know any disabled workers? What kinds of tasks do they perform?
7. What can you do at work to accommodate disabled workers?
8. It is very likely that while doing this exercise, you or your classmates laughed a lot. Talk about why you laughed and whether that is an appropriate reaction.

## Activity 7: The Tolerance Profile

What makes a person tolerant or intolerant? In this activity, you and your classmates will develop two profiles. Look at the following list and put an X next to words that you think describe a tolerant person. Put an O next to words that you think describe an intolerant person. Then discuss the questions that follow the list.

**Team Members**

1.____________________ 2.____________________

3.____________________ 4.____________________

| X or O | Qualities and Characteristics | X or O | Qualities and Characteristics |
|---|---|---|---|
| | Friendly | | Self-confident |
| | Judgmental | | Narrow-minded |
| | Prejudiced | | Frightened |
| | Open-minded | | Compassionate |
| | Suspicious | | Jealous |
| | Willing to listen | | Impatient |
| | Curious | | Bossy |
| | Outgoing | | Focused inward on the self |

*(continued)*

| X or O | Qualities and Characteristics | X or O | Qualities and Characteristics |
|---|---|---|---|
| | Quiet | | Talkative |
| | Brave | | Reasonable |
| | Imaginative | | Miserable |
| | Pushy | | Even-tempered |
| | Patient | | Helpful |
| | Bitter | | Unhappy |
| | Inconsiderate | | Unreasonable |
| | Upbeat | | Thin-skinned |
| | Focused outward to the world | | Perfectionist |
| | Resistant to change | | Unwilling to listen |

## Discussion Questions

1. Which of these characteristics do I admire most in a person?
2. Which of these characteristics do I value the most in myself?
3. What things can I do to achieve the characteristics I most admire and value?
4. Did all of the team members agree on the qualities of a tolerant person? Of an intolerant person? Discuss qualities on which you disagreed.

## Activity 8: Your Turn—Do Something to Improve Tolerance at Work

There are a lot of books and articles that can help you become more tolerant toward those who are different from you. But no one knows your workplace better than you do. Chances are, you can come up with very good ideas to help build tolerance for diversity at your job site. In this activity, you and your classmates will exchange ideas that can help make your workplace pleasant and productive for everyone. Work in groups of three or four and consider the following questions.

**Team Members**

1. ______________________ 2. ______________________

3. ______________________ 4. ______________________

1. Are there groups of people at work that I avoid because I feel prejudice toward them? What can I do to get to know these people better?
2. Do I always take my breaks and eat my meals with the same group of people? What can I do to include other people in our group?
3. Are there any after-work activities that my co-workers and I might participate in that would help us get to know one another better? Can we create such activities?
4. Can we come up with a list of at least 10 things we can do to improve tolerance for diversity at work?

## Activity 9: Dealing with Language Diversity

You may feel that your job is hard enough without having to learn another language, but you may be surprised to find out that you already know a lot of words in another language. On U.S. construction sites today, the most commonly spoken language besides English is Spanish. In this activity, you and your classmates will translate the following words and phrases into English or Spanish. (Note that many Spanish words end in *o* or *a* depending on whether they apply to a man or a woman or whether the word is grammatically masculine or feminine.)

Don't worry if you don't know how to translate the words. The purpose of this exercise is to make you aware of another language. You will review the correct translations with your instructor. After you write those translations down, you will know several words and phrases in English or Spanish.

**Team Members**

1. ______________________ 2. ______________________

3. ______________________ 4. ______________________

| | Translate Into | |
|---|---|---|
| **Word or Phrase** | **English** | **Spanish** |
| Hello | | |
| What is your name? | | |
| ¿Cómo está?<br>(Co-moh) (es-TAH)? | | |
| Adiós<br>(ah-DYOHS) | | |
| Please | | |
| Danger! | | |

| Word or Phrase | Translate Into | |
|---|---|---|
| | English | Spanish |
| ¿Por qué?<br>(pour-KAY)? | | |
| Nuevo<br>(NWAY-vo) | | |
| A little | | |
| More | | |
| Hasta la vista<br>(AH-stah) (lah) (VEE-stah) | | |
| Me llamo<br>(may) (YAH-moh) | | |
| Thank you | | |
| You're welcome | | |
| Muy bien<br>(mwee-bee-YEN) | | |
| Hasta mañana<br>(AHS-tah) (man-YAN-ah) | | |
| Boss | | |
| Problem | | |
| Vamos<br>(VAH-mos) | | |
| Respeto<br>(res-PETT-oh) | | |

## Activity 10: Diversity in the News (optional)

Your instructor may assign this activity as an optional homework assignment. Diversity is in the news every day. You may see it in positive forms, such as when people of various backgrounds work together on a community project or raise funds for a special cause. You will also see it in negative forms, such as hate crimes and demonstrations against certain groups. In this activity, you and your classmates will pull stories that deal with diversity from your local newspaper, a magazine, or the Internet. Bring the stories into class and discuss them with your classmates. Here are some questions to consider:

1. How did this story make me feel?
2. Do I agree or disagree with what the people in the story did?
3. How would I feel if the story involved a friend or relative?
4. How would I feel if hate crimes were directed toward me? Toward a friend or relative? Toward a co-worker?

# Part Two

# Communication Skills

# Communication Skills I: Listening and Speaking

## Self-Assessment

### Are You a Good Listener?

Do you have good listening habits? Take the following self-assessment quiz to find out. Be sure to answer each question honestly.

| | Always | Sometimes | Rarely |
|---|---|---|---|
| 1. I maintain eye contact when someone is talking to me. | ❑ | ❑ | ❑ |
| 2. I pay attention when someone is talking to me. | ❑ | ❑ | ❑ |
| 3. I ask questions when I don't understand something I hear. | ❑ | ❑ | ❑ |
| 4. I take notes when receiving instructions. | ❑ | ❑ | ❑ |
| 5. I repeat instructions my supervisor has given me to make sure I understand them. | ❑ | ❑ | ❑ |
| 6. I nod my head or say I understand to show others that I am listening to them. | ❑ | ❑ | ❑ |
| 7. I let others speak without interrupting. | ❑ | ❑ | ❑ |
| 8. I move to a quieter spot or ask someone to speak up if I am in a noisy location. | ❑ | ❑ | ❑ |
| 9. I put aside what I am doing when someone is speaking to me. | ❑ | ❑ | ❑ |
| 10. I listen with an open mind. | ❑ | ❑ | ❑ |

***Scoring:*** Give yourself 3 points for each "Always" you checked, 2 points for each "Sometimes," and 1 point for each "Rarely." Enter the total for each in the spaces provided. Multiply each by the factors shown, and then add up your total score.

| | | | |
|---|---|---|---|
| Always | ________ | × 3 = | ________ |
| Sometimes | ________ | × 2 = | ________ |
| Rarely | ________ | × 1 = | ________ |
| TOTAL | | | ________ |

***Assessment:***

25–30 points: You already have excellent listening habits. This module will help you review and practice your listening skills.

18–24 points: You have developed some good listening skills but can benefit from the advice presented in this module.

10–17 points: You have developed some undesirable listening habits. The goal of this module is to help you listen more effectively.

## Self-Assessment

## Are You a Good Speaker?

How good are your speaking skills? Although you can use the skills developed in this module to give a speech if necessary, the term *speaking skills* does not refer to your ability to give a speech or make a presentation to a group of people. Instead, it refers to your ability to communicate effectively, one-on-one, to others on the job every day. This self-assessment quiz will help you see your speaking strengths and weaknesses.

| | Always | Sometimes | Rarely |
|---|---|---|---|
| 1. When giving instructions to new co-workers, I explain words they might not understand. | ❑ | ❑ | ❑ |
| 2. When giving instructions for a task with several steps, I organize my thoughts first, then give the instructions. | ❑ | ❑ | ❑ |
| 3. I give more details when explaining a task to inexperienced co-workers. | ❑ | ❑ | ❑ |
| 4. When giving instructions to others, I try to keep from sounding like a know-it-all. | ❑ | ❑ | ❑ |
| 5. When giving instructions to others, I encourage them to ask questions about anything they don't understand. | ❑ | ❑ | ❑ |
| 6. I am patient and will explain instructions more than once if necessary. | ❑ | ❑ | ❑ |
| 7. I try to speak more carefully when giving instructions to a co-worker for whom English is a second language. | ❑ | ❑ | ❑ |
| 8. When speaking on the phone or over a two-way radio, I repeat instructions and spell out words when necessary. | ❑ | ❑ | ❑ |
| 9. If someone asks me a question I don't know the answer to, I admit it and then try to find out the answer. | ❑ | ❑ | ❑ |
| 10. When I give instructions to others, I am confident, upbeat, and encouraging. | ❑ | ❑ | ❑ |

***Scoring:*** Give yourself 3 points for each "Always" you checked, 2 points for each "Sometimes," and 1 point for each "Rarely." Enter the total for each in the spaces provided. Multiply each by the factors shown, and then add up your total score.

| | | | |
|---|---|---|---|
| Always | ________ | × 3 = | ________ |
| Sometimes | ________ | × 2 = | ________ |
| Rarely | ________ | × 1 = | ________ |
| TOTAL | | | ________ |

***Assessment:***

25–30 points: You have developed some excellent speaking skills. This module will help you review and practice your speaking skills.

18–24 points: You have developed some good speaking skills but can benefit from the advice presented in this module.

10–17 points: You have developed some undesirable speaking habits. The goal of this module is to help you speak more effectively.

# Introduction

What's the most important skill needed in your job? Many construction workers would say, "knowing the right way to use tools and equipment." It's true that you need good technical skills to succeed, but you also need good communication skills—listening, speaking, reading, and writing. Here are some examples of why these skills are so important on the job site:

- **Listening:** Your supervisor tells you where to set up safety barriers, but because you did not listen carefully, you miss one spot. Your co-worker falls and is injured.
- **Speaking:** You must train two co-workers to do a task, but you mumble, use words they don't understand, and don't answer their questions clearly. Your co-workers do the task incorrectly, and all of you must work overtime to fix the mistakes.
- **Reading:** Your supervisor tells you to read the manufacturer's basic operating and safety instructions for a new drill press before you use it. You don't really understand the instructions, but you don't want to bug the boss. You go ahead with what you think is correct and damage the drill press.
- **Writing:** Your boss asks you to write up a material takeoff (a supply list) for a project. You rush through the list and don't check what you've written. The supplier delivers 250 feet of PVC piping cut to your specified sizes instead of 25 feet.

As you can see, good communication on the work site has a direct effect on safety, schedules, and budgets. Improving your communication skills will make you a worker every company will want to hire. This module focuses on listening and speaking skills. Module 6 focuses on reading and writing skills.

# How communication works

Before we discuss some of the ways to become a more effective listener and speaker, it is helpful to understand how communication is supposed to work (see *Figure 5–1*). There are two basic steps to clear communication:

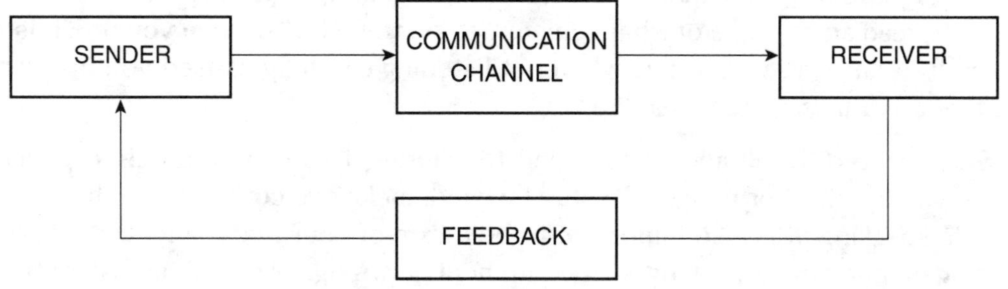


**Figure 5–1. The Communication Process**

**Step 1** A sender sends a spoken or written message through a communication channel to a receiver. (Examples of communication channels include meetings, phones, two-way radios, and email.)

**Step 2** The receiver gets the message and figures out what it means by listening or reading carefully. If anything is not clear, the receiver gives the sender feedback by asking the sender for more information.

This process is called two-way communication, and it is the most effective way to make sure that everyone understands what's going on. It sounds simple, doesn't it? Why is good two-way communication often hard to achieve? When we try to communicate, a lot of things—called noise—can get in the way. Following are some examples of communication noise:

- The sender uses work-related words, or jargon, that the receiver does not understand.
- The sender does not speak clearly.
- The sender's written message is disorganized or contains mistakes.
- The sender is not specific.
- The sender does not get to the point.
- The receiver is tired or distracted or just not paying attention.
- The receiver has poor listening or reading skills.
- Actual noise on the construction site—pneumatic hammers, earth-moving equipment, or drills—makes it physically hard to hear a message.
- There is a mechanical problem with the equipment used to communicate—for example, static on a phone or radio line.

## Becoming an effective listener

Many people think that listening just happens—someone talks and other people hear it. In fact, for effective communication to take place, the listener must take an active role. Here are some tips to help you become an effective listener:

**1. Understand the consequences of not listening.** In the introduction to this module, you read an example of what can happen on the job site when you don't listen carefully. Can you recall a time when not listening carefully caused you problems on the job or in your personal life?

**2. Stay focused.** Don't allow your mind to wander. This can be tough, especially when you are tired or hungry. To stay focused, make eye contact with the person who is speaking. It is also important to be aware of your body language. Are you staring off into space, fiddling with equipment, yawning, or slouching? All of these are signs that you are not listening. To show you are listening, you should nod your head to show agreement or understanding and ask questions if necessary.

**3. Keep an open mind.** When someone starts to say something you already know or something you disagree with, you will automatically stop listening. On a construction site, all communications are important, especially those with your supervisors. Be fair. Don't tune people out before they can get started.

**4. Take an active role to get the information you need.** If you don't understand something someone says, ask questions. If some information seems incorrect to you, question it. If you can't hear what's being said, say so. This problem may be solved by moving to a quieter spot or by simply asking the speaker to speak louder.

**5. Pay attention to the details.** Construction work is specific, so pay close attention to any communication that deals with measurements, amounts, or time. Don't be afraid to question a detail that seems wrong or unclear. Did that supplier on the phone tell you to pick up job supplies at *615* Wyant Street or *650* Wyant Street? Was that *Wyant* Street or *Wyatt* Street? Ask if that was 6-1-5 or 6-5-0 and get the street name spelled out to save yourself a trip to the wrong address.

**6. Take notes.** Get into the habit of jotting down notes to help you recall details. Supervisors appreciate it when you take careful notes. It shows them that you are taking responsibility for your work and approaching the job as a professional.

**7. Don't guess.** Suppose your supervisor tells you to change the tolerance on a machine part. Are you supposed to increase the tolerance or decrease it? By how much? Don't try to guess the answer. Ask.

**8. Ask what words mean.** When you're new on the job, you will hear words and expressions you've never heard before. For example, how would you interpret the following instructions?

- Go to the office and pick up my specs.
- Put a coat of mud on these sections of drywall.
- Rock this room this afternoon.
- The studs should be 16 inches OC.
- Make sure you read the MSDS before you open that can of solvent.

Don't be embarrassed if you don't know what something means. You are going to hear a lot of things you don't understand at first. Your boss knows this and expects you to ask questions. In construction, an unasked question can be hazardous to your health. A good job site motto is "Stay safe. Stay informed."

### *A Note on Terminology*

So what is meant by specs, mud, and rocking a room? Your boss is not asking you to pick up a pair of glasses, dig up mud to put on the wall, or play heavy metal music. What about OC, red tag, and MSDS? In case you don't already know, here is what these terms mean in construction:

**Specs:** An abbreviation for job specifications, which are the detailed descriptions of the job, including the materials needed to complete it.

**Mud:** A term that refers to joint compound, a material used to fill in the thin space (or joint) between pieces of drywall installed next to one another.

**Rock:** An abbreviation for sheetrock, or drywall, which is the material used to build interior walls.

**OC:** An abbreviation for on center, which is the measurement from the center of one stud (wall or ceiling support) to the center of the next.

**Red tag:** The act of placing a red warning tag on equipment. The tag alerts other workers to an unsafe condition.

**MSDS:** An abbreviation for material safety data sheet. An MSDS is a complete description of a product, including any safety hazards and recommendations for safe use. For example, an MSDS for a solvent may recommend wearing a respirator.

**9. Paraphrase what you've heard.** When you paraphrase, you listen to what people say to you and then say it back to them in your own words. Suppose your boss says "Red-tag this scaffold, but set a watch on it first. It's pretty shaky." You listen, then say, "OK, I'll fill out the tag and tie it on the scaffold. I'll get T.J. to keep everyone off 'til I get back." When your supervisor nods, you know you got the message right.

## Barriers to listening

As you have learned, listening well takes some work on your part. However, even when you have mastered effective listening skills, you will still have to overcome some barriers that keep the message from getting through. Following are some of those barriers, along with tips to overcome them.

- **Emotion.** When you're angry or upset, you stop listening. Try counting to 10 or ask the speaker to excuse you for a minute. Go get a drink of water and calm down.
- **Boredom.** Maybe the speaker is dull or overbearing. Maybe you think you know it all already. There is no easy tip for overcoming this barrier. You just have to force yourself to stay focused. Keep in mind that the speaker has important information you need to hear.
- **Distractions.** Anything from too much noise and activity on the site to problems at home can steal your attention. If the problem is noise, ask the speaker to move away from it. If a personal problem is keeping you from listening, concentrate harder on staying focused. In some cases, it may help if you explain to your supervisor why you are having trouble concentrating.
- **Your ego.** Do you finish people's sentences for them? Do you interrupt others a lot? Do you think about the things you are going to say instead of listening? That's your ego putting itself squarely between you and effective listening. Be aware of your ego and try to tone it down a bit so you can get the information you need.

### *Listening in the Classroom*

When you take this class, be aware of things that affect your ability to listen well. Is someone on the other side of the room speaking too softly? Is there noise out in the hall? Did your instructor say something you did not understand? Take action to correct these problems. Ask other classmates to face the class when they speak and to speak loudly. Ask permission to close the door against outside noise. Ask your instructor to explain things you don't understand.

## Becoming an effective speaker

Effective speaking is more than just talking. You have to make an effort to think about what you will say, who you will say it to, and how you will say it. When you are an effective speaker, your listeners never have to wonder what you are talking about. In this section you will learn about speaking face-to-face, speaking to a group, and speaking on the phone.

## Speaking Face-to-Face

Most of the conversations you will have on the work site will be one-on-one. You will talk to your supervisor or to individual members of your team. You can save yourself a lot of time and frustration if you follow these tips:

**1. Give clear directions.** Suppose you are a plumber's apprentice and a more experienced co-worker says, "Hey, go and get me that, uh...the right tee for this fixture. You know what I mean, right? It goes over here." Where are you supposed to go? What are you supposed to get? If your co-worker says the following, you'll know: "Hey, go out to the truck and get a 3-inch tee. Make sure you get the one that's got a 1-1/2-inch inlet on the side."

**2. Consider your listener.** You can take some shortcuts with an experienced co-worker, especially if you've been working together for a while. You must speak more carefully to inexperienced workers or to workers for whom English is a second language. In these cases, use the following tips:

- Explain terms they may not understand.
- Speak a little more slowly and try not to slur your words.
- Encourage questions.
- Demonstrate what needs to be done.
- Ask the worker to paraphrase what you have said.
- Make a sketch if appropriate.

**3. Check your tone of voice.** How you say something is often as important as what you say, so listen to yourself. Do you sound calm or angry, confident or uncertain, patient or impatient, upbeat or negative? When you are calm, confident, patient, and upbeat, your listeners will pay closer attention and respect what you say. Which of the following speakers would you listen to? Which one would you want teaching you?
**Speaker A:** "OK, listen up. I don't want to have to go over this again. I'm a construction worker, not a teacher, see? So pay attention. Let's see, what is this thing here? Is this right? OK. Look. To set this thing up you've got to, uh....hmmm. OK, *now* this looks right. Pay attention so you don't put this thing through your foot. We're gonna bust up some concrete, so listen up!"
**Speaker B:** "I'm going to show you how to set up and use this pavement breaker. This tool can be dangerous, but I'll show you how to stay safe. I'll go over the steps a couple of times first. Be sure to let me know if you have questions or don't understand something. Then I'll turn it on and use it so you can see how it works. Each of you will get a chance to practice after I do the demo, so pay attention, OK? Before we get started, let's check our safety gear."

## Speaking to a Group

At some point in your career, you may be asked to make a presentation to a group. When you make this type of presentation, you will need all of the listening and speaking skills you have learned so far. In addition, keep the following tips in mind:

**1. Get organized.** Outline what you will say and figure out how long it will take you to say it. Be sure to leave time for co-workers to ask questions. Organize any graphs, charts, or illustrations you will use. If you plan to work with a computer program during your talk, practice until you feel comfortable using it. Let your listeners know in advance how much of their time you will need.

**2. Pick a good time.** Try to pick a time when your group will be able to focus best. For example, workers are probably most attentive at the start of a shift. Avoid the hour before a meal break or the end of a shift.

**3. Address your listeners' concerns.** Some of your listeners will tune out because they already know something about your subject. Some will tune out because of other distractions. Almost everyone will tune in to "radio station WIIFM—What's In It For Me?" When you talk about the concerns and questions that are important to your listeners, they will pay closer attention.

**4. Be aware of group dynamics.** Try to address your remarks to the whole group. Avoid one-on-one conversations, and don't allow strong-willed people to take over. When someone asks a question, repeat it so that the entire group can hear what the question was.

**5. Use humor carefully.** In general, it is best to avoid telling jokes. You could offend someone without meaning to. In some cases, certain jokes may be considered harassment.

## Speaking on the Phone

When you communicate by phone, you don't have the advantage of seeing the person you are speaking to. Thus, you'll have to make a greater effort to make sure that you send and receive the right information. Following are some tips to help you do just that:

### *Making calls*

When making phone calls, you will often reach an assistant, voice mail, or an answering machine. Come up with a brief message before you make the call. This technique will save you lots of time. Here are the steps to follow when making calls:

**Step 1** Give your name and your company name and say why you are calling.

**Step 2** Speak clearly and spell out your name and company name if necessary.

**Step 3** If you contact the person you want, take notes during the call to ensure that you get the right information.

**Step 4** If you must leave a message, keep it short, and make sure the message includes your name, your company name, a contact number, and the best time to reach you.

### *Receiving calls*

Some callers may not be good communicators. You may have to ask them to identify themselves completely and state the purpose of their call. Here are some other tips for receiving calls:

- Don't just say "hello." Give your name and company name.
- Avoid leaving callers on hold. If you don't have time to talk, say so, and arrange for a better time.
- Transfer calls courteously. Let the caller know the call is being transferred. Give the caller the number you are transferring the call to in case the call is disconnected.

**Caution**

You must not make cell phone calls while driving or operating heavy equipment. This practice is illegal in many states because it has been shown to cause accidents. If you must make or take such calls, it is best to pull over to a safe spot.

**Note**

Keep cell phone calls short and use them for business only. Cell phone companies charge by the minute for outgoing and incoming calls, and those minutes can add up quickly. If you must take a cell phone call when you are talking to your boss or customers, excuse yourself and step away.

## On-the-Job Quiz

Here's a quick quiz that asks you to apply what you've learned in this module.

1. To accurately define two-way communication, you would say that a _____.
   a. sender sends a message through a communication channel to a receiver
   b. sender sends a message through a communication channel to a receiver, who interprets the message
   c. sender sends a message through a communication channel to a receiver, who interprets the message and gives feedback to the sender
   d. receiver takes detailed notes on any information sent through a communication channel so that everyone will have a record of what's going on

2. When you are listening to instructions, the best way to make sure you get all the information you need is to _____.
   a. take notes and compare them with co-workers' notes
   b. read a book about the topic later on
   c. ask questions, but wait until the person has stopped speaking
   d. take notes, ask questions at appropriate times, and paraphrase instructions
3. You are on a noisy work site when a supplier phones you with questions about your supply list. Some quantities have been left out, and some items you want will have to be substituted. To make sure you get what you need, you should _____.
   a. talk louder or shout if necessary
   b. find a quieter spot so you can hear the supplier better
   c. move to a quieter spot and estimate what you need, figuring you can always return any excess
   d. call the supplier back from a quieter spot with a copy of your supply list in hand
4. While demonstrating a new procedure, your supervisor notices that you are writing in a small pocket notebook. Your supervisor is most likely thinking that you _____.
   a. should be paying more attention, not scribbling in a notebook
   b. are just trying to impress your co-workers
   c. are probably writing a personal letter or doodling
   d. are a professional worker who is taking notes for future reference
5. You're new on the job, and you want to make a good impression. Your supervisor tells you to get a pipe clamp, but you have no idea what that is. You should _____.
   a. ask your supervisor to describe what the pipe clamp looks like and tell you where you can find one
   b. look around the job site and see if you can figure out what a pipe clamp is
   c. ask somebody else, preferably one of the more experienced workers, to get the pipe clamp for you
   d. look up the term "pipe clamp" in a construction dictionary

6. An older, experienced worker is training you and a co-worker. Your trainer acts like a big shot know-it-all and on top of that is boring. You should _____.
   a. respect your trainer's experience and knowledge and force yourself to pay attention
   b. tune out, and then ask your co-worker to recap what the trainer said
   c. think about how you would do a better job of training others
   d. pretend you are paying attention, then read a manual, because you can teach this stuff to yourself
7. You've been working with the same group of people for about five years. You are all friends, and you all know each other's working styles. Today it's your job to explain a new procedure to them. You can assume that your co-workers _____.
   a. will want you to speak very slowly
   b. won't need an explanation of the technical terms you use
   c. probably won't listen very closely because they know a lot already
   d. will resent you for trying to teach them something new
8. Imagine that you are a supervisor. You need your crew to work a lot of overtime to fix a serious problem that affects the safety of the building they are constructing. You need everyone to be cooperative and helpful. To win their cooperation and get their best effort, you should _____.
   a. strongly hint that you will fire anyone who doesn't put in the overtime
   b. order everyone to work overtime, then leave quickly so you don't have to deal with any complaints or arguments
   c. say that you are all in this together and now is the time for the team to step up and do the right thing to demonstrate their professionalism and team spirit
   d. explain how the problem happened, answer workers' questions, and address their concerns about schedules, pay, or planned leave

**9.** You have been asked to demonstrate your company's new web site to a work crew, many of whom have 10 to 15 years of experience. The web site will allow workers online access to permits, specifications, drawings, surveys, schedules, and change orders. The site is expected to save the company money and time. To get the work crew interested in learning the new system, what is the best thing you could say?

a. "This is going to be so cool. The webmaster's used lots of gifs, jpegs, and frames. You can highlight, cut and paste, use auto-fill, and download PDFs."

b. "Look, I'm just the messenger. I don't like this computer stuff any more than you do, but we haven't got a choice, so let's just learn how to use this thing."

c. "The system will save you a lot of time, and it's easy to learn—takes most workers about 45 minutes or so. Best part—you don't have to learn how to type!"

d. "Don't worry. I am going to chain this big user manual right next to the terminal, so if you don't know what to do, you can look it up."

**10.** Your boss has asked you to call a subcontractor about mistakes made on a recent delivery. You know that this subcontractor is often hard to reach, and you will have to leave a message on voice mail. You want the subcontractor to deliver the correct materials on time. What is your BEST course of action?

a. Plan what you will say before you make the call.

b. Ask for a return call so you can discuss the problem.

c. Tell the contractor to report to your boss ASAP.

d. Make the call without thinking too much about it, because you know what to say.

# Individual Activities

## Activity 1: Listening Actively and Asking Questions

Your supervisor does not always speak clearly and often uses words or phrases that are vague or confusing. Read each of the following instructions, then write the question or questions you would have to ask to get the specific information you need. Then pretend you are the supervisor, and write out an answer next to supervisor's response.

1. **Supervisor's instruction:** Adjust the thermostat.

   Your question(s): ______________________________

   Supervisor's response: ______________________________

2. **Supervisor's instruction:** Get the MSDS for that coating and make sure everyone reads it.

   Your question(s): ______________________________

   Supervisor's response: ______________________________

3. **Supervisor's instruction:** Tell a few of the workers to meet with me later this afternoon.

   Your question(s): ______________________________

   Supervisor's response: ______________________________

4. **Supervisor's instruction:** Anybody who comes to the job inebriated will be terminated PDQ. We do not put up with dipsomaniacs at this company.

   Your question(s): ______________________________

   Supervisor's response: ______________________________

## Activity 2: Identifying Poor Listening Habits

The following are some signs of poor listening habits. Check any boxes that you think apply to you. Be honest in your self-assessment! Once you are aware of some problems you may have with your listening skills, you can create an action plan for things you can do to improve.

| Check All That Apply | Actions That Show Poor Listening Skills |
|---|---|
| ❑ | Making jokes when the other person is trying to be serious |
| ❑ | Arguing with everything another person says |
| ❑ | Interrupting others constantly |
| ❑ | Rolling your eyes when you doubt what someone says |
| ❑ | Thinking about other things while someone else is speaking |
| ❑ | Fiddling around with things or fidgeting when someone else is speaking |
| ❑ | Disagreeing constantly with another person's suggestions |
| ❑ | Finishing another person's sentences |
| ❑ | Changing the subject to something you're more interested in |
| ❑ | Saying things like "Cool" or "No kidding" instead of paraphrasing |
| ❑ | Looking at your watch while somebody is talking to you |
| ❑ | Jumping to conclusions before the other person is finished |

My action plan for improving my listening skills:

1. ______________________________
2. ______________________________
3. ______________________________
4. ______________________________
5. ______________________________

## Activity 3: Understanding How Communication Works

The goal of this activity is help you see how two-way communication works in real-life situations. Read each situation, then identify the sender, receiver, and the communication channel used. In addition, identify whether any noise is present. (Recall that noise is anything that blocks the flow of information.) For each situation, complete the grid that follows.

### *Situations*

**1.** Suppose you and three team members have to solve a difficult drainage problem. You want everyone to concentrate, so you arrange to meet at lunch away from the noise and distractions on the work site. You describe the problem and the past attempts to fix it. Then you ask your team for suggestions. You notice that one team member seems more interested in eating than in focusing on the problem. You notice that another team member keeps yawning and gazing off into the distance.

| Sender(s) | Receiver(s) | Communication Channel | Is noise present? If so, what is it? |
|---|---|---|---|
| | | | |

**2.** Suppose that your job requires you to fly in a helicopter over a natural gas pipeline to inspect it for problems. You spot a damaged pipe support and notice that the vegetation around the support is flattened. You radio the control center and say, "Looks like we've got a problem down there." The control center operator asks you to describe the problem and the exact location, but you don't hear that because of static. You repeat what you just said, and the control center operator, a little annoyed, again asks you to describe the problem and the exact location. This time you hear the control center's message and provide a more detailed description of the problem and the exact location.

| Sender(s) | Receiver(s) | Communication Channel | Is noise present? If so, what is it? |
|---|---|---|---|
| | | | |

**3.** During a pressure test on a newly installed plumbing system, you detect a leak. You call your boss, who is solving a problem elsewhere on the site, and say, "Boss, there's a leak in the system." Your boss is standing near some trucks that are backing up to unload supplies. There is also a crew of laborers nearby who are breaking up an old driveway. Your boss asks you to repeat your message and to speak up so that you can be heard over the backup beeps and jackhammers. You repeat your message and your boss tells you to keep the water running, trap the leaking water, and trace the source of the leak by checking upstream. A jet leaving from a nearby airport roars overhead, drowning out the last part of your boss's message.

| Sender(s) | Receiver(s) | Communication Channel | Is noise present? If so, what is it? |
|---|---|---|---|
| | | | |

## Group Activities

### Activity 4: Listening and Following Directions

***Materials Required***

- Paper (at least two sheets per team) and pencil
- Two drawings (provided by your instructor)

In this activity you will see how hard it can be to communicate well. You will also get a chance to practice your speaking and listening skills. Work in teams of two. One team member will be the communicator and the other will be the receiver. (When you complete the activity once, you will switch roles so that everyone gets a chance to both send and receive information.)

To complete this activity, follow these steps:

**Step 1** Sit back-to-back with your teammate.

**Step 2** Your instructor will give a copy of the finished drawing only to the communicator. The receiver is not allowed to see the drawing.

**Step 3** The communicator describes the drawing, and the receiver completes a drawing based on the description. The receiver may not ask any questions and can ask for an instruction to be repeated only one time.

**Step 4** The receiver stops drawing when the instructor says to and turns the drawing over.

**Step 5** Teammates switch roles. The instructor will hand out a new drawing to the new communicators, and teammates will repeat steps 1 through 4.

**Step 6** Teammates compare their drawings with the original drawings and discuss the following questions:

1. Were the receivers able to reproduce the drawings?
2. How could the communicators improve their speaking skills?
3. How could the receivers improve their listening skills?

(Our thanks to R. P. Hughes of Guilford Technical Community College, Jamestown, NC, for contributing the idea for this exercise.)

### Activity 5: Listening and Following Directions (Alternate Activity)

This activity may be used as an alternate for or in addition to Activity 4. It will also help you improve your listening skills.

To complete this exercise, you will need two sheets of lined paper, a ruler, and a pencil with an eraser. Your instructor will read each set of directions to you twice.

You must listen carefully and draw or write things based on the instructions. You are not allowed to ask any questions. When everyone is finished, your instructor will show you how the completed pages should look. Then you and your classmates can discuss the following questions:

1. What instructions were easy to understand?
2. What instructions were hard to understand?
3. What could the instructor have done to make the instructions easier to follow?
4. Do you think this exercise would be easier if you were allowed to ask questions?

### *Directions: Set 1*

1. Take out one sheet of lined paper. Very lightly, draw lines to divide your paper roughly into four map sections: north, south, east, and west.
2. In the center of the southeast section, print the name of the only month that has three letters.
3. Count down three lines from the top of the northeast section. Between lines three and four, in the center of the space, write the year you were born.
4. In the center of the southwest section, draw a circle with a diameter of about 1 inch. Draw a vertical diameter inside the circle.
5. Count down nine lines from the top of the northeast section. On the ninth line, centered horizontally in the section, write in words the sum of three plus two.
6. In the southwest section, locate the circle you drew. Place your pencil at a point on the top left side of the circle and draw a line upward and to the left until it meets the top line on the left-hand side of your paper.
7. Turn your paper upside down and locate the center of the page. Draw a 1-inch square in the center of the page. Next, draw a triangle centered inside the square. No line of the triangle should touch any line of the square.
8. Turn your paper right side up. In the northeast section, locate the line where you wrote the sum of three plus two. Count down four lines. In the center of the line, print your last name.
9. Locate the line where you wrote the year you were born. Move your pencil over to the far left-hand side of the page. Draw a 2-inch arrow pointing northeast.
10. In the northwest section, count down six lines. At about 1/2 inch from the left-hand edge of your paper, print the fifth and tenth letters of the alphabet in reverse order. Place a period after each letter.

### *Directions: Set 2*

1. Take out another sheet of lined paper. Very lightly, draw a line to divide your paper into a right-hand section and a left-hand section.
2. Locate the second line from the bottom on the right-hand side of the page. Print your full name preceded by the last four numbers of your Social Security number.

3. Count down three lines from the top of your paper on the left-hand side. Print your complete mailing address.
4. Locate the line where you wrote the last four numbers of your Social Security number. On the second line directly above that number, print the name of any high school.
5. Locate the lines where you wrote your address. To the right of your address, write your present age in months to the nearest month. Write your month age in numbers.
6. Did you attend the high school you wrote down earlier? Print your answer four lines above the last four numbers of your Social Security number.
7. In the center of the page, use your ruler to draw a rectangle that measures 2 inches vertically and 4 inches horizontally.
8. Inside the rectangle, on the left-hand side, draw a circle. The circle should touch the rectangle's left-hand side and the top and bottom of the rectangle.
9. Inside the circle, draw two curved arrows. Draw one arrow on the right side of the circle and draw one on the left side. The arrows should show a clockwise direction.
10. Count up three lines from the bottom of the page on the far left-hand side. Print a number and words to describe the area of the rectangle you drew.

## Activity 6: Role-Playing Exercise—Paying Attention on the Job

As you learned in an earlier module, not all communication is heard. In this activity, you will see how both spoken and unspoken communication (body language) can affect your career. To complete this activity, you will need five people: a supervisor and four workers. You may find it helpful to read through the script before acting it out. Write the names of the classmates who will play the following roles:

Supervisor: ____________________

H.T.: ____________________

J.C.: ____________________

C.Q.: ____________________

R.P.: ____________________

Those who have been assigned roles will read the script that follows and act out the directions in parentheses. After the role-play, the whole class will work on the discussion questions.

### *Props*

- A magazine
- A couple of pipefittings of slightly different sizes (Optional: If fittings are not available, classmates can pretend to be holding fittings.)
- A ruler with a piece of masking tape on it (Place the ruler on the floor.)

### *Script*

The workers are standing together waiting for instructions from their supervisor. H.T. is slouching against a wall leafing through a magazine. C.Q. keeps looking off to the left and fidgeting.

**Supervisor:** *(You are a little rushed. Some promised deliveries have not arrived. Three workers have not yet shown up. You've just gotten off the phone with the owner, who is upset about schedule delays.)* "H.T., you and J.C. take these two fittings—this one and this one—and go up to the compressor deck. C.Q.! Hello? You and R.P. go get a come-along and bring it up there. I'll meet you on the compressor deck with the permit. Don't forget about your safety gear. And C.Q., go by the trailer before you get the come-along and pick up the MSDS for that solvent. I don't think the guidelines are any different than what we're used to, but it's a new product, so...better safe than sorry. Let's see, what else? The owner will be on site today, so everybody look sharp, got it? Any questions?"

**H.T.:** *(Keep your magazine in one hand and hold the fitting loosely in the other. Roll your eyes and shrug your shoulders.)*

**J.C.:** *(Look directly at the supervisor and nod, then look at the fitting in H.T.'s hand.)* "OK. But boss, I think one of these fittings is the wrong size. Don't both of these have to be the same size?"

**Supervisor:** "Oh boy. What else is gonna go wrong today? Let's see. Well, you're right. Good catch! H.T., go back down to the supply truck and get another fitting. And get the right size this time!"

**H.T.:** *(Jump a little and drop the magazine.)* "Huh?"

**Supervisor:** *(Sound annoyed.)* "I said go down to the truck and get the right size fitting!"

**H.T.:** *(Look confused, then shrug your shoulders, and slowly walk away.)*

**C.Q.:** *(As soon as the supervisor starts talking, bend down and pick up the ruler. Keep peeling off and pressing down the tape. When the boss finishes speaking, look off to the left again. Nudge R.P. and whisper.)* "Who's that? You know whose truck that is?"

**R.P.:** *(Frown at C.Q. Then turn and look at the supervisor.)* "Boss, OK if I go get the MSDS instead? I need to get a replacement filter, so I'll pick up both at the same time."

## Discussion Questions

1. Do you think that H.T. knows what size fitting to pick up? What should H.T. have asked the supervisor?
2. How could the supervisor tell that C.Q. and H.T. were not listening?
3. Do you think the boss should have to remind workers to keep their minds on the job?
4. Which of these workers can the supervisor rely on to be professionals? Why?
5. Which members of the crew will the supervisor recommend for a raise or a promotion? Why?

## Activity 7: Role-Playing Exercise—Leaving Phone Messages

No one likes to play phone tag. It wastes a lot of time during the workday, so it's important to limit the number of times you have to call people and the number of times they have to call you. In this exercise, four of your classmates will role-play different ways to use a cell phone. Record their names here:

**Team Members**

| | |
|---|---|
| 1.______________________ | 2.______________________ |
| 3.______________________ | 4.______________________ |

After each classmate finishes reading his or her script, discuss these questions:

1. What did the caller do correctly?
2. What did the caller do incorrectly?
3. What tips for improvement would you give this caller?

As a group, come up with an action plan for leaving messages that are clear and to the point.

### *Script 1*

Hey T.J., how're you doing? Look, we need those permits, you know? Hey! Do you want to go to the game next weekend? Give me a call. I got tickets. Oh...so OK, don't forget those permits, right? Oh, uh, did I say we needed them by Monday? Well, we do. So, like, don't forget, OK?

### *Script 2*

Hi T.J., this is T.L. over at Rocket Construction. We're starting that Basin Street project and need the plumbing permits you promised. We've got to have them on

Monday morning before 11:00, so can you drop them off at 404 Mercants Avenue? That's M-e-r-c-a-n-t-s. Go east on Highway 20, to the stadium exit. Our office is two miles down on the right. Call me if you have questions. I'm at 703-555-1212. Take care, and thanks.

### *Script 3*

T.J.! Why don't you ever answer the phone yourself? You can't be that busy. You know who this is, right? Look, you better drop off those permits for the Basin Street project by Monday A.M. or the boss will be steamed! You know where we are. If not, call me.

### *Script 4*

T.L. here. I'll make this short 'cause my cell phone bill's going through the roof. You won't believe what it was last month! I should own stock in the phone company or something. Then I could quit working, ha, ha, ha. That would be cool, no more work! In my dreams, right? Ha, ha! So here goes. Short and sweet. Plumbing permits. By Monday morning or else! Got it? Catch you later.

## Activity 8: Being Specific and Getting to the Point

We often fail to be specific when speaking to others. We assume that they will know exactly what we mean. Quite often they do, but not always. Write down what you think are the right answers to the following questions. Then break into groups of three or four to see what your classmates wrote. Did everyone give the same answer to each question?

**Team Members**

1. ______________________ 2. ______________________

3. ______________________ 4. ______________________

1. A supplier phones to say you will get your siding at the *end of the week.* This means that your siding will arrive _________.
2. Your boss says to turn in your time sheet at the *end of the day.* This means that you should turn your time sheet in by _________.
3. Your boss tells you to come to the office *first thing Monday morning.* This means you should go to the office at _________.
4. A subcontractor leaves this message on your voice mail: "I need those permits *ASAP*!" This means that you must get the permits to the subcontractor on or by _________.
5. Your boss walks through the work site and tells you to clean up an area *when you can get to it.* When should you clean up the area?
6. You tell your boss that a wall should be finished in *a little while.* When should your boss come by to see the finished wall?

7. A co-worker needs a ride and arranges to meet you *around 7:00 over by the ballpark.* Is this enough information for you to pick up your co-worker?
8. Say you are a supervisor and a crewmember says the following to you: "Boss. Hey. How are you? You know, I have been working real hard and there has been more overtime than usual. I am not complaining or anything. This is a good job and all. But there has been a lot of work lately, you know? I have this problem to tell you about if you have a minute, OK? The problem I have is this. My brother is getting married next month. Man, is he excited! So, like, he wanted to know if I would be best man, you know? This is a big honor for me. So, my brother is counting on me, OK?"

   Based only on what this worker has said, do you know what the worker wants and what you are supposed to do?

   ______________________________________________

   ______________________________________________

9. You are taking a break with a co-worker who says the following: "We're gonna have to get with the program, know what I mean? 'Cause like I said to the boss, I said, 'Like, you know we are putting in some heavy-duty overtime here, you know?' So the boss looks at me like this, right? But I'm not gonna be an ice cube and melt, right? I mean, what's the story going to be—that's what I want to know. You know what I'm saying? So, are you with me or what?"

   Based only on what your co-worker has said, what are you supposed to do?

   ______________________________________________

   ______________________________________________

10. A co-worker tells you not to inhale a solvent, and you ask why. Your co-worker says "Ooooh. You don't wanna know. Trust me. Don't even go there!"

    Based only on what your co-worker has said, do you know what actually will happen if you inhale the solvent?

    ______________________________________________

    ______________________________________________

When you have finished discussing your answers, go back and rewrite each statement so that someone hearing it knows exactly what is meant.

## Activity 9: Test Your Speaking Ability

In this activity, you will make a short presentation to three or four classmates. (You may also present the instructions to the entire class.) Choose a topic you know fairly well or use one of the suggestions shown below. Then do the following:

- Organize your thoughts. For example, if you are giving step-by-step instructions, which instruction must come first? Which must be last?

- Think about the words you will use. Are there some words you think your classmates might not understand? Explain difficult words or come up with simpler ones.
- Make things clear by using examples or making a sketch.
- Focus on safety. Tell your classmates how to carry out the instructions safely. Make sure they understand exactly what will happen if they don't follow the safety rules.
- Leave time for and encourage questions.

### *Suggestions*

1. How to change a tire on a car that is parked on a hill.
2. How to pour scalding hot water from one pan into a drain pan.
3. How to operate a circular saw.
4. How to build a simple toolbox.
5. How to show up for work on time.
6. How to set up a scaffold.
7. How to use a builder's level.
8. How to build a sawhorse.
9. How to fix a leaking pipe.
10. How to use a sledgehammer.

### *Rate the Speaker*

Rate your classmates on their speaking ability. Use the following rating table.

| | Outstanding | Good | Could Use Some Work |
|---|---|---|---|
| 1. Gave clear instructions. | ❑ | ❑ | ❑ |
| 2. Demonstrated self-confidence. | ❑ | ❑ | ❑ |
| 3. Demonstrated knowledge of the subject. | ❑ | ❑ | ❑ |
| 4. Answered questions clearly. | ❑ | ❑ | ❑ |
| 5. Gave clear definitions or examples. | ❑ | ❑ | ❑ |
| 6. Made me feel confident that I could do the task described. | ❑ | ❑ | ❑ |

### *Rate Yourself as a Listener*

Recall that the best communication is two-way. Rate yourself as a listener using the following table.

| | Outstanding | Good | Could Use Some Work |
|---|---|---|---|
| 1. I looked at the speaker except when taking notes. | ❑ | ❑ | ❑ |
| 2. I took notes. | ❑ | ❑ | ❑ |
| 3. I asked questions about things I did not understand. | ❑ | ❑ | ❑ |
| 4. I asked for something to be repeated if I did not hear it clearly. | ❑ | ❑ | ❑ |

Each time you check "Outstanding" or "Good," be prepared to state why. Each time you check "Could Use Some Work," be prepared to give constructive suggestions to the speakers or for yourself as a listener. As a group or as a class, list five qualities that you think make someone a good communicator.

1. ______________________________
2. ______________________________
3. ______________________________
4. ______________________________
5. ______________________________

## Activity 10: Finding Ways to Reduce Communication Noise

In this module you learned about communication noise and other barriers to effective listening. In this activity you will come up with an action plan for dealing with communication noise. Choose one or more of the following situations, then work with three or four classmates to develop an action plan.

**Team Members**

1. ______________ 2. ______________

3. ______________ 4. ______________

1. You owe money for several purchases. You've been making payments on schedule, but you had to lend money to a relative. Then your car needed some expensive repair work. Now you are behind on several payments. Worry is keeping you awake nights and taking your mind off the job during the days. Yesterday, you did not hear some instructions your boss gave you and made several mistakes. You need a plan to deal with your money problems and concentrate at work.

______________________________

______________________________

______________________________

2. You get excellent grades in your classroom work and have been told that you are the best trainee at your company. You have even been asked to teach other trainees how to do certain tasks. You get so much admiration, in fact, that you start to believe that you can do anything. Your boss tells you to sit in on a safety retraining session, but you've "been there and done that," so you skip it and miss

out on some important updates. You need a plan to help you deal with your ego getting in the way of listening and learning.

3. Your boss has teamed you with an experienced co-worker to enhance your on-the-job training. Your co-worker is nice enough until the training starts. Then it's lecture, lecture, lecture. Your trainer never gives you a chance to ask a question or say what you already know how to do. The training is boring, and after a while you just start to tune out. However, the boss expects you to learn from your co-worker. You need a plan for staying focused and getting the most out of the training.

4. Your boss chews you out because you've been making a lot of mistakes lately and showed up late three times this week. Then your boss goes on to give you instructions for completing a task. You are angry because you feel that your boss is not being fair. In addition, you don't like the fact that some other workers heard the boss yelling at you. While the boss is giving you instructions, you are thinking about all the times when your work has been good and all the times you showed up on time. You spend so much time thinking about what you are going to say in your defense that you don't hear the instructions. You need a plan for dealing with your emotions and for getting those instructions repeated without making your boss even angrier.

## Activity 11: "Pass It On"

In this activity, you and your classmates will participate in an old, but effective party game. The game is designed to show how hard it is to keep information accurate as it moves from one person to another. You can work in groups of four, or your instructor may decide to divide the class into two larger groups.

### *Instructions*

1. One class member should quietly read the information printed below. (The rest of the class must close their books.)
2. In a voice low enough so that other class members can't hear, the class member who read the instructions should then state (not read) the information to another class member.
3. The person hearing the information must listen carefully and, in a low voice, repeat the information to the next person. Listeners are not allowed to ask questions or take notes.
4. The last person to receive the information should repeat it out loud while the rest of the class checks it against their books.

### Discussion Questions

1. What surprised you about this activity?
2. What could you have done to make sure you stated the information accurately?
3. What could you have done to make sure you heard and understood the information accurately?

### *Information for Activity 11*

To stay safe on the job site, you have to wear safety gear. That gear includes a hard hat, gloves, appropriate footwear, eye and ear protection, and equipment to protect you from falling. If you don't wear the appropriate safety gear, you could get into trouble with the boss. The main point, however, is that you can be injured or even killed if you don't wear it.

# Communication Skills II: Reading and Writing

## Self-Assessment

### Are You a Careful Reader?

Do you read closely and carefully? Take this self-assessment quiz to find out. Read the following information carefully and then answer the questions.

### *When do construction injuries happen?*

It may surprise you to learn that most construction injuries happen at certain times of day, during certain seasons of the year, and on certain days of the week. The following table summarizes when most injuries happen and provides some tips on how to avoid injuries.

| When do most injuries occur? | Why? | Suggestions to avoid injury |
|---|---|---|
| Between 10 A.M. and 11 A.M., and between 2 P.M. and 3 P.M. | These are the peak work hours. During peak hours, more workers are on the job, and they are working at their highest level of intensity. That is when most mistakes can occur. | Think safety first. If you begin to feel tired or start to lose concentration, tell your supervisor. You may just need to take a short break to refocus. Never take shortcuts to finish a job early. Always wear your safety gear. |
| On Mondays. There are fewer accidents on other days of the week, with the fewest on Fridays. | Getting back to work after the weekend is difficult, and many workers have trouble concentrating the first day back at work. (Note that although shift work may make a day other than Monday the start of the workweek, most construction workers start the workweek on Mondays.) | On Sunday evening, get your work clothes and gear ready so you won't feel rushed on Monday. Then get a good night's sleep. On Monday, get up early, exercise, and eat a good breakfast. Regular exercise will help you meet the demands of your job. A good breakfast will give you the energy you need to get going. |
| The day after payday. | Many workers celebrate until late at night and are not alert the next day. For some workers, payday means a chance to go out and have drinks with friends. Workers who are hung over cannot concentrate very well. | Do not party or stay out late on a work night. Save the good times for a day when you don't have to report to work the next day. You'll be healthier and live longer if you learn to eat and drink in moderation. |
| In summer, especially in August. | Most heavy construction is done in warm weather. Work slows during the colder months and over the winter holidays. The lowest number of injuries occurs between December and February. | When it's hot outside, you must drink plenty of water to prevent dehydration or heat exhaustion. If you feel dizzy or faint, stop working and let your supervisor know that you need a break. Wear a sweatband or bandanna to keep sweat from dripping into your eyes. |

Source: Adapted from *Construction Safety.* Jimmie W. Hinze. Upper Saddle River, NJ: Prentice Hall, 1997, pp. 31–39.

## *Reading Comprehension Questions*

1. Most injuries on construction sites occur _____.
   a. after the holidays
   b. on Mondays
   c. on Fridays
   d. during the winter months
2. During the workday, one of the heavy work activity periods is _____.
   a. between 10:00 P.M. and 11:00 P.M.
   b. just after lunch
   c. between 10:00 A.M. and 11:00 A.M.
   d. first thing in the morning
3. Most work in the construction industry is done _____.
   a. during the summer months
   b. during the winter months
   c. between Tuesdays and Thursdays
   d. on Mondays
4. According to the information in the table, you should exercise regularly because _____.
   a. it will help you meet the demands of your job
   b. it will help you overcome the effects of staying up late
   c. it will help you stay awake during the workday
   d. it will make you hungry enough to eat a good breakfast to get ready for work
5. Accidents tend to occur during peak work hours because _____.
   a. most workers are on site and working at their most intense level
   b. workers are hung over from partying the night before and cannot concentrate on work
   c. workers are overcome by heat and have sweat dripping into their eyes
   d. most workers are rushing to get the job done and don't pay attention to safety
6. The lowest number of injuries occurs _____.
   a. between March and April
   b. between December and February
   c. between September and October
   d. between June and August

**7.** Suppose you get paid on a Tuesday night. You don't have to work on Wednesday, but you do have to work from Thursday until next Tuesday. According to the table, the best night for you to stay out late with friends is _____ night.

a. Tuesday
b. Wednesday
c. Thursday
d. Friday

**8.** It is most important to drink plenty of water on the job _____.

a. when it's hot outside
b. at lunchtime
c. whenever you take breaks
d. before you start any task

**9.** To avoid injury on the job, it is best to _____.

a. always get plenty of sleep
b. exercise because strong muscles are injured less often
c. drink strong coffee to keep your focus sharp
d. always wear safety gear

**10.** If you feel dizzy or faint at work, it is best to _____.

a. lie face down and rest for about five minutes
b. drink cold water until the dizziness goes away
c. stop working and let your supervisor know you need a break
d. ask co-workers to cover for you while you go get something to eat

***Scoring:*** Enter the number of questions you got right. __________

***Assessment:***

8–10: You pay attention to detail and are already a good reader. This module will help you review your reading skills and develop them even further.

6–7: You have developed some good reading skills, but you'll benefit from further study. This module will help you increase your reading skills.

0–5: You need to pay closer attention to what you read. This module will help you focus on what you're reading so that you can understand more and do better on the job.

## Are you a careful writer?

Can you write a set of clear, simple instructions for a co-worker? Take this self-assessment quiz to find out.

Write a simple set of step-by-step instructions for any one of the following tasks:

- Using a power tool
- Installing plumbing for a sink or dishwasher
- Installing and testing electrical outlets
- Framing a closet
- Laying tile
- Painting a room
- Making a peanut butter and jelly sandwich

Be sure to include safety tips in your instructions. When you are finished, exchange papers with a classmate, and discuss the following questions:

### *Discussion Questions*

1. Were the instructions clear and simple?
2. Were the instructions given in a logical order?
3. What did not make sense to you? Why?
4. Do you think you could actually follow the instructions?
5. What could you do to improve the instructions?

If some of your instructions were not too clear, the information and exercises in this module will help you improve. Keep this self-assessment quiz in mind as you work on improving your business writing skills.

## Introduction

To be successful at any job, you need good reading and writing skills. Take a look around your job site. A lot of the information you need every day is written down. Being able to read and understand such things as work orders or maintenance instructions is an important part of your job. You must also have good writing skills so that you can produce written information for your co-workers, your supervisors, and, when necessary, for suppliers and clients. In this module, you will learn how to read more effectively and write more clearly. You will also learn some good basic reading and writing habits.

## Reading on the job

A lot of the reading that you will do on the job site is related to your safety. To make the workplace safer, Congress passed legislation in 1970 to create the Occupational Safety and Health Administration (OSHA). This agency has created many safety rules and regulations. In fact, one of the first things you will probably read on the job site is the OSHA poster. This poster outlines your rights and safety responsibilities on the job site. It is your responsibility to read and understand the information on the poster.

What other types of things will you have to read at work? Here's just a sample:

- Work orders
- Work permits
- Change orders
- Supply lists
- Bills
- Codes
- Material safety data sheets
- Operating instructions
- Blueprints
- Maintenance manuals
- Information about company rules, pay, benefits, and leave policies

To read effectively and well, you must develop some basic reading habits. The following habits will help you read and understand all types of material, from basic instructions to more complex material.

**1. Learn how to find the information you need.** To help you concentrate and understand what you are reading, follow these tips to make complicated material easier to understand:

- Look for cues to help you find what you are looking for. Examples of cues include tables of contents, boldface type, italic type, section headings or chapter titles, numbered lists, bulleted lists, illustrations, tables, references, and indexes. For example, most employee manuals have a table of contents that you can use to quickly find the information you need on company benefits and rules.

- Ask yourself, "Does this apply to me and the work I am doing?" "Is there information I need to know to do a task safely?" "Are there directions that I must follow to complete a form?" If the answer is yes, focus on reading the parts that apply to you and the task at hand. If the answer is no, you can usually skip that part. For example, part of an employment application may be printed inside a box with the heading "For Office Use Only." You can ignore the information inside that box.
- Make a note of any words or phrases you don't understand. You can look up unfamiliar words in a dictionary (there are dictionaries written specifically for the construction industry). However, especially when a question involves safety, it's best to ask your supervisor.

More information on how to find what you are looking for in books and technical manuals is included in *Appendix A* of this module. More information on reading plans and blueprints is included in *Appendix B*.

**2. Take notes.** Write down the main points as you read. This technique will help you to concentrate better and remember more of what you have read.

**3. Adjust your speed.** Read at a speed that allows you to understand what you are reading. If you don't understand something, slow down and try reading it again.

**4. Visualize.** Create a mental picture as you read. This technique is especially helpful when you are reading step-by-step instructions. Try to see yourself doing each step, and you'll find the instructions much easier to remember. You will also be able to perform the task better.

**5. Read all the directions first.** This technique is also helpful when following step-by-step instructions. Don't try to complete any task by reading and completing one instruction at a time. Reading all the directions will give you a clear picture of what you must do. It will also save you a lot of time and trouble.

**6. Ask for help when you need it.** Some of the things you must read for work won't be clear even if you read them a second time. In those cases, don't hesitate to ask your supervisor or a more experienced co-worker for help.

**7. Help yourself.** Don't let a problem with reading hold you back. If you find reading difficult, take action to help yourself improve. You can look up definitions to words you don't know in the dictionary. You can take a reading course at a community college or through a local adult education program.

### Study Tip

You may have to get special training to use certain tools or perform certain tasks. That training may require you to read textbooks or training manuals. To read and recall the material successfully, set aside time each day for study, read in a quiet place that is free from distractions, and take careful notes or highlight important information. Following these study tips will help you to better understand and recall what you have studied.

### *Example: On-the-Job Reading*

Let's take a look at one type of reading you may have to do on the job: the material safety data sheet, or MSDS. Companies that make products containing hazardous chemicals must provide an MSDS so that people can use these products safely. An MSDS looks hard to read because it contains a lot of information, but only some of that information applies to you. Consider the following example.

Suppose your boss says to use paint thinner to clean up after a painting job, but tells you to read the MSDS first. Let's use some of the basic reading skills to figure out how the following MSDS on paint thinner applies to you (see *Figure 6–1*).

- **Find the information you need.** Look at the boldface headings to find sections that apply to you and your task. For example, you probably don't need to read the information under the heading **"2 Ingredient Composition Information,"** but you should read the section titled **"4 Fire and Explosion Hazard Data."** What other sections should you read? Look at the boldface headings and boldface words to find the sections that apply to your task.
- **Define words or phrases you don't understand.** For example, under the heading **"6 Health Hazard Data,"** you will see the phrase "gastrointestinal irritation." If you don't know what this phrase means, you might be able to figure it out by reading the words around it, by looking in a dictionary, or by asking your supervisor. Recall that asking your supervisor is especially important for safety matters.
- **Adjust your speed, visualize, and take notes.** Look under the heading **"7 Precautions for Safe Handling and Use."** Read the instructions carefully. Read them again if you need to, and imagine yourself cleaning up spills as directed. You can jot down some notes as well. For example, you might write, "Don't smoke! Can blow up!"
- **Read all the directions first.** For example, if you have to clean up a small spill, the directions in the MSDS tell you to use absorbent material and to place the material in a closed container. Before you start this task, you must know what type of absorbent material you will use and what type of container you'll need. If you don't know, check with your supervisor. Then, if a small spill happens, you'll be ready to handle it quickly and safely.

It takes only a few minutes to carefully read and understand the information you need on the job. The few minutes you spend at the beginning of a task will save you lots of time and headaches later on. They may even save your life.

#### A Special Note on References

Be aware that some of the work-related material you read may refer you to other publications. For example, government regulations often contain references to other regulations. Building codes may refer you to an earlier version of the code. References are used to avoid repeating information that readers can find elsewhere. It will take you a while to learn the system of references, but once you learn it, you will be able to find the information you need.

*Series 76000, 76600 includes 76001, 76005, 76055, 76601, 76604*

# Material Safety Data Sheet

# Series 76000, 76600

## 1 Company and Product Identification

| | |
|---|---|
| Manufacturer s Name: | STAR BRONZE COMPANY, INC.<br>PO Box 2206<br>Alliance, Ohio 44601-0206 |
| Emergency Telephone: | 330-823-1550 |
| Information Telephone: | 330-823-1550 |
| Identity: | 76000 Zip-Strip Quality Paint Thinner (Mineral Spirits)<br>76600 Zip-Strip Quality Paint Thinner (Mineral Spirits) |
| Date Prepared: | April 11, 2001 (Revised) |

## 2 Ingredient Composition Information

| *Ingredient* *CAS No.* | *% by volume* | *---- PPM ----* *OSHA PEL* | *ACGIH TLV* |
|---|---|---|---|
| Stoddard Solvent 8052-41-3 | > 90 | 100 | 100 |
| 1, 2, 4 - Trimethylbenzene 95-63-6 | < 5 | 25 | 25 |
| 1, 3, 5 - Trimethylbenzene 108-67-8 | < 5 | 25 | 25 |

Section 313: Supplier Notification. This product contains the following toxic chemicals, subject to the reporting requirements of Section 313 of the Emergency Planning & Community Right to Know Act of 1986, and of 40 CFR 372. **1,2,4 - Trimethylbenzene.**

This information must be included in all Material Safety Data Sheets that are copied and distributed for this material.

## 3 Physical and Chemical Properties

| | |
|---|---|
| **Boiling Range:** | 310°F - 390°F |
| **Evaporation Rate:** | (Ether = 1) 70.0 |
| **Percent Volatile:** | 100% |
| **Appearance and Odor:** | clear liquid,<br>typical Hydrocarbon odor |
| **VOC:** | 772 grams/liter |
| **VOS:** | 6.44 lbs./gal. |
| **Vapor Density:** | (Air = 1) 4.9 |
| **Weight per Gallon:** | 6.44 lbs. |
| **Solubility in Water:** | negligible |
| **Specific Gravity:** | 0.773 |
| **Vapor Pressure:** | 2.00 MM Hg @ 20°C |
| **Solvent Density:** | 0.77 |

## 4 Fire and Explosion Hazard Data

**Flash Point:** 100°F **Flammable Limits:**

**LEL:** 0.8% **UEL:** 5.0%

**Extinguishing Media:** Regular foam, carbon dioxide, or dry chemical.

**Special Fire Fighting Procedures:** Wear self contained breathing apparatus with a full face piece operated in the positive pressure demand mode, with appropriate turn out gear & chemical resistant personal protective equipment.

**Unusual Fire and Explosion Hazards:** Vapors are heavier than air and may travel along the ground or be moved by ventilation and ignited by heat, pilot lights, other flames, sparks, heater, smoking, electric motors, static discharge or other ignition sources at locations distant from material handling point. Keep away from heat, sparks, pilot lights and other sources of ignition. Closed containers may explode when exposed to extreme heat.

**HMIS Codes:** Health 0, Flammability 2, Reactivity 0

**NFPA Codes:** Health 1, Flammability 2, Reactivity 0

## 5 Reactivity Data

**Stability:** Stable

**Conditions to Avoid:** N/A

**Incompatibility:** Avoid contact with strong oxidizing agents.

**Hazardous Decomposition of By-products:** May form toxic materials: carbon dioxide and carbon monoxide, various hydrocarbons.

**Hazardous Polymerization:** Cannot occur

## 6 Health Hazard Data

**Routes of Entry:** Inhalation - Yes, Skin - Yes, Ingestion - Yes

**Health Hazard Acute and Chronic:**

**Inhalation:** Excessive inhalation of vapors can cause nasal and respiratory irritation; central nervous system effects, including dizziness, weakness, fatigue, nausea and headache, and possible unconsciousness; or in extreme cases, death. Intentional misuse by deliberately concentrating and inhaling the contents may be harmful or prove fatal.

**Skin:** Prolonged or repeated contact can cause moderate irritation, defatting, dermatitis.

**Eyes:** Can cause severe irritation, redness, tearing and blurred vision.

**Ingestion:** Can cause gastrointestinal irritation, nausea, vomiting, diarrhea. Aspiration of material into the lungs can cause chemical pneumonitis, which can be fatal.

Star Bronze Company, Inc 76000, 76600 Zip-Strip Paint Thinner Page 1 of 2

**Figure 6-1. Material Safety Data Sheet (1 of 2)**

*Series 76000, 76600 includes 76001, 76005, 76055, 76601, 76604*

**Chronic Overexposure**: Excessive exposure may cause permanent brain and nervous system damage.

**Medical Conditions Aggravated by Exposure**: unknown

**Carcinogenicity**: Not presently listed as a carcinogen. IARC - not listed; NTP - not listed; OSHA - not listed.

**Emergency First Aid Procedures:**

**Inhalation**: If affected, remove individual to fresh air. If breathing is difficult, administer oxygen. If breathing has stopped, give artificial respiration. Keep person warm and quiet, and get medical attention.

**Skin**: Thoroughly wash exposed area with soap and water. Remove contaminated clothing. Launder contaminated clothing before reuse.

**Eyes**: Immediately flush thoroughly with large amounts of water, occasionally lifting upper and lower lids. Get medical attention.

**Ingestion**: Do not induce vomiting. Keep person warm and quiet, and get medical attention immediately. Aspiration of material into lungs due to vomiting can cause chemical pneumonitis, which can be fatal.

## 7 Precautions for Safe Handling & Use

**Steps to be taken in case material is released or spilled**

**Small Spill**: Absorb liquid on paper, vermiculite, floor absorbent or other absorbent material and transfer to vent hood or closed container.

**Large Spill**: Eliminate ignition sources (flares, flames, pilot lights, electrical sparks). Contain liquid, stop spill at source. Ventilate area, avoid breathing vapors. Clean up with absorbent material and place in closed container for disposal.

**Waste Disposal Method:**

**Small Spill**: Allow volatile portion to evaporate away from inhabited areas or in ventilated hood. Dispose of remaining material in accordance with applicable regulations.

**Large Spill**: Dispose of by sending to licensed reclaimer or permitted incinerator in accordance with local, state and federal regulations.

**Precautions to be taken in handling and storing**: Store in cool, dry area. Avoid flames and high temperatures. Store upright to prevent leaks. Keep container tightly closed.

**Other precautions**: None

## 8 Control Measures

**Respiratory Protection:** If workplace exposure limits of product or any component are exceeded, a NIOSH/ MSHA approved air supplied respirator is advised in absence of proper environmental control. OSHA regulations also permit other NIOSH/ MSHA respirators (negative pressure type) under specified conditions (see your safety equipment supplier). Engineering or administrative controls should be implemented to reduce exposure.

**Ventilation**: Provide sufficient mechanical (general and/or local exhaust) ventilation to maintain exposure below PEL & TLV.

**Protective Gloves:** Wear resistant gloves such as nitrile rubber, neoprene, polyvinyl alcohol.

**Eye Protection**: Chemical splash goggles in compliance with OSHA regulations are advised. However, OSHA regulations also permit other types of safety glasses (consult your safety equipment supplier).

**Other Protective Clothing or Equipment**: Where prolonged or frequently repeated contact could occur use protective clothing impervious to this material. Selection of specific items, such as gloves, boots or aprons will depend upon operation.

**Work/ Hygienic Practices:** Avoid contact with eyes, skin and clothing. Avoid breathing vapors or spray mist. Wash thoroughly after handling and before eating, drinking or smoking. Remove any contaminated clothing promptly and clean before reuse.

## 9 Transportation Data

Note: In containers of 119 gallons capacity or less, this product is not regulated by DOT.

| *Proper Shipping Description* | *Hazard Class* | *ID#* | *Pkg Group* | *Label Req.* |
|---|---|---|---|---|
| Quart | | | | |
| Paint Related Material | none | none | none | none |
| Gallon | | | | |
| Paint Related Material | none | none | none | none |
| 5 Gallon Pail | | | | |
| Paint Related Material | none | none | none | none |
| 55 Gallon Drum | | | | |
| Paint Related Material | none | none | none | none |

## 10 Regulatory Information

**Toxic Substances Control Act:** All ingredients are listed on TSCA Inventory

**SARA 311/312 Hazard Categories:** Health - Immediate Health, Delayed health, Fire

**SARA 313 Components**: 1,2,4 Trimethylbenzene

**California Proposition 65 Warning**: This material contains a chemical known to the State of California to cause cancer and birth defects or other reproductive harm. (benzene)

The information and recommendations contained herein have been compiled from sources believed to be accurate and reliable. The information herein is given in good faith, but no warranty, expressed or implied, is made.

Page 2 of 2 76000, 76600 Zip-Strip Paint Thinner Star Bronze Company, Inc

**Figure 6-1. Material Safety Data Sheet (2 of 2)**

## Are you a good business writer?

What does it mean to be a good business writer? When you write well, you think about the people who have to read what you write, so you do the following things:

- Use words your readers are likely to understand.
- Get to the point quickly and stay there.
- Don't write anything that is rude or nasty or that might offend your readers.
- Follow the reader rules. Your writing must answer these questions for the reader:
  - Who wrote this?
  - Why I am reading this?
  - What am I supposed to do when I finish reading this?
  - When am I supposed to do it?
  - Where am I supposed to do it?
  - Who can I contact if I have questions?

The reader rules always apply, even if you are writing something short and pretty simple. Read the following true story. Then consider the discussion questions that follow.

### *Jargon*
### *+ Not Thinking about the Reader*
### *= One Upset Customer*

Being careful about the words you use when writing is especially important when dealing with clients. To appreciate the humor in this story, you have to know a couple of terms used in the electrical construction industry. Two types of electrical wires enter a building: *drops* (overhead wires) and *laterals* (underground wires).

A power-company customer called to report a power outage. The service technician looked at the problem, wrote up the work order, gave the customer a copy, and left. The customer took one look at the work order, got angry, and called the company to complain that its service technician was rude. What made the customer angry? Here is what the service technician wrote on the work order:

**INVESTIGATED POWER OUTAGE—DROP DEAD**

The technician described the problem accurately, but the customer took it as a personal insult!

(Our thanks to Don Gumieny of Electrical Concepts, Inc., Waukesha, WI, for sharing this story.)

## Discussion Questions

1. What could the technician have done to avoid insulting the customer?
2. What terms do you use in your job that clients might not understand?

## Types of Business Writing

In this section, we will discuss some of the job-related writing you will most likely be doing. Before we do, let's take a look at the basic types of communication used in the business world: memos and business letters.

### *Memos*

People use a memo (short for memorandum) mainly to communicate information within an organization. A memo may be printed on paper and distributed by hand, mailed, or sent via email on a company's intranet (internal network) or through the internet. People use memos to do the following:

- Give instructions
- Ask or answer questions
- Explain new policies
- Call meetings
- Summarize decisions
- Ask for information
- Remind people about upcoming tasks or events

Study the example of a memo in *Figure 6–2.* Does this memo answer all of the questions a reader might have?

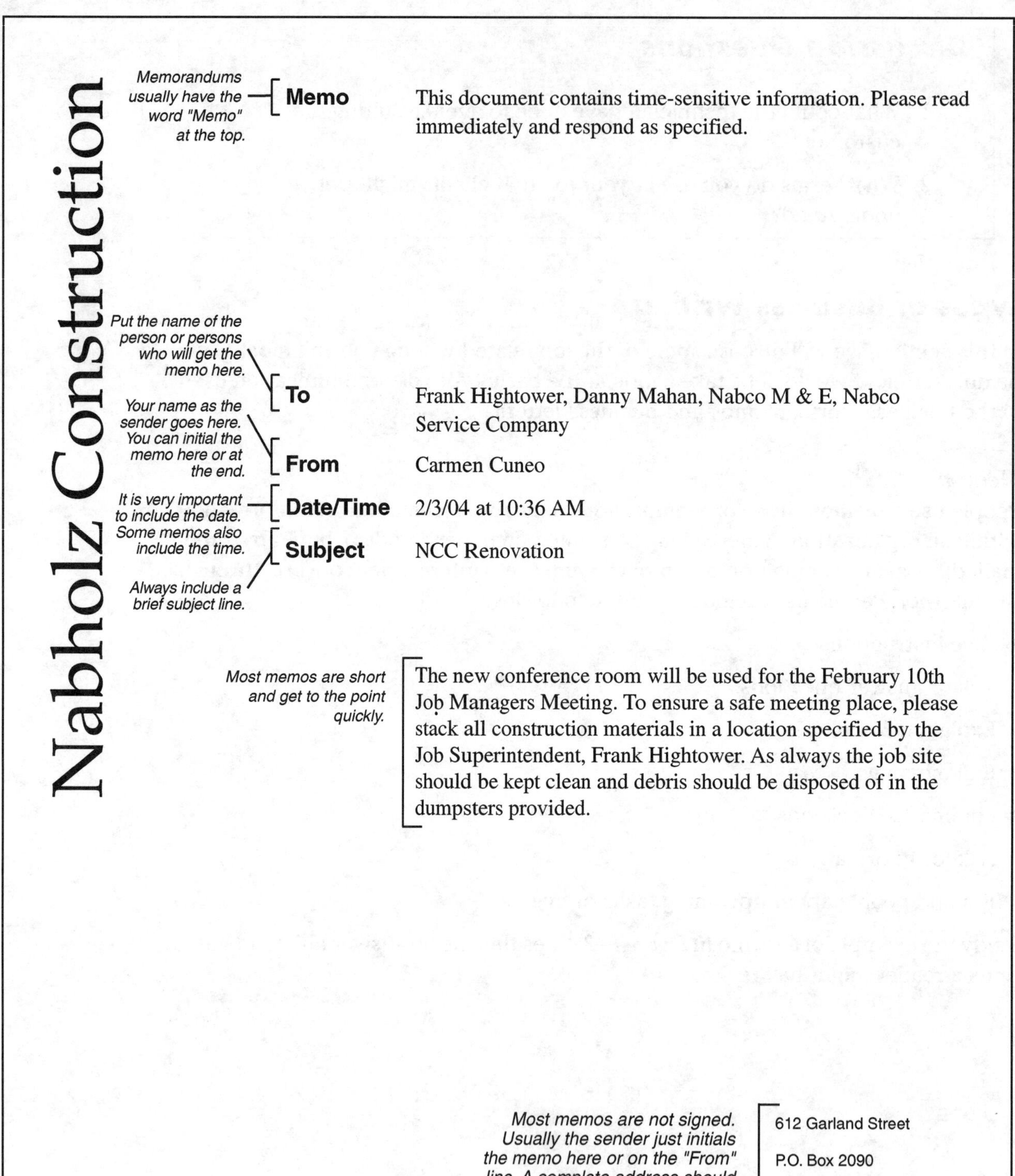

Nabholz Construction

Memorandums usually have the word "Memo" at the top.

**Memo** This document contains time-sensitive information. Please read immediately and respond as specified.

Put the name of the person or persons who will get the memo here.

**To** Frank Hightower, Danny Mahan, Nabco M & E, Nabco Service Company

Your name as the sender goes here. You can initial the memo here or at the end.

**From** Carmen Cuneo

It is very important to include the date. Some memos also include the time.

**Date/Time** 2/3/04 at 10:36 AM

Always include a brief subject line.

**Subject** NCC Renovation

Most memos are short and get to the point quickly.

The new conference room will be used for the February 10th Job Managers Meeting. To ensure a safe meeting place, please stack all construction materials in a location specified by the Job Superintendent, Frank Hightower. As always the job site should be kept clean and debris should be disposed of in the dumpsters provided.

Most memos are not signed. Usually the sender just initials the memo here or on the "From" line. A complete address should be included in the memo.

612 Garland Street

P.O. Box 2090

Conway, AR 72032

(501) 327-7781

(501) 327-8231 Fax

Carmen_Cuneo@Nabholz.com

Source: Nabholz Construction Corporation, Conway, AR

**Figure 6-2. Sample Memorandum**

The speed, flexibility, and convenience of email make it a very popular business communication tool (see *Figure 6–3*). The sender can attach text and image files and send them in far less time than it would take to type, photocopy, assemble, and distribute a paper memo.

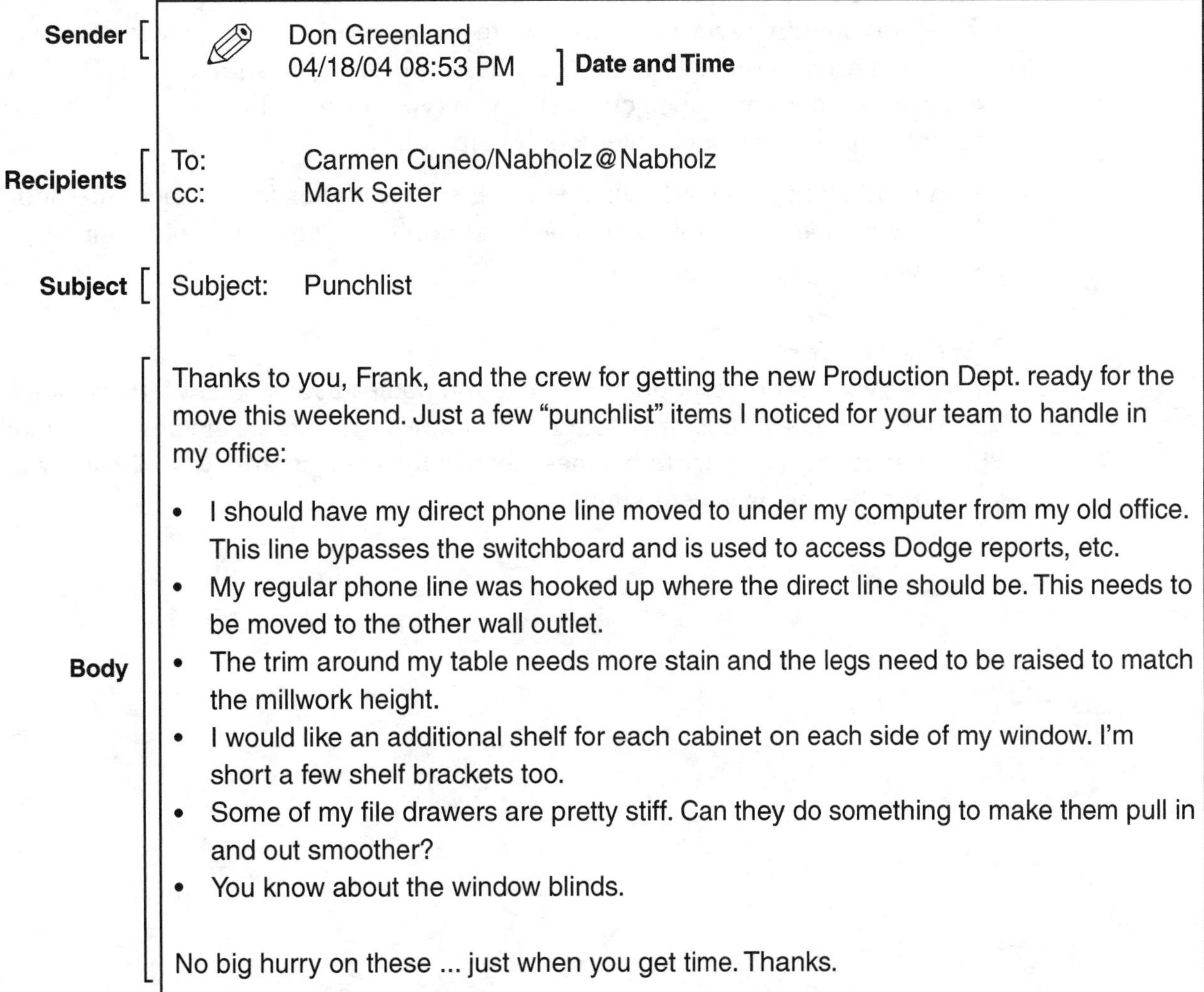

**Sender** [ Don Greenland
04/18/04 08:53 PM ] **Date and Time**

**Recipients** [ To: Carmen Cuneo/Nabholz@Nabholz
cc: Mark Seiter

**Subject** [ Subject: Punchlist

**Body**

Thanks to you, Frank, and the crew for getting the new Production Dept. ready for the move this weekend. Just a few "punchlist" items I noticed for your team to handle in my office:

- I should have my direct phone line moved to under my computer from my old office. This line bypasses the switchboard and is used to access Dodge reports, etc.
- My regular phone line was hooked up where the direct line should be. This needs to be moved to the other wall outlet.
- The trim around my table needs more stain and the legs need to be raised to match the millwork height.
- I would like an additional shelf for each cabinet on each side of my window. I'm short a few shelf brackets too.
- Some of my file drawers are pretty stiff. Can they do something to make them pull in and out smoother?
- You know about the window blinds.

No big hurry on these ... just when you get time. Thanks.

Source: Nabholz Construction Corporation, Conway, AR

**Figure 6–3. Sample Email**

There are many advantages to email, but there are some drawbacks as well. Here are some tips to help you use this communication tool wisely:

- **Write business email the same way you would write a formal business letter or memo.** Because email is fast and easy to use, people tend to be very casual with subject lines, sentence structure, and punctuation. If you treat business email as you would any other business communication, you won't make these mistakes. You also won't use emoticons (smiley faces, frowning faces, etc.), type in all capital letters, or pepper your email with abbreviations that your reader might not understand, such as IMHO (in my humble opinion), LOL (lots of luck or laugh out loud), or TAFN (that's all for now).

- **Email is not private.** Anyone, including your boss, can read it. In addition, anyone who gets your email can forward it to many other people. Never write or attach anything sensitive, personal, rude, or pornographic. Unless you know that you have a secure connection, avoid including personal information.
- **There is no "undo" on the send button.** Once you press send, your email is gone, so carefully review what you write. Make sure dates and amounts are correct. Make sure you've typed a good description in the subject line. Don't rely entirely on your email spell checker. If you type "furnace flu" or "flew" when you meant "flue," the spell checker won't help you.
- **Don't hide behind email.** Email is not a substitute for face-to-face interaction. Never send bad news through email, and don't use email to avoid your responsibilities.

### *Business Letters*

For some types of correspondence, most companies use business letters (see *Figure 6–4*). In general, business letters are more formal than memos and emails. When you are asked to write business letters for your company, you'll know that you've reached management status!

**NABHOLZ CONSTRUCTION CORPORATION**

| | |
|---|---|
| **Date** | May 6, 2004 |
| **Inside Address** | Chris Little, Project Manager<br>Nabco Mechanical & Electrical Contractors, Inc.<br>P.O. Box 1547<br>Conway, Arkansas 72033 |
| **Subject** | RE: CRMP Banister-Lieblong |
| **Salutation** | Dear Chris: |
| **Body** | A pre-construction meeting has been scheduled for the Banister-Lieblong Building, Monday, May 17, 2004, at 1:30 PM. The meeting will be held at Nabholz Construction Corporation s Conway office in the main conference center.<br><br>Your attendance at this meeting is required. Please make every effort to send at least one representative from your firm to attend this meeting. You may contact my assistant, Gaye Hayes, to confirm your attendance.<br><br>We look forward to working with you on this project. |
| **Complimentary Close** | Sincerely,<br>Nabholz Construction Corporation |
| **Signature** | *Carmen Cuneo* |
| **Name and Title** | Carmen Cuneo<br>Project Manager |
| **Initials** | cc/hs |
| **Copy list** | Cc: Gary Dean/Williams and Dean Associated Architects<br>Kay Ponthieux/Conway Regional Medical Center<br>Don Greenland/Nabholz Construction Corporation<br>Mark Seiter/Nabholz Construction Corporation<br>David Nabholz/Nabholz Construction Corporation<br>Perry McGinty/Nabholz Construction Corporation<br>Danny Mahan/Nabholz Construction Corporation |

General Contractors ■ Construction Managers

612 Garland Street ■ P.O. Box 2090 ■ Conway, Arkansas 72033-2090 ■ Phone (501) 376-1581 or 327-7781
Fax (501) 327-8231 ■ Email conway@nabholz.com

Source: Nabholz Construction Corporation, Conway, AR

**Figure 6–4. Sample Business Letter**

## Writing on the job

No matter what job you have in the construction industry, you'll have to write something, sometime. However, you don't have to be an expert in grammar or have a degree in writing. To communicate with others in writing, you just have to develop some basic writing skills. In fact, once you have mastered the basic reading skills, you have already developed some of the basic writing skills.

**1. Give your readers the information they need.** Recall how you were able to use cues such as boldface type to make reading the MSDS easier. When you write something, try giving your reader cues. For example, let's say that you want to let a client know about the choices of paint and fixtures available on a bathroom remodel. Both of the following examples are well written, but the second example makes it easier on the reader. A reader can quickly scan the boldface type, bulleted lists, and column headings for information.

***Example 1***

Here are the paint colors and faucets available for your bathroom: Color # 1415, Soft Jade; Color # 1416, Garden Moss; and Color #1417, Forest Glen. All are available in semi-gloss or eggshell finish. There are also three faucet sets: the Meridian (single handle) $109.88; the Mermaid (dual handles) $83.50; and the Monitor (dual handles) $95.75. All are available in polished brass or polished chrome. I've included paint samples and photos of the faucets. Please tell me your choices by Friday. If you have any questions, call me at 703-555-1212.

***Example 2***

Here are the paint colors and faucets available for your bathroom (paint samples and photos are enclosed). Please tell me your choices by Friday. If you have any questions, call me at 703-555-1212.

**Paint Colors** (Available in semi-gloss or eggshell finish)

- # 1415 Soft Jade
- # 1416 Garden Moss
- # 1417 Forest Glen

**Faucet Sets** (Available in polished brass or polished chrome)

| | Model | Price | Handle Style |
|---|---|---|---|
| • | Meridian | $109.88 | Single |
| • | Mermaid | 83.50 | Dual |
| • | Monitor | 95.75 | Dual |

**2. Define words or phrases readers might not understand.** Or better yet, avoid using words that are hard to understand. If you are writing something for a co-worker, supervisor, or supplier, you can use construction jargon. However, as you saw in the true story earlier, using jargon with clients is not a good idea.

**3. Visualize.** If you can see something in your head, you can describe it to someone else. Let's say you have to write down and fax driving instructions for a supplier who is on the other side of town. Here is what you would do:

- Imagine yourself driving the route.
- Write down the directions, including all the turns and street names in order.
- Read over your directions and mentally drive the route again. Ask yourself this question: If I were from out of town, could I follow these directions?

**4. Review your writing before you send it anywhere.** Get in the habit of looking over your writing, whether it's a handwritten note, a supply list, an email, or a business letter. Use this checklist:

- Have I identified myself to the reader?
- Have I said why I am writing this?
- Will the reader know what to do and, if necessary, how to do it?
- Will the reader know when to do it?
- Will the reader know where to do it?
- Will the reader know whom to call with questions?

Sometimes it is helpful to ask a friend or co-worker to review something you have written. Another reader can usually spot any mistakes or problems. For example, you might ask a friend to review your job application or resume. You can ask a co-worker to check over a work permit or material takeoff to make sure you haven't left out any information or made any mistakes in math. Don't be embarrassed to ask for this type of help, and don't be upset if your friend or co-worker spots a mistake. Professionals are always glad to catch mistakes before those mistakes create bigger problems.

## On-the-Job Quiz

Here's a quick quiz that asks you to apply what you've learned in this module.

1. It's your first day on the job, and you've been given a copy of the employee manual. You're interested in finding information on the company's health benefits. To find the information you need quickly, it is best to _____.
   a. flip through the manual until you see the words "health benefits"
   b. read the entire manual in a quiet spot until you find the section on health benefits
   c. look in the table of contents to locate the page where health benefits are described
   d. ask your boss or an experienced co-worker about the company's health benefits
2. Your boss tells you to read the manufacturer's safety instructions for operating a reciprocating saw. The safety instructions include words you don't understand. To operate the saw safely, what is your best course of action?
   a. Look up the words in a construction dictionary.
   b. Figure that if you don't understand the words, the instructions probably don't apply to you.
   c. Ask your supervisor for help.
   d. Go ahead and use the saw, figuring if you know how to use one type of saw, you know how to use all of them.
3. You're looking in a large manual for information on how to operate a sheet metal brake. The manual includes step-by-step instructions for safely operating the brake. It also includes a lot of technical information and information about other metal-forming machines. What is the best way to remember the instructions?
   a. Read the step-by-step instructions three times.
   b. Read the step-by-step instructions and visualize yourself doing the tasks.
   c. Read in a quiet spot that is free from distractions.
   d. Photocopy the instructions and paste them on a wall near your work site.

4. Your boss authorizes you to set up a scaffold. The manufacturer's guidelines include setup instructions, safety instructions, and tagging instructions. What is your best course of action?
   a. Read only the setup instructions to complete the task you were assigned.
   b. Perform each instruction in order as you read.
   c. Read both the setup and safety instructions before setting up the scaffold, and after the scaffold is set up, go back and read the tagging instructions.
   d. Read all of the instructions, get answers to any questions you have, and determine if you need any tools before setting up the scaffold.
5. You should always carefully review your email before sending it because _____.
   a. email is an expensive way to communicate
   b. email is very fast
   c. the spell checker is completely unreliable
   d. there is no "undo" on the send button
6. You have to send an email to get answers to questions about a task and to request supplies. To write an email that follows the reader rules, you should _____.
   a. say who you are, why you are writing, what you are writing about, when you need an answer, and where and when you need the supplies
   b. number each question carefully and also use the opportunity to pass along some interesting company gossip
   c. say who you are, ask your questions, give complete delivery information, and attach a funny cartoon about construction you found on the Internet
   d. create one table for your questions and another table showing all the supplies you need; then send each table as a separate attachment
7. You have decided to go into business for yourself as a painting contractor, and you have to come up with a way to show clients what services your company will perform and how much each service costs. The best way to present this information to your clients is to create a _____.
   a. legal document that is several pages long and that says who is responsible for what
   b. table showing services in one column and prices in the next column
   c. memorandum including the date, your name, a description of your company, and some biographical information about your skills
   d. formal letter introducing yourself and describing your company and its services

8. If you are writing to a co-worker or supplier, it is OK to use construction jargon.
   a. True
   b. False
9. Your boss tells you to fax directions to a construction site in a nearby town to several suppliers who are all located in the same part of your city. What is the best way to complete your task?
   a. Send a fax giving the main cross streets nearest to the construction site and let the suppliers figure out the best way to get there.
   b. Visualize the route from the area nearest the suppliers, write down the directions in order, and, before sending the fax, check your directions by visualizing the route again.
   c. Use a bright yellow or orange highlighter on a map to trace the route and fax the map to the suppliers.
   d. Send a fax that gives the main cross streets and includes your supervisor's cell phone number in case anyone has questions.
10. You decide to put together a resume of your work experience and construction skills and send it to three companies you are interested in working for. What is your best course of action?
   a. Print your resume on expensive paper so it will look really good.
   b. Use lots of words so that your resume fills three or more pages, making you look more experienced.
   c. Include bulleted lists, boldface type, italic type, a table, and a photo of yourself.
   d. Have a friend or co-worker check it over for mistakes before you make copies and mail it.

## Individual Activities

### Activity 1: Understanding What You Read

In this activity, you will check your ability to read closely and carefully. Following are two reading exercises. One deals with the safe use of fire extinguishers. The other is a sample company memo. Read each carefully and answer the questions that follow.

#### *Reading Exercise 1*

**Fire Extinguishers**
Four classes of fuels can be involved in fires. Each fuel class requires a different kind of fire extinguisher.

- *Class A fires*: Paper, wood, or other common combustibles. Class A fire extinguishers are filled with water. Because water can cause other types of fire to spread, you must never use Class A extinguishers on any other class of fire.
- *Class B fires*: Liquids and gases. Class B fire extinguishers are filled with carbon dioxide ($CO_2$). The $CO_2$ smothers the fire.
- *Class C fires*: Electrical equipment. Because electrical currents are so dangerous, Class C extinguishers are designed to protect against possible electric shock. Like Class B extinguishers, Class C extinguishers put out fires by smothering them.
- *Class D fires*: Metals that burn. Class D extinguishers contain a special powder that prevents oxygen from reaching the fire. Because fires need oxygen to continue burning, the lack of oxygen will put the fire out.

**Using a Fire Extinguisher**
There are eight simple steps to using a fire extinguisher properly. You must always match the fire extinguisher to the type of fire.

**Step 1** Hold the extinguisher upright.

**Step 2** Pull the pin. The plastic seal will break.

**Step 3** Stand at least 10 feet from the fire. The extinguishing material will shoot from the nozzle with a certain amount of force. If you stand too close you may blow burning objects into the air, thus spreading the fire.

**Step 4** Aim at the base of the fire.

**Step 5** Squeeze the handle to discharge the contents. Sweep the extinguisher from side to side.

**Step 6** When the fire is out, move closer to look for any remaining burning residue.

**Step 7** When the fire is completely out, quickly check to make sure it has not restarted.

**Step 8** Leave the area quickly. Fumes and smoke can be harmful, even deadly.

## Reading Exercise 1 Questions

1. The article includes several features that make this material easier to read. The features include _____.
   a. italic type, boldface type, a glossary, and charts
   b. boldface type, italic type, bulleted lists, and numbered lists
   c. boldface type, italic type, and numbered lists
   d. numbered lists, figures, a chart, and bulleted lists
2. An important point is repeated twice, in slightly different ways, in the article. The point is that _____.
   a. fires need oxygen to keep burning
   b. smoke and fumes can cause serious harm to people
   c. it is important to match the type fire extinguisher to the type of fire
   d. carbon dioxide can be used to put out Class B fires
3. Under the heading "Using a Fire Extinguisher," you will find step-by-step instructions for fighting a fire. The best way to remember this material is to _____.
   a. read it backwards, starting with Step 8 and going backwards until you reach Step 1
   b. visualize the steps in your mind as you read them
   c. send an email to your boss outlining the steps
   d. cut the steps out and tape them in a notebook
4. Which types of fires are put out by smothering?
   a. Class B and Class C
   b. Class A and Class B
   c. Class C and Class D
   d. Class A and Class D
5. According to the article, when using an extinguisher you should stand at least 10 feet from a fire because _____.
   a. you probably won't be wearing fireproof clothing
   b. the smoke can damage your sense of smell
   c. the fire extinguisher won't work if you stand closer
   d. the force that pushes out the foam can blow burning material into the air

### *Reading Exercise 2*

MEMO

All State Construction Company

#350 King Street, New Orleans, LA

Phone: (504) 555-8980 Fax: (504) 555-6542

Email: **AllState@aol.com**

To: Hourly Employees of All State Construction

From: Human Resources Dept.

Date: May 5, 2004

Subject: Employee Meeting

A meeting will take place on May 12, 2004, at 8:30 A.M. The location is 450 Dauphin Street, second floor, Room 203. All hourly employees are required to attend. Workers who need to remain on the job site for safety purposes must inform their managers that they will not be able to attend. There will be a make-up meeting for those employees, at the same address, at 4:30 P.M. on the same day.

We will discuss the following important points at the meeting:

1. The absenteeism policy. Absenteeism has been very high lately.
2. Safety policies, especially with respect to working in confined spaces. We have seen many violations of good safety procedures.
3. Tardiness policy. Our records show that workers are routinely punching in 15 to 20 minutes late in the morning and are returning from lunch 10 minutes late.

The meeting will take approximately one hour. All employees must report back to the job site as soon as the meeting is over.

### Reading Exercise 2 Questions

1. Who must attend the meeting?
2. What is the only acceptable reason for missing the meeting?
3. You have promised to call a contractor at 11:00 A.M. on May 12. Will you be able to do so without missing the meeting?
4. You are a salaried employee of All State Construction. That is, you are not paid by the hour. Do you have to attend the meeting?
5. What do you think would happen if you showed up to the meeting late?

## Activity 2: Reading Tables

Writers often use tables to summarize important information or to make certain types of information easier to read. In this exercise, you will test your ability to read a table. Review the following table, then answer the questions that follow.

**Types of Wood and Their Properties**

| Type | Color | Weight | Workability | Holding Power: Screws and Nails | Holding Power: Glue |
|---|---|---|---|---|---|
| Ash | Light brown | Heavy | Hard | Average | Average |
| Balsa | Light brown | Light | Easy | Poor | Good |
| Birch | Medium brown | Heavy | Hard | Good | Good |
| Cedar | Red | Light | Easy | Good | Good |
| Cherry | Light to dark red | Medium | Good | Excellent | Good |
| Fir | White to medium red | Medium | Good | Good | Average |
| Hemlock | Buff or tan | Light | Easy | Good | Good |
| Mahogany | Red to dark brown | Medium | Easy | Good | Good |
| Maple | Light brown or tan | Heavy | Fair | Average | Good |
| Oak | Tan to red | Heavy | Hard | Good | Average |
| Pine (Eastern) | Light brown | Light | Easy | Good | Good |
| Redwood | Reddish brown | Light | Good | Good | Good |
| Walnut | Deep dark brown | Heavy | Good | Good | Good |

### Table Questions

1. Of the woods listed, _____ has the best holding power for screws and nails and _____ has the worst holding power for screws and nails.
2. The five lightest woods are _____.
3. You want a wood that is red, light, and easy to work, so you choose _____.
4. You want a light-brown wood that can hold both glue and nails, so you choose _____.
5. True or false: Mahogany is easy to work with.

## Activity 3: Filling Out Employment Forms

To get a job, you'll have to fill out an application and give the company and the government some personal information. Following are some tips for filling out employment forms. After you've read through the tips, complete the employment application form (*Figure 6–5*) and the I-9 form (*Figure 6–6*). The U.S. Bureau of Citizenship and Immigration Services (a division of the Department of Homeland Security) requires the I-9 form for anyone (citizens and noncitizens) hired for employment in the United States.

### *Tips for Filling Out the Employment Application and I-9 Forms*

**1. Take your time.** Always read through the whole form before you begin filling it out. (Note that on some forms, such as the I-9, your employer fills out part of the form for you.)

**2. Ask for help.** If there is something about the form you don't understand, don't be shy about asking for help.

**3. Follow directions exactly.** On some forms you must write your first name first. On others you must write your last name first. Almost all employment applications require you to list your experience staring with your most recent employer.

**4. Look before you write.** Take a look at how much space you have to write in. Some forms don't give you very much space, so you may have to print a bit smaller than usual.

**5. Think before you write.** You must complete printed forms in ink. You'll have to cross out any mistakes, and there won't be much room to squeeze in corrections. Pay special attention to boxes that you must check, especially any that are next to the words "Yes" and "No." Be sure to check the right box. (Note that some companies may allow you to complete an application online.)

**6. Print clearly and neatly.** Think about the person who has to read your application. Make it as easy to read as possible. The person who reads your application may one day be your boss.

**7. Don't leave blanks.** To avoid leaving blanks on an application, bring a copy of your resume with you. If you don't have a resume, bring along a folder or a piece of paper with information about you, your education, and your work experience. Here are some examples of information you will need:

- The names and addresses of any schools you attended and when you attended them
- Information about military service
- Former addresses (some companies want this information if you've lived at your current address for less than five years)
- Names, addresses, and phone numbers of former employers
- Names, addresses, and phone numbers of references

**8. Be truthful.** Many forms related to getting jobs include a penalty if you don't tell the truth about your experience or background.

**9. Review the form.** Check over what you have written to make sure it is accurate and that you have not left anything out.

**10. Sign.** Most employment forms require a signature and date. Don't forget this last step.

*Building Integrity*

612 Garland Street ▪ Conway, Arkansas 72032 ▪ Ph 501-327-7781 ▪ Fax 501-327-8231 ▪ www.nabholz.com

NOTICE TO ALL APPLICANTS

RE: DRUG & ALCOHOL ABUSE POLICY

Employers have certain necessary and valid conditions of employment which must be met to ensure a safe workplace. Due to the nature of our operation, employees must be able to exercise good judgment, react properly in unexpected situations and perform tasks efficiently and safely.

We care about the safety and health of our employees, including you, if you are employed with us. Therefore, as a condition for employment, ALL applicants must be drug screened before they can be considered for employment.

In our continued effort to maintain a safe and healthy workplace, as required by Federal Law, we plan to include both scheduled and unscheduled drug/alcohol testing of employees, as well as programs with which to assist our employees who may have or develop these substance abuse problems. Our substance abuse policy and consent and release form are included in this application for employment.

If you use illegal drugs or if you excessively drink alcoholic beverages, you may NOT want to complete this application; rather, you may want to seek employment elsewhere.

Thank you for your interest in working for Nabholz.

The Nabholz Companies
Employee Services Department

"Nabholz...we will be the best. We care about people."

ACTIVE EMPLOYEE CERTIFICATE AGREEMENT

This certificate becomes part of the active employee's personnel file.

NABHOLZ COMPANIES 

I do hereby certify that I have received and read the NABHOLZ COMPANIES substance abuse and testing policy and have had the drug-free workplace program explained to me. I understand that if my performance indicates it is necessary, I will submit to a drug and/or alcohol test. I also understand that failure to comply with a drug and/or alcohol testing request or a positive, confirmed result for the illegal use of drugs and/or alcohol may lead to discipline up to and including termination of employment and/or loss of workers compensation benefits, pursuant to Nabholz Company Policy.

Employee Signature

Employee Name (Print)

Date

Source: Nabholz Construction Corporation, Conway, AR

**Figure 6–5. Employment Application (1 of 4)**

*Building Integrity*

612 Garland Street ▪ Conway, Arkansas 72032 ▪ Ph 501-327-7781 ▪ Fax 501-327-8231 ▪ www.nabholz.com

# APPLICATION FOR EMPLOYMENT

*AN EQUAL EMPLOYMENT OPPORTUNITY EMPLOYER M/F*

Note: *This application is valid for 60 days. If you wish to be considered for employment after this 60-day period, a new application must be completed.*

**PERSONAL INFORMATION** DATE:______

Name:______ SS#:______

Present Address:______
Street City State Zip

Permanent Address:______
Street City State Zip

Phone No:______ Are you 18 years or older? YES____NO____

**EMPLOYMENT DESIRED**

Position:______ Date You Can Start______Salary Desired______

Are You Employed Now?______ If So, May We Inquire of Your Present Employer?______

Ever Applied to This Company Before?______If so, where?______When?______

| EDUCATION | Name & Location of School | No. of years Attended | Did You Graduate? | Subjects Studied |
|---|---|---|---|---|
| Grammer | | | | |
| High School | | | | |
| College | | | | |
| Trade or Business | | | | |

**GENERAL**

Subjects of special study or research work:______
Military or Naval Service:______ Rank:______
Present Membership in National Guard or Reserves:______

**FORMER EMPLOYERS** (List last four, starting with last one)

| Date/Month/Year | Name &Address | Supervisor | Salary | Position | Reason for Leaving |
|---|---|---|---|---|---|
| 1. to | | | | | |
| 2. to | | | | | |
| 3. to | | | | | |
| 4. to | | | | | |

**Figure 6–5. Employment Application (2 of 4)**

**REFERENCES**
(Give the names of three persons not related to you, whom you have known at least one year.)

| Name | Address | Business | Year Acquainted |
|---|---|---|---|
| 1. | | | |
| 2. | | | |
| 3. | | | |

In case of Emergency, notify: ______________________________
Name Address

Phone: ______________________

Have you ever been convicted of a crime, other than minor traffic offenses: ______________
If so, please explain ______________________________

Note: A prior conviction will not necessarily bar you from employment; however the type of conviction and when it occurred will be considered.

CERTIFICATION

"I certify that the information in this application is true and understand that misrepresentations of false or omitted facts may result in my termination, regardless of the time of discovery by the company. I also understand that, if hired, my employment is for no definite period and may be terminated at any time without written notice and that, absent a written contract signed by the President of the company, I will remain an at-will employee and can be terminated at any time without any notice.

I authorize investigation of the statements contained herein and the references listed above to give you any and all information concerning my previous employment and any pertinent information such references may have, personal or otherwise, and release all parties from all liability for any damage that may result from furnishing same to you.

I understand that if the company decides to engage an investigative consumer reporting agency to report on my credit and personal history, the company will provide me, at my request, with the name and address of the agency so that I can obtain from them the nature and substance of the information contained in the report.

______________________________
Date Signature

**DO NOT WRITE BELOW THIS LINE**

Interviewed By: ______________________ Date: ______________

Hire: Yes_____ No______ Position: ______________
Department: ______________ Salary: ______________
Date Reporting to Work: ______________________
Approved: 1.____________ 2.____________ 3.____________

**Figure 6–5. Employment Application (3 of 4)**

*Building Integrity*

612 Garland Street ■ Conway, Arkansas 72032 ■ Ph 501-327-7781 ■ Fax 501-327-8231 ■ www.nabholz.com

It is the policy of the Nabholz Construction Corporation, Inc. to ensure and maintain a working environment free of harassment, intimidation, and coercion at all sites, and in all facilities, at which our employees are assigned to work. Specific attention will be given to ensure that minorities and women are provided with a work environment free of harassment, intimidation and coercion at all times. Any harassment, intimidation, or coercion observed by any employee should be reported immediately to your supervisor or the Company EEO Officer. This policy will be rigidly adhered to by all personnel of the Nabholz Construction Corporation.

It is the policy of this organization to provide equal employment opportunity to all qualified applicants for employment without regard to race, color, religion, national origin, sex, age, veteran status or disability.

*I have read the above Company Policy and have been provided other information, related to Company and Affirmative Action Procedures. As a condition of my employment, I hereby agree to comply with the above policy and report any violations of this policy to the Company EEO Officer, and/or my supervisor.*

____________________________ ____________________

Employee Signature Date

To help us comply with Federal/State Equal Employment Opportunity record keeping, reporting and other legal requirements, please answer the questions below. **This form is confidential and will be maintained separately from your application form.**

NAME:
(print) ____________________________________________
LAST FIRST MIDDLE

ADDRESS: ____________________________________________
Street City State/Zip Code

TELEPHONE: (__) ________________ BIRTHDATE ____________ AGE ________

SEX: ( ) Male ( ) Female

MARITAL STATUS: ( ) Single ( ) Married ( ) Divorced ( ) Widowed

RACE/ETHNIC GROUP: ( ) White ( ) African-American ( ) Hispanic
( ) American Indian/Alaskan Native ( ) Asian/Pacific Islander

Are you a Disabled Veteran? ( ) Yes ( ) No If yes what is your VA Disability Rating? __________%
*A person entitled to disability compensation under laws administered by the Veterans Administration for disability rated at 30% or more, or a person whose discharge or release from active duty was for a disability incurred or aggravated in the line of duty.*

Are you a Vietnam Veteran? ( ) Yes ( ) No
*A person who served on active duty for a period of more than 180 days any part of which occurred between 8/5/64 and 5/7/75, and was discharged or released there from with other than a dishonorable discharge or for a service connected disability.*

**Figure 6–5. Employment Application (4 of 4)**

U.S. Department of Justice
Immigration and Naturalization Service

OMB No. 1115-0136

## Employment Eligibility Verification

### INSTRUCTIONS

PLEASE READ ALL INSTRUCTIONS CAREFULLY BEFORE COMPLETING THIS FORM.

**Anti-Discrimination Notice.** It is illegal to discriminate against any individual (other than an alien not authorized to work in the U.S.) in hiring, discharging, or recruiting or referring for a fee because of that individual's national origin or citizenship status. It is illegal to discriminate against work eligible individuals. Employers **CANNOT** specify which document(s) they will accept from an employee. The refusal to hire an individual because of a future expiration date may also constitute illegal discrimination.

**Section 1 - Employee.** All employees, citizens and noncitizens, hired after November 6, 1986, must complete Section 1 of this form at the time of hire, which is the actual beginning of employment. **The employer is responsible for ensuring that Section 1 is timely and properly completed.**

**Preparer/Translator Certification.** The Preparer/Translator Certification must be completed if Section 1 is prepared by a person other than the employee. A preparer/translator may be used only when the employee is unable to complete Section 1 on his/her own. However, the employee must still sign Section 1.

**Section 2 - Employer.** For the purpose of completing this form, the term "employer" includes those recruiters and referrers for a fee who are agricultural associations, agricultural employers or farm labor contractors.

Employers must complete Section 2 by examining evidence of identity and employment eligibility within three (3) business days of the date employment begins. If employees are authorized to work, but are unable to present the required document(s) within three business days, they must present a receipt for the application of the document(s) within three business days and the actual document(s) within ninety (90) days. However, if employers hire individuals for a duration of less than three business days, Section 2 must be completed at the time employment begins. **Employers must record: 1)** document title; **2)** issuing authority; **3)** document number, **4)** expiration date, if any; and **5)** the date employment begins. Employers must sign and date the certification. Employees must present original documents. Employers may, but are not required to, photocopy the document(s) presented. These photocopies may only be used for the verification process and must be retained with the I-9. **However, employers are still responsible for completing the I-9.**

**Section 3 - Updating and Reverification.** Employers must complete Section 3 when updating and/or reverifying the I-9. Employers must reverify employment eligibility of their employees on or before the expiration date recorded in Section 1. Employers **CANNOT** specify which document(s) they will accept from an employee.

- If an employee's name has changed at the time this form is being updated/ reverified, complete Block A.
- If an employee is rehired within three (3) years of the date this form was originally completed and the employee is still eligible to be employed on the same basis as previously indicated on this form (updating), complete Block B and the signature block.
- If an employee is rehired within three (3) years of the date this form was originally completed and the employee's work authorization has expired **or** if a current employee's work authorization is about to expire (reverification), complete Block B and:
  - examine any document that reflects that the employee is authorized to work in the U.S. (see List A **or** C),
  - record the document title, document number and expiration date (if any) in Block C, and
  - complete the signature block.

**Photocopying and Retaining Form I-9.** A blank I-9 may be reproduced, provided both sides are copied. The Instructions must be available to all employees completing this form. Employers must retain completed I-9s for three (3) years after the date of hire or one (1) year after the date employment ends, whichever is later.

**For more detailed information, you may refer to the INS Handbook for Employers, (Form M-274). You may obtain the handbook at your local INS office.**

**Privacy Act Notice.** The authority for collecting this information is the Immigration Reform and Control Act of 1986, Pub. L. 99-603 (8 USC 1324a).

This information is for employers to verify the eligibility of individuals for employment to preclude the unlawful hiring, or recruiting or referring for a fee, of aliens who are not authorized to work in the United States.

This information will be used by employers as a record of their basis for determining eligibility of an employee to work in the United States. The form will be kept by the employer and made available for inspection by officials of the U.S. Immigration and Naturalization Service, the Department of Labor and the Office of Special Counsel for Immigration Related Unfair Employment Practices.

Submission of the information required in this form is voluntary. However, an individual may not begin employment unless this form is completed, since employers are subject to civil or criminal penalties if they do not comply with the Immigration Reform and Control Act of 1986.

**Reporting Burden.** We try to create forms and instructions that are accurate, can be easily understood and which impose the least possible burden on you to provide us with information. Often this is difficult because some immigration laws are very complex. Accordingly, the reporting burden for this collection of information is computed as follows: **1)** learning about this form, 5 minutes; **2)** completing the form, 5 minutes; and **3)** assembling and filing (recordkeeping) the form, 5 minutes, for an average of 15 minutes per response. If you have comments regarding the accuracy of this burden estimate, or suggestions for making this form simpler, you can write to the Immigration and Naturalization Service, HQPDI, 425 I Street, N.W., Room 4034, Washington, DC 20536. OMB No. 1115-0136.

**EMPLOYERS MUST RETAIN COMPLETED FORM I-9**
**PLEASE DO NOT MAIL COMPLETED FORM I-9 TO INS**

Form I-9 (Rev. 11-21-91)N

**Figure 6–6. I-9 Form (1 of 3)**

U.S. Department of Justice
Immigration and Naturalization Service

OMB No. 1115-0136

**Employment Eligibility Verification**

**Please read instructions carefully before completing this form. The instructions must be available during completion of this form. ANTI-DISCRIMINATION NOTICE: It is illegal to discriminate against work eligible individuals. Employers CANNOT specify which document(s) they will accept from an employee. The refusal to hire an individual because of a future expiration date may also constitute illegal discrimination.**

**Section 1. Employee Information and Verification.** To be completed and signed by employee at the time employment begins.

| Print Name: Last | First | Middle Initial | Maiden Name |
|---|---|---|---|
| Address *(Street Name and Number)* | | Apt. # | Date of Birth *(month/day/year)* |
| City | State | Zip Code | Social Security # |

**I am aware that federal law provides for imprisonment and/or fines for false statements or use of false documents in connection with the completion of this form.**

I attest, under penalty of perjury, that I am (check one of the following):
- ☐ A citizen or national of the United States
- ☐ A Lawful Permanent Resident (Alien # A__________
- ☐ An alien authorized to work until ___/___/___
  (Alien # or Admission #)__________

Employee's Signature | Date *(month/day/year)*

**Preparer and/or Translator Certification.** *(To be completed and signed if Section 1 is prepared by a person other than the employee.) I attest, under penalty of perjury, that I have assisted in the completion of this form and that to the best of my knowledge the information is true and correct.*

| Preparer's/Translator's Signature | Print Name |
|---|---|
| Address *(Street Name and Number, City, State, Zip Code)* | Date *(month/day/year)* |

**Section 2. Employer Review and Verification. To be completed and signed by employer. Examine one document from List A OR examine one document from List B and one from List C, as listed on the reverse of this form, and record the title, number and expiration date, if any, of the document(s)**

| | List A | OR | List B | AND | List C |
|---|---|---|---|---|---|
| Document title: | ________ | | ________ | | ________ |
| Issuing authority: | ________ | | ________ | | ________ |
| Document #: | ________ | | ________ | | ________ |
| Expiration Date *(if any)*: | ___/___/___ | | ___/___/___ | | ___/___/___ |
| Document #: | ________ | | | | |
| Expiration Date *(if any)*: | ___/___/___ | | | | |

**CERTIFICATION - I attest, under penalty of perjury, that I have examined the document(s) presented by the above-named employee, that the above-listed document(s) appear to be genuine and to relate to the employee named, that the employee began employment on** *(month/day/year)*___/___/___ **and that to the best of my knowledge the employee is eligible to work in the United States. (State employment agencies may omit the date the employee began employment.)**

| Signature of Employer or Authorized Representative | Print Name | Title |
|---|---|---|
| Business or Organization Name | Address *(Street Name and Number, City, State, Zip Code)* | Date *(month/day/year)* |

**Section 3. Updating and Reverification** To be completed and signed by employer.

| A. New Name *(if applicable)* | B. Date of rehire *(month/day/year) (if applicable)* |
|---|---|

C. If employee's previous grant of work authorization has expired, provide the information below for the document that establishes current employment eligibility.

Document Title:________ Document #:________ Expiration Date (if any):___/___/___

**I attest, under penalty of perjury, that to the best of my knowledge, this employee is eligible to work in the United States, and if the employee presented document(s), the document(s) I have examined appear to be genuine and to relate to the individual.**

| Signature of Employer or Authorized Representative | Date *(month/day/year)* |
|---|---|

Form I-9 (Rev. 11-21-91)N Page 2

**Figure 6-6. I-9 Form (2 of 3)**

## LISTS OF ACCEPTABLE DOCUMENTS

### LIST A

**Documents that Establish Both Identity and Employment Eligibility**

1. U.S. Passport (unexpired or expired)
2. Certificate of U.S. Citizenship *(INS Form N-560 or N-561)*
3. Certificate of Naturalization *(INS Form N-550 or N-570)*
4. Unexpired foreign passport, with *I-551 stamp or* attached *INS Form I-94* indicating unexpired employment authorization
5. Permanent Resident Card or Alien Registration Receipt Card with photograph *(INS Form I-151 or I-551)*
6. Unexpired Temporary Resident Card *(INS Form I-688)*
7. Unexpired Employment Authorization Card *(INS Form I-688A)*
8. Unexpired Reentry Permit *(INS Form I-327)*
9. Unexpired Refugee Travel Document *(INS Form I-571)*
10. Unexpired Employment Authorization Document issued by the INS which contains a photograph *(INS Form I-688B)*

**OR**

### LIST B

**Documents that Establish Identity**

1. Driver's license or ID card issued by a state or outlying possession of the United States provided it contains a photograph or information such as name, date of birth, gender, height, eye color and address
2. ID card issued by federal, state or local government agencies or entities, provided it contains a photograph or information such as name, date of birth, gender, height, eye color and address
3. School ID card with a photograph
4. Voter's registration card
5. U.S. Military card or draft record
6. Military dependent's ID card
7. U.S. Coast Guard Merchant Mariner Card
8. Native American tribal document
9. Driver's license issued by a Canadian government authority

**For persons under age 18 who are unable to present a document listed above:**

10. School record or report card
11. Clinic, doctor or hospital record
12. Day-care or nursery school record

**AND**

### LIST C

**Documents that Establish Employment Eligibility**

1. U.S. social security card issued by the Social Security Administration *(other than a card stating it is not valid for employment)*
2. Certification of Birth Abroad issued by the Department of State *(Form FS-545 or Form DS-1350)*
3. Original or certified copy of a birth certificate issued by a state, county, municipal authority or outlying possession of the United States bearing an official seal
4. Native American tribal document
5. U.S. Citizen ID Card *(INS Form I-197)*
6. ID Card for use of Resident Citizen in the United States *(INS Form I-179)*
7. Unexpired employment authorization document issued by the INS *(other than those listed under List A)*

**Illustrations of many of these documents appear in Part 8 of the Handbook for Employers (M-274)**

Form I-9 (Rev. 10/4/00)Y Page 3

**Figure 6–6. I-9 Form (3 of 3)**

### Just Starting Out? More Tips for Completing the Job Application

Many people, especially when they are just staring out, feel at a disadvantage because they don't have real work experience or work-related references. If you are just beginning your career, here are some things you should include on your application:

1. **Summer jobs.** If you worked for anyone during summer vacation, be sure to include that information on your application. Summer jobs, just like full-time jobs, require you to show up for work on time, do your job responsibly, and demonstrate your ability to do a job well. Don't overlook work you may have done for a relative or a neighbor.
2. **Ability to use tools and machines.** Be sure to write down every tool and machine you know how to operate. Don't overlook your ability to operate machines such as photocopiers, calculators, cash registers, or computers. Think about every job you have done and the tools or machines you know how to operate safely and well. Add those to your list of skills.
3. **Volunteer work.** This type of work gives you experience you can use on a future job. It also shows a prospective employer that you are a responsible person. Examples of volunteer projects include Habitat for Humanity, Christmas in April, food or clothing drives, and youth group projects.
4. **References.** Of course you'll include anyone you worked for over summer vacation, but don't forget to include volunteer coordinators, a school or youth group counselor, or your instructors. You can also include a priest, minister, rabbi, or other religious advisor.

## Activity 4: Reading a Project Manual

A project manual is a book that is produced for large construction projects. The manual includes detailed information about every part of the project, from the size and type of construction materials to the color and type of paint. The following is an excerpt from a project manual for a medical clinic. Read the excerpt carefully and answer the questions that follow.

## *Project Manual—Excerpt*

| | |
|---|---|
| **Project:** | **Banister-Lieblong Clinic of the Conway Regional Medical Center, Conway, Arkansas** |
| **Architect:** | **Williams and Dean Associated Architects** |
| **Structural engineers:** | **Professional Engineering** |
| **Mechanical engineers:** | **Mike Trusty Engineering** |
| **Electrical engineers:** | **Harp Consulting Engineers** |

**Section 16471**

**Telephone Service Entrance**

**Part 1 General**

**1.01 Summary**

A. This section covers the work necessary to provide and install a complete raceway system for the building telephone system. The system shall include telephone service entrance raceway, equipment and terminal backboards, and empty 3/4" conduits to telephone outlets.

**1.02 Related Sections of the Project Manual**

| A. Section No. | Item |
|---|---|
| 09900 | Painting and Staining |
| 16111 | Conduit |
| 16130 | Boxes |
| 16195 | Electrical Identification |

**1.03 Quality Assurance**

A. Telephone Utility Company: Southwestern Bell Telephone Company
B. Install work in accordance with Telephone Utility Company's rules and regulations.

**Part 2 Products**

**2.01 Telephone Termination Backboard**
A. Material: Plywood
B. Size: 4' × 8', 3/4" thick

*(continued)*

**Part 3 Execution**

**3.01 Examination**

A. Verify that surfaces are ready to receive work.
B. Verify that field measurements are as shown on the drawings.
C. Beginning of installation means installer accepts existing conditions.

**3.02 Installation**

A. Finish paint termination backboard with durable enamel under the provisions of Section 09900 prior to installation of telephone equipment. Color to match wall.
B. Install termination backboards plumb, and attach securely at each corner. Install cabinet trim plumb.
C. Install galvanized pull wire in each empty telephone conduit containing a bend of over 10 feet in length.
D. Mark all backboards and cabinets with the legend "TELEPHONE" under the provisions of Section 16195, Electrical Identification.

END OF SECTION 16741—TELEPHONE SERVICE ENTRANCE

Source: Courtesy of Nabholz Construction Corp., Conway, AR

## *Project Manual Questions*

**1.** Look in section _____ of the project manual to find information on electrical identification.
a. 16130
b. 16195
c. 19651

**2.** _____ utility company provides telephone service to the Banister Lieblong Clinic.
a. Southwestern Bell
b. Pacific Utility Company
c. Conway Telephone, Inc.

**3.** _____ will *not* be part of the complete raceway system for the building telephone system.
a. Terminal backboards
b. Conduits measuring 1/2" to telephone outlets
c. Telephone service entrance raceway

**4.** The rules and regulations of _____ should be followed when installing the telephone service entrance.
   a. Southwestern Bell
   b. The Conway Medical Center
   c. Harp Consulting Engineers

**5.** The telephone termination backboard should be constructed of _____.
   a. 3/4"-thick plywood
   b. 1/2"-thick plywood
   c. 3/4"-thick medium-density fiberboard

**6.** _____ should be used to paint the termination backboard.
   a. Semi-gloss latex
   b. Durable enamel
   c. Flat latex

**7.** The backboards and cabinets must all be marked with the legend _____.
   a. COMMUNICATIONS
   b. RACEWAY RELAY
   c. TELEPHONE

**8.** _____ is the name of the electrical engineering firm working on this project.
   a. Mike Trusty Engineering
   b. Professional Engineering
   c. Harp Consulting Engineers

**9.** Galvanized pull wire is to be installed in each empty telephone conduit containing a bend of over _____ in length.
   a. 10 inches
   b. 10 feet
   c. 4 feet

**10.** To find more information on conduits, you would look in section _____ of the project manual.
   a. 16110
   b. 16111
   c. 16112

## Activity 5: Completing Workplace Forms

At work, you will have to fill out forms for lots of different activities. Examples of forms you will complete include time cards, work permits, safety tags for equipment, injury reports, and requests for equipment or to take leave. All forms share certain things in common. You must follow all directions on a form, fill out the form completely, and sign and date it.

This activity will give you practice in filling out two forms common in construction jobs: the weekly time card and the safe work permit.

### *Weekly Time Card*

Your pay (regular and overtime), leave, and benefits are all based on the number of hours you work each week. It is important to complete your time card carefully and accurately (see *Figure 6–7*). Use the following instructions to complete the time card.

#### Instructions for Completing a Time Card

1. Complete the top part of the form by printing your name, Friday's date, and your Social Security number.

2. Fill in each day based on the following information. On Monday you spent 10 hours welding. Eight of those hours were regular time; two of those hours were overtime. On Tuesday you spent six hours of regular time welding, and on Wednesday you spent three hours of regular time welding. The job number for welding is 14. The cost code for welding is A335.

3. You didn't work on Thursday—it was your day off.

4. On Friday, Saturday, and Sunday, you welded for eight hours each day. You worked two hours of overtime on both Friday and Saturday to help the framing crew meet a deadline. The job number for carpentry work is 22, and the cost code is C625.

5. Total your hours for the week in the far right column and check your math.

6. Sign your name.

7. Ask a classmate to check your time card, make sure your addition is correct, and sign the time card for you as your supervisor.

### *Safe Work Permit*

Safe work permits are issued by a qualified person; for example, a company's safety representative or the local fire marshal. These permits are required for certain types of tasks on a construction site. Examples of tasks that require safe work permits include the following:

- Welding or cutting operations that require the use of torches
- Tasks that involve the possibility of fire or explosion
- Tasks that must be done in confined spaces, such as pits or tanks

Emp. Name:____________________________

Week Ending:____________________________

**NABHOLZ CONSTRUCTION CORP.**
**LABOR DISTRIBUTION**

Soc. Security #:____________________________

| Job Number | Cost Code | Monday | | Tuesday | | Wednesday | | Thursday | | Friday | | Saturday | | Sunday | | Total | |
|---|---|---|---|---|---|---|---|---|---|---|---|---|---|---|---|---|---|
| | | Reg | O/T | Reg | O/T | Reg | O/T | Reg | O/T | Reg | O/T | Reg | O/T | Reg | O/T | Reg | O/T |
| | | | | | | | | | | | | | | | | | |
| | | | | | | | | | | | | | | | | | |
| | | | | | | | | | | | | | | | | | |
| | | | | | | | | | | | | | | | | | |
| | | | | | | | | | | | | | | | | | |
| | | | | | | | | | | | | | | | | | |
| | | | | | | | | | | | | | | | | | |
| | | | | | | | | | | | | | | | | | |
| | | | | | | | | | | | | | | | | | |
| | | | | | | | | | | | | | | | | | |

Employee Signature: ____________________________ Supt. Signature:____________________________

Source: Nabholz Construction Corporation, Conway, AR

**Figure 6-7. Weekly Time Card**

Authorized personnel must review and sign the permit. The permit allows authorized personnel to identify hazards, take steps necessary to safeguard workers, and make sure that the proper safety equipment is available and in good working order. Permits cover only the people identified in the permit for specific tasks and for specific dates and times.

In this activity, you will practice reading and completing a safe work permit (see *Figure 6–8*). Use the following information to complete this activity.

**Information Needed to Complete the Safe Work Permit**

**A note on terminology:** This permit involves hot work and lockout/tagout. Here is what these terms mean:

**Hot work:** Maintenance or repair tasks done on or near electrically energized or flammable equipment. Examples include electrically operated equipment and pipes that transport natural gas or petroleum.

**Lockout/tagout:** This two-step method ensures the safety of workers performing routine maintenance or repairs. Workers place approved locking devices on the equipment so that it cannot be accidentally turned on. They then affix a tag that states who authorized the lockout and why and how long the equipment will be locked.

**Section 1**

- The permit is issued for May 22, 2004, from 8:00 A.M. until 8:00 P.M.
- The work to be performed is the repair of an electrical service that has shorted out.
- The building number where the work will be done is 7C.
- The building supervisor is M.K. Gold.
- The specific equipment is Electrical Panel #3.
- The specific location of the work to be done is Floor 1, Room 106.
- The company performing the work is Electrical Concepts, Inc.
- The workers performing the work are P. White (entrant), J. Green (entrant), and T. Brown (attendant).

**Sections 2–13**

(2) Type of permit issued: hot work

(3) Protective equipment required: gloves and goggles

(4) Preparation required: lockout/tagout and work-area barricades

(5) General instructions: Workers must report hazards or accidents immediately and must stop work if any alarm sounds.

(6)–(11) Special precautions: Workers must remove all combustibles (items that can catch fire) from the area before they begin working. They must also cover all floor and wall openings and sprinkler heads and keep a water hose running.

## SAFE WORK PERMIT
## (1) GENERAL INFORMATION

Safe Work Permits are valid only during the shift (8 or 12 hours) for which issued. A new permit is needed for each shift.

This permit is Issued for: ______________ (date) from ______________ AM PM to ______________ AM PM

| Work To Be Performed: | Work Order Number: |
|---|---|

| Building Number or Department Name: | Building or Department Supervisor: |
|---|---|
| Specific Equipment or Object of the Work: | Specific Location of the Work: |

Name of Company Performing Work:

| Names of Employees Performing Work: | | Circle if appropriate: (Confined Space) | | |
|---|---|---|---|---|
| | 1– | | Entrant | Attendant |
| | 2– | | Entrant | Attendant |
| | 3– | | Entrant | Attendant |
| | 4– | | Entrant | Attendant |
| | 5– | | Entrant | Attendant |
| | 6– | | Entrant | Attendant |

| (2) TYPE PERMIT ISSUED | Yes | No | Initials |
|---|---|---|---|
| **Confined Space Entry** | | | |
| **Hot Work** | | | |
| **Line/Equipment Opening** | | | |
| **High Work** | | | |
| **Close Proximity Work** | | | |
| **Radioactive Device** | | | |
| **Other (specify):** | | | |
| **Insulation Removal—Separate Permit Required (IH PROCEDURE 7)** | | | |
| **Excavation—Separate Permit Required (SAFETY PROCEDURE 16)** | | | |
| **Hot Tapping—Separate Permit Required (SAFETY PROCEDURE 4)** | | | |

| (3) PROTECTIVE EQUIPMENT REQUIRED | Yes | No | Initials |
|---|---|---|---|
| Ear Protection | | | |
| Gloves (Specify Type: ) | | | |
| Acid Suit | | | |
| Protective Coveralls | | | |
| Respirator (Specify Type: ) | | | |
| Goggles | | | |
| Faceshield | | | |
| Lifeline and Body Harness | | | |
| Safety Net | | | |
| Other (list) | | | |

| (4) PREPARATIONS REQUIRED | Yes | No | Initials |
|---|---|---|---|
| Lockout/Tagout | | | |
| Drain/Empty Line/Equipment | | | |
| Vent/Purge Line/Equipment | | | |
| Valve Off/Isolate Line/Equipment | | | |
| Blind/Disconnect Line/Equipment | | | |
| Barricade Work Area | | | |
| Barricade Floors Below | | | |
| Other (specify) | | | |

| (5) GENERAL INSTRUCTIONS | Yes | No | Initials |
|---|---|---|---|
| Instructed on Sign In/Sign Out | | | |
| Instructed on Hazardous Materials Involved in Work | | | |
| Instructed on Fire Extinguisher Location/Operation | | | |
| Instructed on Shower/Eyewash Location/Operation | | | |
| Instructed on Sounding Alarm/Evacuations | | | |
| Instructed to Stop Work If Any Alarm Sounds | | | |
| Instructed to Report Hazards/Accidents Immediately | | | |
| Instructed on Permit Requirements | | | |

| (6) SPECIAL PRECAUTIONS—HOT WORK (SAFETY PROCEDURE 5) | Yes | No | Initials |
|---|---|---|---|
| Inertize Equipment | | | |
| Remove Combustibles in Area | | | |
| Cover Combustibles in Area | | | |
| Cover Floor/Wall Openings | | | |
| Cover Trenches/Sewer Drains | | | |
| Cover Conveyor Systems | | | |
| Cover Sprinkler Heads | | | |
| Cover Combustibles—Floor Below | | | |
| Wet Down Floor/Floor Below | | | |
| Water Hose Running | | | |
| Type ABC Extinguisher at Work Site (10 lb. minimum) | | | |
| Instructions on Fire Watch Duties | | | |

| (7) SPECIAL PRECAUTIONS—CONFINED SPACE ENTRY (SAFETY PROCEDURE 2) | Yes | No | Initials |
|---|---|---|---|
| Outside Fresh Air Supply Blower/Vacuum | | | |
| Bottom Outlet Valve Open Position | | | |
| 12 Volt Lighting or Ground Fault Interrupter | | | |
| Ladder Extended to Bottom and Tied Off | | | |
| Supplied Air Respirator w/ Built-In Escape | | | |
| Confined Space Watch/Attendant | | | |
| CPR & Rescue Personnel Available/Notified | | | |
| Entrants/Attendants Identified Above | | | |
| 2 SCBAs, 2 Lifelines w/ Harness at Job Location | | | |
| Communications Device to Summon Help | | | |
| Management Approval for Off-Hour Entries | | | |
| Safety Dept. Approval when Hazards Can Develop | | | |

| (8) SPECIAL PRECAUTIONS—LINE OPENING (SAFETY PROCEDURE 4) | Yes | No | Initials |
|---|---|---|---|
| Support/Hanger Conditions OK | | | |
| Opening Lines Under Pressure | | | |
| Opening Lines w/ Combustibles | | | |
| Opening Lines from Ladder | | | |
| Opening Common/Shared Lines | | | |

| (9) SPECIAL PRECAUTIONS–HIGH WORK (SAFETY PROCEDURE 23) | Yes | No | Initials |
|---|---|---|---|
| Instructed not to Walk on Tank Tops/Pipes | | | |
| Instructed not to Walk on Cable Trays | | | |
| Instructed not to Walk on Fiberglass/Plastic | | | |
| Instructed to Inspect Safety Harness/Lanyard/Lifeline | | | |
| Permission Given to Enter Roof | | | |

| (10) SPECIAL PRECAUTIONS—CLOSE PROXIMITY (SAFETY PROCEDURE 23 & 27) | Yes | No | Initials |
|---|---|---|---|
| Lifting/Hanging Objects Over Lines/Equipt. | | | |
| Lifting/Rigging w/i 15 ft of Electrical Line | | | |
| Moving Equipment w/i 10 ft. of 50 Kv Line | | | |
| Moving Equipment w/i 20 ft. of >50 Kv Line | | | |
| Other (specify) | | | |

| (11) SPECIAL PRECAUTIONS—RADIOACTIVE DEVICES (SAFETY PROCEDURE 22 & 24) | Yes | No | Initials |
|---|---|---|---|
| Procedure for Removing Radiation Device Reviewed | | | |
| Procedure for Industrial Radiography Reviewed | | | |
| Safe Perimeter Established/Barricaded/Signs Posted | | | |
| Restricted Area Cleared of Personnel | | | |
| Approval of Radiation Safety Officer Obtained | | | |

| (12) TESTS REQUIRED | Yes | No | Results | Initials |
|---|---|---|---|---|
| **Test Equipment Calibrated** | | | | |
| Initial Oxygen Meter Test (must be >18.5% and <22%) | | | | |
| Continuous Oxygen Meter Test (must be >18.5% and <22%) | | | | |
| Initial Explosion Meter Test (must be zero) | | | | |
| Continuous Explosion Meter Test (must be zero) | | | | |
| Toxic Substances (must be zero) | | | | |
| **Other (specify)** | | | | |

| (13) OTHER TEST RESULTS (ie., after breaks) | Time | Result | Initials |
|---|---|---|---|
| Oxygen [ ] Explosion [ ] Toxic (list) [ ] | | | |
| Oxygen [ ] Explosion [ ] Toxic (list) [ ] | | | |
| Oxygen [ ] Explosion [ ] Toxic (list) [ ] | | | |
| Oxygen [ ] Explosion [ ] Toxic (list) [ ] | | | |
| Oxygen [ ] Explosion [ ] Toxic (list) [ ] | | | |
| Oxygen [ ] Explosion [ ] Toxic (list) [ ] | | | |
| Oxygen [ ] Explosion [ ] Toxic (list) [ ] | | | |

(14) REMARKS

(15) APPROVAL SIGNATURES INDICATING JOB INSPECTION AND PERMIT REQUIREMENTS HAVE BEEN MET FOR WORK TO PROCEED

| Radiation Safety Officer (If Required) | Building Manager (Off–Hour Confined Space) | Safety Department (Variance Request) |
|---|---|---|

| Responsible Person for Maintenance or Contractor: | Responsible Person for Building or Department: |
|---|---|
| Print: Sign: | Sign: |

(18) SIGNATURES VERIFYING WORK COMPLETED AND WORK SITE READY FOR USE

| Responsible Person for Maintenance or Contractor: | Responsible Person for Building or Department: |
|---|---|
| Print: Sign: | Print: Sign: |

**PLANT EMERGENCY PHONE NUMBER IS**

Source: BE & K Construction Company, Birmingham, AL

**Figure 6–8. Safe Work Permit**

(Notice that the permit has six sections for special precautions, one for each type of permit issued. You must fill out only the section for the type of permit requested here.)

(12) Tests required: None

(13) Other test results: None

**Sections 14–18**

(14) Remarks: The job was completed in two hours.

(15) and (18) Approval signatures: For this permit, no signature from a radiation safety officer is required. Signatures are required from the building manager, the safety department representative, the person responsible for maintenance, and the person responsible for the building. (For this activity, you can pretend that you are these people. Print and sign their names. On an actual job, of course, only authorized personnel may sign the permit.)

## Activity 6: Getting to the Point in Writing

Because businesspeople are always busy, business writing has to be clear, direct, and to the point. Read the following email and answer the questions that follow.

From: You

To: The Boss

Re: Warehouse on Industrial Way

Date: May 12, 2004

Boss. How are things? I know you are busy, but I hope you read this email soon. I'm sending it to tell you about the new warehouse that we are putting up over on Industrial Way. We're swamped, but I think we can stay on schedule. As you know, my crew is scheduled to start working there next Monday. I only hope that everyone shows up. We've been having some tardiness problems. But nothing for you to worry about (I hope). This is going to be a big job, and I've already put in a lot of overtime. I've got things under control and I think we're going to be OK on the schedule, but there are a few things worrying me. Probably what's worrying me the most is that we don't have the permits yet. I know that we absolutely, positively cannot start until we have the permits. Anyway, hope your weekend goes well. I think the rain will hold off, which will be good for the startup on Monday (if everyone shows up on time). By the way, I should be freed up in about three weeks, and I'd like to take some time off.

## Questions

1. After reading this email, your boss will _____.
   a. think you want to be congratulated for staying on schedule
   b. think you want to be thanked for working overtime
   c. understand that you have things under control
   d. not know for certain what you actually want
2. To understand your email, your boss _____.
   a. should reread the email several times to find out what you want
   b. should highlight the main points of your email
   c. will probably have to guess what you want
   d. will probably have to call you or send an email asking what you want
3. If you were the boss in this example, you should probably ask your employee to _____.
   a. never send you an email again
   b. take a course in business writing
   c. give you information in person only
   d. stop wasting your time and get to the point
4. You wrote that "a few things" were worrying you. After reading your email your boss will know what all of those things are.
   a. True
   b. False
5. After reading this email, your boss will know what day you want to start your leave and how many days off you want.
   a. True
   b. False

## Activity 7: Writing a Resume

Your resume is one of the most important work documents you will write. In many cases, the appearance and content of your resume will determine whether you even get seen for a face-to-face interview. (See the sample resume format in *Figure 6–9.*) In this activity, you will collect information to write a resume for yourself. Here are some guidelines for writing a good resume:

- Keep it brief. Businesspeople are very busy and prefer resumes that are only one or two pages long.
- Spelling, grammar, and neatness count. Have a friend or instructor check over your resume for mistakes. Make sure your finished resume looks neat and clean.
- Tell the truth. Don't lie about or exaggerate your education, skills, or experience.
- Keep it up to date. As you gain more experience and training, add this information to your resume.

Use the following format to create your resume.

| Questions to Ask Yourself | Statements or Information to Include on Your Resume |
|---|---|
| Name, address, phone number, email address | |
| 1. What type of job are you hoping to get? | |
| 2. Who have you worked for already? (Include company names, addresses, and phone numbers) | |
| 3. What types of work have you done? | |
| 4. What types of skills do you have? | |
| 5. What type of education have you received? (Include your apprenticeship training plus any certification programs you attended.) | |

Your Name

Address

Phone number

Email address

**EMPLOYMENT OBJECTIVE**

Seeking a construction job where I can use my carpentry and custom woodworking skills.

**EXPERIENCE**

From May 2000 to present. Journeyman carpenter. LJL Construction, 123 Hammer Heights Rd., Fairfax, Va. 800-222-2222. Built custom cabinets, closet systems; framed single-family homes.

From June 1996 to May 2000. Carpenter. Hammer Company, 456 Lathe Lane, Philadelphia, Pa. 900-456-4566. Built closets and storage systems for commercial storage units.

From February 1994 to June 1996. Carpenter. Blue Ridge Builders, 789 Mountain Way, Fresno, Ca. 888-123-4567. Framed condo units, built fences and raised wood walkways.

**SKILLS**

Practical knowledge of carpentry hand and power tools, measuring tools, and woodworking tools. Qualified to read residential and commercial blueprints. Experience with both stick and modular frames, including steel frames. Working knowledge of roofing and residential plumbing. Trained and certified to use powder-actuated tools.

**CONSTRUCTION EDUCATION**

Apprenticeship. Carpentry. MK Builders Inc., Fresno, Ca. Certificate, 1996.

Professional carpentry certification program. ABC Training Corp., Philadelphia, Pa. Certificate, 2000.

Powder-actuated tools certification program. All States Community College, Fairfax, Va. Certificate, 2001.

**Figure 6-9. Sample Resume Format**

# Group Activities

## Activity 8: Making an Email Easier to Understand

In this activity, you will practice writing clearly and to the point. First read the following email. With the skills you have developed in this course, you and your classmates will rewrite it so that it is clear and easy for readers to understand. Discuss how you can make this email easier to read. What information can you take out? What information must be left in? (Hint: Remember the reader rules, and don't forget to use reader cues, like boldface type or bulleted lists.) Choose one team member to write down your group's suggestions.

**Team Members**

1. ______________________________ 2. ______________________________

3. ______________________________ 4. ______________________________

### *Email to a Supplier*

From: bk@waterworld.com

Subject: Plumbing supplies

Hi L.J.: I am in the process of getting the crew ready to begin work on the new Westside Hospital clinic. There will be a need for plumbing supplies, of course, and I hope you will be able to get us the supplies at prices like the ones we had on that elementary school job last summer. You remember that one, right? The plumbing supplies I will need are 24 stainless steel lavatories, 24 single lever faucets (also stainless), 28 water closets (electronic eye flushometers). I understand you now stock other finish fixtures as well. This is good news as it will be good to get all my supplies in one spot. Of course, I hope the prices will also be good for my budget. So I will also need 12 square wall-mount soap dispensers, 8 "hands free" hand dryers, and 8 baby-changing stations (the pull-down, molded plastic kind). You might as well include a unit price on a roller towel dispenser, too. Let me know prices and when I can get these supplies. On those sinks, make sure you price out both the 24 inchers and the 30 inchers. I also need the manufacturer's specs on those changing stations regarding any reinforcing we might have to do on the wall. And don't forget the grab bars. Hope you are having a great summer. Looking forward to that fishing trip this fall.

## Activity 9: Writing a Memo to Complain about a Problem

A lot of workplace communications involve identifying and describing problems. Often, people who write memos to complain let their emotions get in the way of clear communication. They're mad and they want everyone to know it. Venting your emotions in workplace communications is not professional, and those emotions can get in the way of stating your problem clearly. This activity will give you practice in writing a complaint memo and in separating emotions from facts. Follow the directions for setting up the memo, and read the tips. When you have completed your memo, exchange it with a classmate and answer the discussion questions.

### *Instructions for Writing the Memo*

- Use your name (as the sender) and today's date.
- Address the memo to your boss.
- Choose a subject line based on the following information.

### *Background Information for the Memo*

You are writing the memo to let your boss know about a mistake made on your most recent paycheck. You worked 10 hours of overtime on the weekend (which caused you to miss your child's soccer game) but were not paid for it. You had to go to the payroll office on your meal break to get the problem corrected and were late getting back to work because there was only one staff person on duty. The members of your work team were annoyed because you were late and put them behind. This is the second time in two months that a mistake has been made in overtime hours on your paycheck. The last time this happened, a big overtime check you were counting on for a family party was delayed for a week, so you had to borrow money from a relative. You have copies of your time sheets that clearly show the number of overtime hours worked. You feel that you have done a good job reporting your hours. You want to be paid for the overtime missed on this paycheck, and you want to let your boss know that you think the payroll office is not doing a good job.

### *Tips for Writing the Memo*

- Keep your cool. You feel pretty angry, but remember to be respectful.
- Stay on track. Say exactly what you want and what you think should be done to correct the problem now and in the future.
- Read your memo before exchanging it with your classmate, and don't forget to check your spelling.

### Discussion Questions

1. Is your classmate's memo respectful?
2. Based only on what your classmate has written, do you know what the problem is?
3. If you were your classmate's boss, would you know what your employee wants you to do?
4. What things did your classmate do well? How could your classmate's memo be improved?

## Activity 10: Paying Attention to Details

Details count, especially in construction work. Work with three or four of your classmates. Read each of the following situations and figure out what, if any, details are missing.

**Team Members**

1. ____________________ 2. ____________________

3. ____________________ 4. ____________________

**1.** For a fire to start, three things must be present in the same place at the same time: heat and oxygen.

Are all details present? ❑ Yes ❑ No

What's missing? ______________________________

**2.** You must follow four steps when using an orbital sander: Get a good grip on the tool before you turn it on. Let the sander come up to full speed before you set it against the surface to be sanded. When finished, don't set the sander down right away.

Are all details present? ❑ Yes ❑ No

What's missing? ______________________________

**3.** You must never wear contact lenses while welding. The ultraviolet rays might dry the moisture beneath the contact lens, causing it to fuse to your eye. If you then try to pull out the contact lens, you could rupture your cornea and go blind.

Are all details present? ❑ Yes ❑ No

What's missing? ______________________________

4. You will see four types of fire extinguisher labels: Class A (green), Class B (red), Class C, and Class D. Each stands for a different type of combustible fuel: A for ordinary combustibles, B for liquids, and C for electrical equipment.

   Are all details present? ❑ Yes ❑ No

   What's missing? ______________________

5. To get to the new job site, travel on Interstate 95 for 10 miles. Take the exit marked "Glades." Turn at the end of the ramp, and you'll see the new site in a little while.

   Are all details present? ❑ Yes ❑ No

   What's missing? ______________________

# Appendix A: Finding Information Fast in Books and Manuals

Suppose you want to find safety information on fire extinguishers in a 400-page manual. Flipping through all those pages would take a really long time! To quickly find the information you need, use one or more of the following features: table of contents, section headings, index, and glossary.

You will find the table of contents at the front of the manual. When you scan the table of contents, you will probably see the following:

Chapter 12 Preventing and Fighting Fires .............................. 35

You can now turn to page 35 and scan the section headings in Chapter 12 until you find one that reads "Fire Extinguisher Safety." What if you want to find the information even faster? Start at the table of contents and find the page number where the index starts. All the topics covered in the manual are listed in alphabetical order in the index. If you look under "F" for "fire extinguishers," you will find an entry that looks like this:

Fire extinguishers
  Safety, 142
  Types of, 145

While you read the safety information on page 142, you see the word ***accelerant*** in boldface type. The boldface type is a clue to you that the word is defined in a glossary (a mini-dictionary), which you will find by checking its location in the table of contents.

The table of contents, section headings, index, and glossary are the most common keys to finding information in a book or manual. Here are three more keys that will also help you find information fast:

- **Tables.** Examples of information commonly found in tables include statistics, weights and measures, pipe sizes, abbreviations, machine tolerances, machine parts, and load specifications. Many books and manuals have a special table of contents that lists only the tables.
- **Figures.** Many books and manuals also list figures in a special table of contents. Figures can include photographs, maps, and line drawings.
- **Section tabs.** Publishers sometimes add tabs to section dividers. The tabs project a little beyond the pages, so you can quickly spot the section you need when the book is closed.

# Appendix B: A Quick Guide to Reading Plans and Blueprints

Most blueprints today are not actually blue, but because these plans were at one time shown as white lines on a blue background, they are still called blueprints. Learning how to read blueprints takes time, and you will learn more about this topic in other training. For now, however, here is a quick guide to finding your way around most blueprints:

- **Know what type of blueprint you are looking at.** All blueprints include a title that describes the drawing. Here are some examples of titles: Roof Framing Plan, Floor Plan, Front Elevation, Finish Detail, Plumbing Plan, and Electrical Plan.
- **Figure out where you are in relation to the drawing.** Sometimes a drawing shows what a structure will look like if you are standing right in front of it (an elevation). To understand some drawings, like floor plans, you have to imagine that you have removed the roof from a structure so that you can look down into the rooms. Some plans show you a side view of a structure. Some drawings show only a part (section) of a structure, and some drawings show a close-up view (detail).
- **Know where to look for the meaning of symbols and abbreviations.** Blueprints contain a lot of information, so much of it is shown as tiny symbols or abbreviations. Symbols and what they mean are included on a list called a legend. Abbreviations are spelled out on an alphabetical list. Legends and lists may appear right on the drawing or be included in separate pages in a set of plans.
- **Know where to look for the scale of the drawing.** You will usually find this information next to or below the title of the drawing.
- **Know where to find additional information about the plans.** All sets of plans include general notes that give additional information about how the structure will be built, what materials will be used, and what building codes will be followed.
- **Know what to do if you have a question about a blueprint.** If you can't figure out a drawing or if something looks wrong to you, always talk to your supervisor. If there is an error in the drawing, your company will have a process in place to deal with it.

# Part Three

# Resolving Workplace Issues

# Managing Stress on the Job

## Self-Assessment
## How stressed are you?

How much stress do you have in your life? Although we all need a certain amount of stress, too much stress can make you ill. Stress is sneaky. You may not know how much stress you are feeling on a daily basis. For example, do you know how much stress you have recently experienced? Take this self-assessment quiz to find out. Put a checkmark next to any of the situations you have experienced over the past two weeks. Then count the number of boxes you checked.

**Stress Indicators**

*Note:* Everyone reacts to life events differently. The items in this table may not cause stress for everyone.

| | | |
|---|---|---|
| ❑ Was stuck in traffic | ❑ Didn't have the right tools | ❑ Had to go to the doctor or dentist |
| ❑ Waited in a long line | ❑ Was discriminated against | ❑ Was fired |
| ❑ Was put on hold on the phone for a long time | ❑ Was cursed at | ❑ Was treated rudely |
| ❑ Argued with someone | ❑ Got into a fistfight | ❑ Bought something that did not work |
| ❑ Felt jealous | ❑ Got cut off on the road | ❑ Had problems with my car |
| ❑ Called someone who did not call me back | ❑ Had money problems | ❑ Did not get enough sleep |
| ❑ Lost my temper | ❑ Drank too much alcohol | ❑ Ran out of supplies |
| ❑ Took illegal drugs | ❑ Worked under a tight deadline | ❑ Had too many events on my calendar |
| ❑ Waited for someone who was late or did not show up | ❑ Was late for work | ❑ Changed jobs |
| ❑ Had to discipline children | ❑ Got a promotion | ❑ Was nagged or harassed |
| ❑ Disagreed with a co-worker | ❑ Got married or divorced | ❑ Lost money |
| ❑ Felt pressure at work | ❑ Moved | ❑ Was the victim of a crime |
| ❑ Was kept awake by noise | ❑ Experienced the death of a friend or relative | ❑ Was ill |
| ❑ Could not find a parking spot | ❑ Saw someone else take credit for my work | ❑ Was delayed on a trip |
| ❑ Made a large purchase | ❑ Had to work in extreme temperatures or bad weather | ❑ Lost my wallet or keys |
| ❑ Lost information because my computer crashed | ❑ Worked a lot of overtime | ❑ Was upset by something I saw on the news |

***Scoring:*** Total checked ________

***Assessment:***

0–4 boxes checked: You haven't experienced much stress in the past two weeks. This module will help you learn to cope with stress when you do encounter it.

5–10 boxes checked: You may be experiencing moderate amounts of stress. You'll feel healthier and happier on the job if you find ways to lessen the stress you're under. This module will help you do exactly that.

More than 10 boxes checked: You may be experiencing a fairly high level of stress. This module offers tips, suggestions, and techniques for helping you reduce the stress you feel.

*Note:* For this self-assessment quiz, you must also consider the type of stress. You might have experienced only four stress indicators, but they might be high-stress ones. For example, the death of someone close to you, divorce, losing money, and being the victim of a crime are all fairly high-level stresses.

## Introduction

We all have many demands on our time. There are lots of things we have to do and lots of things we want to do. Fitting them all in is what makes life interesting. As you learned in the self-assessment quiz, even little things or joyful events can cause stress. Too much stress can make you sick. The good news is that you can manage stress. In this module, you will learn some techniques you can use to manage your stress and stay healthy.

## Recognizing stress

You won't always know when you are under too much stress. You will move from one thing to another, thinking that you can handle everything. Others may notice, however. For example, a co-worker may notice that you are rubbing your temples or clenching your fists or your jaw a lot. You may notice that someone else is acting distracted and not focusing on the job. A friend may notice that you are acting differently and tell you that you look stressed out. Following are some warning signs of stress:

- Can't sleep or sleep too much
- Have trouble concentrating or remembering things
- Feel tired all the time
- Frequently feel depressed, hopeless, or anxious
- Frequently have headaches or chest, back, or stomach pain

**Caution**

Be aware that many of the warning signs of stress are also warning signs of other health problems. Take responsibility for your health and know when to contact your doctor.

## Tips for managing stress

People feel the most stressed when they feel like victims of circumstances. To help reduce stress, try one or more of the following techniques. As you read, you'll see that all these suggestions have one thing in common—they all require you to take positive action.

**1. Solve problems that cause you stress.** If you know what causes stress in your life, you can find ways to stop that stress from happening. In fact, you can reduce certain types of stress with simple solutions. Here are some examples.

- Are you frustrated because the soda machine at work always seems to be out of soda or change? Try bringing in your own sodas in a cooler. It will save you time and money.
- Do you hate waiting in line? Bring along a book or magazine to help pass the time. Try calling ahead with your order. This is especially helpful when ordering job supplies.
- Are you feeling pressured because there is too much to do in a short time? Come up with a plan to help spread the workload around to meet the deadline, and show the plan to your supervisor.
- Are you dreading an upcoming test or job interview? Prepare as much as you can, then exercise, do something to take your mind off the event, and get a good night's sleep.

**2. Keep tools and equipment in good working order.** There's nothing more stressful than when a tool or machine breaks at a critical time. You can't prevent every breakdown, but you can head off most of them. Periodically check your tools and machines. Perform the manufacturer's recommended maintenance. When tools or equipment do break down, make repairs immediately or find another tool so that you can finish your task.

**3. Be as neat as the job allows.** A messy work area makes it difficult to find what you need, and that can be frustrating and stressful. It can also create stress for the people around you. In addition, a messy work area can be unsafe. To have a stress-free, safe work site, put away your tools, keep floor and work surface areas clear, and dispose of waste material promptly.

**4. Plan ahead.** Before you start a project, gather all the necessary tools and supplies and put them in one place. You'll have everything you need nearby, and you won't be frustrated by having to stop work to get needed supplies. If you have to pick up supplies, call or fax your order ahead of time so it will be ready for pickup.

**5. Do the hardest tasks first.** The longer you wait to do something difficult and the more time you spend thinking about it, the more stress builds up. Whenever possible, do the hardest part of a task first. You'll be amazed at how much stress you can avoid by tackling the hardest part of a task first.

**6. Eat right and exercise.** When you are fit, you can more easily handle stress. Many people smoke, eat junk food, take drugs, or drink alcohol to calm down. The calming effects don't last very long, however, and often result in cravings that actually cause more stress.

Many construction workers think they get enough exercise on the job. However, most construction tasks don't provide you with aerobic exercise. Aerobic exercise gets your heart rate up, helps to release stored-up tension, and helps you to sleep better. When you are feeling stressed, aerobic exercise will help you to relax.

**7. Get rid of negative thoughts.** Negative thinking is often the product of low self-esteem or worry. Instead of focusing on things you cannot do well, focus on the things you can do well, and figure out a plan to help you work on your weak areas. Believing in yourself is a great stress buster.

**8. Be flexible.** If you always expect everything to go perfectly, you'll always feel frustrated, because things rarely go 100 percent according to plan. If you can roll with the punches and adapt to changing situations, you'll experience much less frustration and stress. Keep in mind that most of these situations are temporary.

**9. Manage your money wisely.** Many people point to money, or the lack of it, as their number-one worry. Here are some tips to help you manage your money wisely:

- Make a budget so you will know how much money you need to pay your bills each month.
- Before you buy anything, ask yourself if you really need it or just want it.
- Limit your credit card use and try to pay off balances each month.
- Shop for bargains and sales.
- Limit the number of times you eat out or go out drinking.
- Get in the habit of saving some money from every paycheck.

**10. Keep work stress separate from home stress.** Sometimes it's hard to separate your job from your home life. However, try to leave work problems at work and home problems at home. Remember that work is only part of your life; it's not your whole life. Keep things in perspective, and recognize that almost all stressful situations are temporary. Focus on tasks you must accomplish as you work through a stressful situation.

**11. Hang on to your sense of humor.** Laughter is an instant muscle relaxer. You won't always be able to laugh your troubles away, but a healthy sense of humor can help you out of a lot of stressful situations. As the old saying goes, laughter really is the best medicine.

**12. Breathe deeply.** When you're stressed, you tend to breathe in short, shallow breaths, which increases muscle tension. To head off this problem, take several slow, deep breaths. You'll find that it is very hard to stay tense when you breathe deeply.

### A Special Tip
### Don't Fret over Small Things

Some people worry a lot about small things that really shouldn't matter. So what if you have to wait in line for 10 minutes? So does everyone else. So what if the car in front of you is going five miles under the speed limit? It will probably turn off the road soon anyway. When you decide not to get stressed, you will see your stress level go down or disappear completely.

**13. Improve your appearance.** It's true that when you look good you will feel good. So when you are feeling down, spruce yourself up.

**14. Do something for someone else.** A good way to take your mind off your own problems is to help someone else with theirs. Help out a friend in need. Volunteer to help others in your community. You'll get a lot of satisfaction from your efforts, and you'll see your own problems in a new light.

## Stress busters

This section includes some activities to help you relax and manage stress better. Also included are a few examples of stressful situations and suggestions for dealing with them.

A good way to keep stress in perspective is to find some time to do something you enjoy. Think of it as your reward for working hard. Consider the following stress busters:

- Participate in a sport or exercise.
- Do volunteer work.
- Take up a hobby.
- Relax your mind with a favorite book, movie, video, or CD.
- Relax your muscles by taking a nap, hot bath, or shower.
- Play with your children or your pet.

Each of the following examples offers suggestions for dealing with stress. However, because everyone reacts to stress differently, each person will also handle stress differently. Before you read each suggested stress buster, ask yourself how you would deal with the each of the following situations.

***Example 1:*** You and a co-worker are building a wall on a hot day. Sweat keeps dripping into your eyes and you are having trouble hanging on to your tools. To make matters worse, mosquitoes keep buzzing around and biting. You are scheduled to take a break, but you're a little bit behind, so you skip your break and keep working. Your co-worker accidentally steps on your foot and you start shouting and cursing.

***Suggested stress buster:*** Take that break. It will give you time to drink some water, wipe off the sweat, and apply insect repellent. Tie a bandanna on your forehead to soak up the sweat and keep it out of your eyes. Get a cloth to wipe sweat off your hands so you can handle your tools safely. Apologize to your co-worker and get on with the job.

***Example 2:*** Your co-worker constantly makes jokes about the way you talk. At first, you just shrugged it off; but lately, the comments are starting to bug you. Today, your co-worker seems determined to get you angry and pokes you in the ribs to see if you are listening to the jokes. You are tired of being treated disrespectfully and feel your fists clenching. You'd like to punch your co-worker.

***Suggested stress buster:*** Learn to control your anger and frustration. Don't let them control you. When you sense your anger level rising, close your eyes, take a deep breath, and count to 10 or 20 if necessary. That little break will help you calm down and refocus your energy. If you still feel like you're going to blow up, walk away. Later, when you are calm, talk to your co-worker. Say that you think the constant joking is unprofessional and that you want to be treated with respect.

***Example 3:*** You are in a money jam. You owe three creditors and only have enough money in your budget to make the minimum payment to two of them. Every Friday, your co-workers go out for drinks, and you are spending $15 to $20 each time you join them. You are not a heavy drinker but wind up spending more because the group always divides the bill up evenly. You feel guilty about time spent away from your child and want to buy a nice toy to make up for that. Your money problems are eating you up, and you are considering taking on a part-time job, even though your current job is very tiring.

***Suggested stress buster:*** Talk to a credit counselor who can help you figure out a more workable payment plan. Explain to your co-workers why you can't afford the Friday drinking parties every week, and cut back on the number of times you go. Look for other ways to keep from spending money, like bringing lunch from home instead of eating out. Use the free time you now have on Friday nights to spend more time with your child.

## Making the most of your time

Often, people who experience stressful lives think, "I wish there were more than 24 hours in a day. That's the only way I'd be able to get everything done." In truth, you don't need additional time; you just need to become a better time manager. You'll experience less anxiety if you attack each day with a game plan for accomplishing your tasks. Here are some tips to help you do just that:

**1. Make a plan, and stick to it.** A construction site is a busy place, and the final deadline for completing a project depends on all workers meeting their individual deadlines. As you leave work each day, plan what you'll do the next day. You can keep your plan in your head, but you may find it more satisfying to write it down and cross off items as you finish them. As you write the plan, identify your priorities. Ask yourself, "What are the most important tasks I need to accomplish tomorrow?" The next day, tackle those tasks with vigor.

**2. Don't procrastinate.** When you procrastinate, you put off doing the tasks that you have to do. People procrastinate when they don't enjoy doing a task, when they think it will take a lot of time, or when they feel they cannot handle the task. Not every task on a construction site is enjoyable, but they all need to get done on time. Try tackling the things you least like to do first (if possible) to get them out of the way.

**3. Don't waste time.** It's easy to get distracted on the job. Talking about your weekend, problems you have at home, or your upcoming plans can eat up an amazing amount of time. No one expects you to be a machine, but you should keep social conversations at work brief and focus on your tasks.

**4. Look for ways to use time wisely.** Say your workday includes the following tasks: going downtown to pick up some permits, hanging some doors, delivering supplies to another work site, taking some bags of garbage to a nearby dump, and shingling a roof. What order would you do these tasks in? It's usually best to do the most difficult or most time-consuming tasks first and to group similar tasks together. Here's one suggestion:

- Shingle the roof in the morning when the temperature is coolest.
- Load the supplies and the garbage bags into your truck. Drop off the garbage on your way to deliver the supplies.
- Drive downtown to pick up the permits.
- Hang the doors.

On the job site, of course, you have to take into account the schedules of other workers as well as the tasks your supervisor schedules. Whenever possible, try to figure out the best way to use your time each day.

## On-the-Job Quiz

Here's a quick quiz that asks you to apply what you've learned in this module.

1. One of your co-workers says to you, "Wow, you look really stressed out." What might you be doing to make your co-worker say this?
   a. Acting distracted and not focusing on the job.
   b. Drinking a lot of coffee.
   c. Writing down a long list of your plans for your workday.
   d. Looking off into the distance and breathing deeply.
2. A row of coat hooks is located near the break area at work. There aren't enough hooks for everyone, so workers just double or sometimes triple up on the hooks. At day's end, workers waste time cursing and looking for their jackets, and some jackets always fall on the ground. It's a small, but annoying and somewhat stressful, problem. To solve this problem in a positive way, you should _____.
   a. remove all the hooks and let workers find their own spots to hang up their jackets
   b. put up a sign that says when all the hooks are filled, workers have to find another place for their jackets
   c. make a rule that only the most senior workers can use the hooks
   d. install some more hooks

3. You are in the middle of ripping clapboards for a custom siding job when your circular saw jams and stops working. What is the least stressful way to deal with this problem?
   a. Mentally kick yourself for failing to maintain your saw.
   b. Take a short break, breathe deeply, and wonder how you will fix your saw.
   c. Fix the problem or find a replacement saw and do a better job of maintenance in the future.
   d. Tell your supervisor that the saw is broken and you won't be able to stay on schedule.
4. You've had a tough day on the job. You're exhausted and a little bit behind schedule, so you are feeling really stressed out. You don't want to take out your frustrations on your family. What is the best way to deal with your stress?
   a. Go to the gym and work out.
   b. Go to a bar with friends and relax with a couple of drinks.
   c. Ask your boss for permission to work overtime so you can get caught up.
   d. Complain to your boss or a co-worker about the stress you are feeling.
5. You are worrying a lot about your job. You have to do some detailed woodwork next week, and it's going to take a lot of time and skill. You've been feeling tired, and you're afraid you're going to make a lot of mistakes and get fired. Then who will feed your family? Who will pay the bills? What is the best way to deal with this situation?
   a. Go out for a nice dinner and see a movie.
   b. Believe in your ability, exercise to relax, and get more sleep.
   c. Tell your boss you are not up to doing this job and ask that it be assigned to someone else.
   d. Drink more coffee or soda to increase your caffeine levels so that you will be alert when doing the work.
6. You are scheduled to do roofing today. You enjoy roofing, and it's a nice cool day for the work. However, your boss tells you that you have to help complete some trenching work, which you dislike doing, instead. What is your best course of action?
   a. Recognize that the situation is temporary, be flexible, and do a good job.
   b. Explain to your boss that trenching is really not your job and someone else should do that task.
   c. Do the trench work, but make sure your boss knows how much you dislike it so that you won't be assigned to do trench work again.
   d. Do the trench work, but take an extra half hour for lunch to reward yourself for working hard.

7. You earn a good salary, but unexpected expenses land you with more bills than you can pay. The best way to manage the stress caused by your money problems is to _____.
   a. join a local gym and exercise regularly to reduce the stress you feel
   b. talk to a credit counselor to find a manageable way to pay your debts
   c. take a vacation so that you can forget your troubles and get rid of stress
   d. volunteer to help the needy so that you can put your problems in perspective

8. Your supervisor, who is normally easygoing and reasonable, is getting a divorce and has been very critical of your work lately. You recognize that your boss is letting stress at home affect the job. Now you are feeling stressed, too. What is your best course of action?
   a. Show your supervisor this module and state that it is best to keep home stress separate from the workplace.
   b. Tell your supervisor's boss about the problems your boss is causing.
   c. Recognize that the situation is temporary and focus on doing a good job.
   d. Offer to act as a sounding board for your boss and give advice on how to handle the divorce.

9. A co-worker who has a foul mouth and a rotten temper curses at you for no reason. You feel angry and insulted and want your co-worker to know that you should be treated with respect. What is your best course of action?
   a. Curse back to let off steam and reduce your stress, but don't physically attack your co-worker.
   b. Count slowly to 10 before you say anything, and walk away if you're still angry.
   c. Wait until after work when you are off the job site to settle the matter.
   d. Make fun of your co-worker, because laughter is the best medicine.

**10.** Your boss tells you that you must accomplish the following four tasks:

- Sweep the floors of the house your team is building.
- Hang four doors in the house.
- Drive across town to pick up supplies needed by the end of the workweek.
- Place a large order for lumber.

Assuming that no other people on the job are affected by any of these tasks, in what order should you do the tasks?

a. Order the lumber, hang the doors, sweep the floors, pick up the supplies.
b. Hang the doors, pick up the supplies, order the lumber, sweep the floors.
c. Pick up the supplies, hang the doors, order the lumber, sweep the floors.
d. Sweep the floors, hang the doors, pick up the supplies, order the lumber.

## Individual Activities

### Activity 1: Eliminating Your Time Wasters

Managing your time effectively will help you control the stress in your life. To manage your time well, you need to be aware of your own personal time wasters—those people or activities that take up your time and prevent you from accomplishing the tasks you must do.

The following list includes some common time wasters. Check any that apply to you, then develop an action plan for dealing with them.

| Check Here | Time Wasters |
|---|---|
| ❑ | Being disorganized |
| ❑ | Spending time searching for misplaced items |
| ❑ | Trying to do too much in one day |
| ❑ | Getting up late |
| ❑ | Being a perfectionist |
| ❑ | Spending too much time gossiping with co-workers |
| ❑ | Talking on the phone to friends during work hours |
| ❑ | Staying up late at night to party too often |
| ❑ | Failing to plan ahead |
| ❑ | Allowing too many interruptions to your workday |
| ❑ | Procrastinating |
| ❑ | Failing to listen to or read instructions |
| ❑ | Spending too much time fiddling with small, unimportant tasks |
| ❑ | Working too slowly |
| ❑ | Playing computer games or surfing the internet |
| ❑ | Other: |

**Sample Problem:** *Procrastination*

**Sample Action Plan**

1. Divide a big job into small tasks so I don't feel overwhelmed.
2. If possible, do the hardest tasks or tasks I don't like first to get them out of the way.
3. Give myself deadlines for getting each task done.
4. Reward myself for completing the tasks or withhold the reward if I don't complete them.

**My Time Wasters**

Problem: ____________________

Action Plan: ____________________

____________________

____________________

____________________

Problem: ____________________

Action Plan: ____________________

____________________

____________________

____________________

Problem: ____________________

Action Plan: ____________________

____________________

____________________

____________________

## Activity 2: Practicing Relaxation Techniques

When people feel stress, they often take shallow breaths. Shallow breathing, in turn, causes more stress. Fortunately, there are several deep-breathing and muscle-relaxation exercises you can do to lessen physical stress. In this activity, you will practice doing these exercises. You might think that these exercises are silly and you might be embarrassed to try them, but don't be. These exercises are a good way to reduce stress, and they really work. Try one or more of the exercises and then answer these questions:

1. Did you feel more relaxed after trying the exercise?
2. Can you think of a recent situation where these exercises could have helped you relax?

### *Deep-Breathing Exercise*

This exercise will help you get more air into your lungs, which will help relieve stress in your shoulders and back. At first, you may feel more stress than relaxation, but once you learn the exercise, it will work for you. Repeat the exercise five times.

1. Sit up straight in a comfortable chair.
2. Place one hand on your stomach and the other hand on your chest.
3. Breathe in slowly through your nose. When you breathe in, you should feel the hand on your stomach rise before the hand on your chest rises. Practice until this happens.
4. As you continue to inhale, you will feel your shoulders rise a little as your lungs fill with air.
5. Hold your breath for five seconds.
6. Slowly exhale. As you exhale, your shoulders will drop.

### *Muscle-Relaxation Exercises*

These exercises will help you relax when you feel pain or tension in your head, jaw, arms, shoulders, neck, or legs. In each exercise, you will first increase and then relieve the tension. Repeat each exercise 5 or 10 times or until you feel the tension disappear. Focus on doing each exercise smoothly. Don't forget to breathe!

***Forehead:*** Close your eyes, and raise your eyebrows as high as you can. Hold for five seconds and relax.

***Jaw:*** Bite down and pull down the corners of your mouth in an exaggerated frown. Hold for five seconds and relax.

***Arms:*** Push your elbows into the back of your chair just enough to feel tension in your upper arms. Hold for five seconds and relax.

***Shoulders and neck:*** Pull your chin down into your chest as far as it will go. Hold for five seconds and relax. Take a deep breath to release the tension from your shoulders.

***Legs:*** Raise your legs and point your toes. Hold for five seconds and then lower your legs.

## Activity 3: Determining Your Sources of Stress

In this activity, you will use the worksheet provided to list the things that cause you the most stress. Based on what you have learned in this module, come up with a plan of positive actions you can take to reduce stress.

| Personal Stress Worksheet | |
|---|---|
| **Cause of Stress** | |
| **Action Plan** | |
| **Cause of Stress** | |
| **Action Plan** | |
| **Cause of Stress** | |
| **Action Plan** | |
| **Cause of Stress** | |
| **Action Plan** | |

## Activity 4: Creating Your Own Stressometer

Everyone reacts to stress differently. In this activity, you will create your own stress profile on the stressometer (see *Figure 7–1*). Record the things that cause you just a little stress at the lowest temperatures, the things that cause you moderate stress at the middle temperatures, and the things that make you boil over at the highest temperatures. Think about some strategies that you can use to manage or head off the higher-temperature stresses in your life.

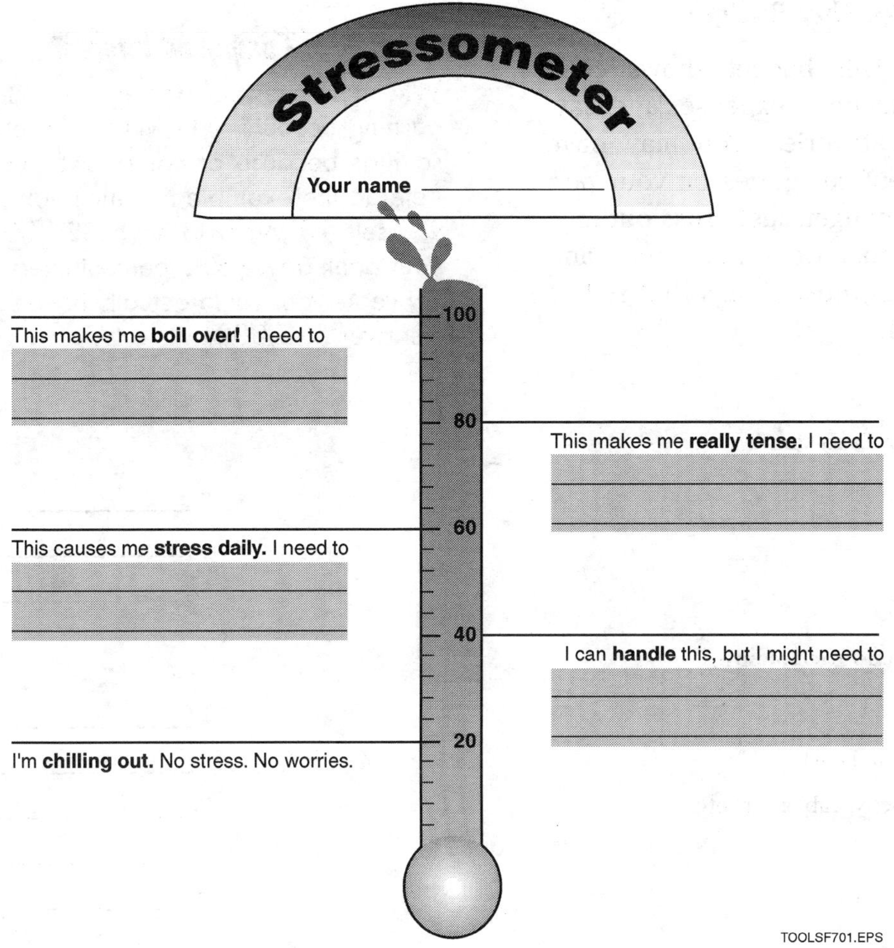


**Figure 7-1. Stressometer**

## Activity 5: Creating Your Own Budget

As you learned in this module, many people say that money—or not enough of it—is a big source of stress. A great way to keep money troubles from stressing you out is to learn how to make and work with a budget. If you have never done this before, this activity will give you the tools and information you need. First, consider a couple of tips:

- To figure out how much money you need to save each month for a future event, divide the total amount needed by the number of months in the time period you have selected. Example: You figure that you will need $20,000 in 10 years. So you would need to save about $167.00 per month. ($20,000 ÷ 120 months = $166.66). Note that if you invest your savings in an interest-earning account, you will reach your savings goal in less time.
- Keep up with credit card payments, pay more than the minimum required by the credit card company, and avoid charging more than you can pay off in six months or a year. If you pay only the minimum, you wind up paying much more than the amount you charged.

### My Monthly Budget

*Note:* This budget shows common income, expense, and savings categories. You may have different categories on your personal budget. Just cross out anything that does not apply, and write in those things that reflect your life.

> **The Magic of Compound Interest**
>
> When you invest your money in an interest-earning account, you will increase your savings because of compound interest. Refer to the example in which you gave yourself 10 years to save $20,000. If your bank pays you 3 percent interest, in 10 years you would actually have saved just over $23,000.

| Category 1: Money Coming in Each Month | |
|---|---|
| My salary | $ ________ |
| Other income | ________ |
| **Total category 1** | $ ________ |

| Category 2: Money I Must Spend Each Month | |
|---|---|
| Rent or mortgage | $ ________ |
| Insurance (life, health, home, and car) | ________ |
| Utilities (phone, water, electricity, cable, gas, etc.) | ________ |
| Car payments | ________ |
| Car upkeep (gas, oil, maintenance) | ________ |
| Food and toiletries | ________ |
| Clothes and shoes | ________ |
| Medical (co-payments, prescriptions, etc.) | ________ |
| Other | ________ |
| **Total category 2** | $ ________ |

| Category 3: Things I Must Save Money for Each Month | |
|---|---|
| Emergencies | $ ________ |
| Retirement | ________ |
| Education for myself or my children | ________ |
| A home purchase | ________ |
| Holiday purchases | ________ |
| Other | ________ |
| **Total category 3** | $ ________ |

| Category 4: Things I Want to Spend Money On | |
|---|---|
| Fun (eating out, entertainment, books, records, hobbies, vacations) | $ ________ |
| Other | ________ |
| **Total category 4** | $ ________ |

To complete your budget, follow these steps:

**Step 1** Add up the numbers to get the totals for categories 1, 2, and 3.

**Step 2** Add the totals of categories 2 and 3 together.

**Step 3** Subtract that answer from the category 1 total.

At this point, it would be nice if you had some money left over for category 4. You may or may not. Keep in mind that when you first start out, your budget will feel a little tight. If you establish good saving habits, you will soon have a pool of money that you can use for both the things you need and the things you want.

## Group Activities

### Activity 6: Turning Negative Thinking into Positive Thoughts and Actions

Negative thinking is pretty harmful. It makes you feel less sure of yourself, which can lead to stress. In this activity, you and three or four classmates will replace negative thinking with positive thinking and affirmative statements or actions. As you work through this activity, keep these tips in mind:

- Focus on the behavior, not on the person. A mistake may, in fact, be stupid, but making one does not mean that you are a stupid person.
- The world will be on your shoulders only if you put it there. Ask for help when you need it.
- Examine thoughts that include the words *never* or *always*. Is it really true that you will *never* learn how to do something? Is it really true that you *always* miss out on the good things in life?
- To get rid of negative thoughts, you have to do more than just change the words in your head. You have to take positive or affirmative actions. Those actions might include getting additional education or training, meeting your challenges, or simply learning to accept yourself for who you are and deciding to be happy about it.

**Team Members**

1. ______________________ 2. ______________________

3. ______________________ 4. ______________________

| Negative Thought | Positive Thoughts and Affirmative Actions |
|---|---|
| I can't believe that I did that wrong again! I'm so stupid! | Example: I am not stupid. I might just need additional training. I'll ask my supervisor about training opportunities. |
| No matter how hard I try, I will never be able to figure out how to do this job. | |
| I just know the boss is going to make me work overtime this weekend. Why is it always me? | |

*(continued)*

| Negative Thought | Positive Thoughts and Affirmative Actions |
|---|---|
| I am tired of the boss telling me what to do. No one has the right to do that. | |
| I don't think I would like being a boss, and besides, I am not good enough to do that job. | |
| I have to baby-sit everybody on this job. Co-workers always bring their troubles to me. Do I have a sign on my forehead that says, "All your problems solved here"? | |
| None of the other workers like me. And I know the boss hates me. No wonder I can't get ahead in this job. | |
| The boss must stay up late nights thinking of ways to make my life miserable. I am always given the cruddy jobs. | |
| This job is too hard. I am not strong enough to do it on my own. Who do these people expect me to be? The Incredible Hulk? | |
| I am drowning in debt. I'll probably get kicked out on the street and starve. Why does this stuff always happen to me? | |
| My co-workers are such jerks. Not one of them is worth anything. I have to fill in for all of them! | |

## Activity 7: Swatting the "Stress Bugs"

Some experts believe that small annoyances—getting stopped at a red light, breaking a shoelace, or missing your favorite TV show—can create more stress than big things like getting married or changing jobs. In this activity, you and three or four of your classmates will make a list of "stress bugs," those small but pesky annoyances that have gotten on your nerves recently. Most people who do this activity enjoy it and wind up laughing as they list each tiny bug. That's a good sign, because it shows that you realize that these things are not worth getting upset about. Try to keep this activity in mind the next time you have to deal with one of these bugs. Remember: only tiny stress bugs are allowed on this list.

**Team Members**

1. ______________________ 2. ______________________

3. ______________________ 4. ______________________

**My Stress Bugs**

1. ____________________
2. ____________________
3. ____________________
4. ____________________
5. ____________________
6. ____________________
7. ____________________
8. ____________________
9. ____________________
10. ____________________

## Activity 8: Your Turn—Telling Inspirational Stories

Almost everyone knows a story about someone who has overcome the odds to succeed in life. These are people who seem to have every reason for being unhappy and stressed but are upbeat and positive instead. Maybe you are one of those people. For this activity, do one of the following:

- Tell your classmates a story about yourself or someone you know who deals with hardships yet faces life optimistically.
- Find a story about such a person in a newspaper, a magazine, or on the internet to share with your classmates.
- Talk about why these people are upbeat. What inspires them and keeps them going?

## Activity 9: Your Turn—Creating Stress Busters at Work

You are the local expert regarding conditions at your work site. Do you think that your co-workers or boss would benefit from some of the stress busters you learned about in this module? Do you think that you can make changes in your workplace to help reduce stress? Here's your chance to create an action plan that you can take back to the job with you. Work with three or four of your classmates to create your workplace stress-busting plan by answering the discussion questions.

**Team Members**

| | |
|---|---|
| 1. ____________________ | 2. ____________________ |
| 3. ____________________ | 4. ____________________ |

## Discussion Questions

1. What activity or exercise could I share with my team that can help all of us deal with stress?
2. If my co-workers like to go out drinking on a regular basis, can I suggest some other enjoyable activities that don't cost as much or that don't always involve alcohol?
3. Is there some little but annoying problem at work that I could help solve to make things better?
4. Can I get a reduced membership fee at a gym if I can get a bunch of my co-workers to sign up with me?
5. Can I convince my co-workers to have a "bring-lunch-to-work day" to help reduce what we all spend on lunches out?
6. Can I get my co-workers interested in doing something nice for others (for example, volunteering for a community project or giving blood) as a way of reducing stress?

## Activity 10: Your Turn—Creating a Rescue Resource List

Doing relaxation exercises and practicing positive thinking will only take you so far. Sometimes you need to reach out for help, especially for the more serious stress-related problems. For example, some people turn to their religion or a workplace counselor for help. Some people join a group of people with similar problems, and some rely on a trusted friend. In this activity, work with three or four classmates to come up with a list of people or agencies that can help you work through serious problems.

**Team Members**

1. ______________________ 2. ______________________

3. ______________________ 4. ______________________

**My Rescue Resource List**

1. ______________________________________________
2. ______________________________________________
3. ______________________________________________
4. ______________________________________________
5. ______________________________________________

## Discussion Questions

1. Do I know what resources are available at my company? How can I find out?
2. Do I know what resources are available in my community? How can I find out?
3. Do I know what resources are available online? How can I find out?

# Thinking Critically and Solving Problems

## SELF-ASSESSMENT
### CAN YOU THINK CRITICALLY?

Do you think before you act? Can you solve problems creatively when they arise? Take the following self-assessment quiz to evaluate your problem-solving abilities. Check whether you agree or disagree with the following statements, then look at your score below.

| | I Agree | I Disagree |
|---|---|---|
| 1. Anything I read in a book, magazine, newspaper, or on the internet must be true. | ❑ | ❑ |
| 2. The old-fashioned way is usually the best way to do something. | ❑ | ❑ |
| 3. The boss is always right. | ❑ | ❑ |
| 4 If I ignore a problem long enough, it will go away. | ❑ | ❑ |
| 5. Something I learn from reading a book is always more reliable than my own experience. | ❑ | ❑ |
| 6 I get the best solutions when I solve problems on my own. | ❑ | ❑ |
| 7. The best way to solve a problem is to just do it. Research and thinking just wastes time | ❑ | ❑ |
| 8. News on television and radio is 100 percent accurate. | ❑ | ❑ |
| 9. There is usually only one good way to solve a problem. | ❑ | ❑ |
| 10. The cause of most problems is usually obvious. | ❑ | ❑ |

***Scoring:*** Total the number of "Disagree" boxes you checked: ________

***Assessment:***

9–10 boxes checked: You have the ability to think critically. This module will help you fine-tune your skills.

7–8 boxes checked: You have the ability to think critically, but you may tend to accept some information without evaluating it. This module will help you to further develop your critical thinking and problem-solving skills.

1–6 boxes checked: You tend to accept information at face value. This means that you don't think about information you receive or evaluate it. This module will help you learn to evaluate information and develop critical-thinking skills.

## Introduction

Construction work is challenging. During your career, you will frequently deal with new problems, new techniques, new machinery, new materials, and new technology. To be successful, you must be ready, willing, and able to handle these challenges and help solve any problems that arise. Although it is sometimes stressful or frustrating to deal with workplace problems, they do make your job more interesting. You will get a lot of satisfaction when you tackle a difficult problem and figure out how to solve it.

In this module, you will learn about and practice two skills: critical thinking and problem solving. Being able to think critically will help you develop the skills you need to become a better problem solver.

## Critical thinking

What is critical thinking? When you think critically, you do the following things:

- You pay close attention to information that you hear or read.
- You evaluate the information based on what you already know or what you can discover by doing some research or asking some questions.

The goal of critical thinking is to help you make the best possible decisions about information that you receive. When you learn to think critically, you will look beyond the surface and dig deeper to understand why something is happening. That means you won't make hasty or snap decisions or jump to conclusions before you think things through.

**Note**

The word *critical* in *critical thinking* means focusing on information that is important. It does not mean *negative*. As you will see in a later module, criticism is not always negative.

Consider this example: You can't figure out your co-worker. Sometimes everything seems fine. At other times, your co-worker ignores you when you speak, doesn't return your greetings, or doesn't answer your questions. What's going on? Is your co-worker mad at you or just rude? Maybe. But there might be other reasons that could explain your co-worker's behavior. Can you think of any? Once you have thought of other possible reasons, how will you check to see if these reasons are accurate?

### Using the Critical-Thinking Tools

The critical-thinking tools are a series of questions that you can ask to evaluate information or situations. Read the following example, and then see how the critical thinking tools are applied to the information provided.

### Learn Construction Math in Just Two Days!

Could your construction career use a boost? This easy, fun-filled course will make you a more valuable employee. In almost no time, you will learn everything you need to know about the following topics:

- Applying basic math functions to construction work
- Converting fractions to decimals and decimals to fractions
- Measuring with hand- and computer-assisted tools
- Using the standard and metric measuring systems and making conversions
- Applying geometry to construction problems
- Working with nominal sizes
- Using simple algebra to solve construction problems

Yes! In just two fun-filled days you will master all these topics and more! Impress your boss with your math wizardry. Astonish your co-workers. Using our proven and tested methods, you will learn instantly and without effort. Call today!

XYZ Learning, Inc.

P.O. Box 001

Richmond, VA 00001

800-000-0000

**Tool 1. Can I trust the source of this information?** You will get information from many sources. Which of those sources can you trust? Generally, you can trust sources with one or more of the following characteristics:

- An established track record of telling the truth
- Proven experience in an area
- A record of knowledge or expertise in an area

Who is the source of the information in this example? Do you think you can trust this source? Why or why not? What can you do to check out this source? Note that some people or companies won't have a track record. People who are just starting out or brand-new companies must work hard to earn the trust of others. In these situations, you must evaluate the source based on your own knowledge and experience.

**Tool 2. How does this information measure up against my own knowledge and experience?** Your own knowledge and experience are important parts of critical thinking. Look at the example again. Do you think that it is possible to learn all of the subjects listed in two days? Why or why not? Do you think it is possible to learn the topics instantly and without making any effort? Why or why not?

**Tool 3. How do I feel about this information, and why do I feel this way?** Sometimes your personal feelings can get in the way of your ability to critically evaluate information. Consider the example again. If you really dislike math courses, you might be tempted to take this "easy, fun-filled" course, even though all of your critical-thinking skills are telling you this offer is probably too good to be true. Your desire to learn a difficult subject without making any effort might overcome your critical-thinking skills. When you think that your emotions—good or bad—might affect your judgment, put emotions to one side and think over the facts before doing anything.

**Tool 4. What other sources can I consult about this information?** Even when you apply your critical-thinking skills and put your emotions to one side, you might still be undecided. Who knows? Unlikely as it may seem, maybe these people have discovered an easy way to learn math. If you are unsure about information, it is a good idea to talk to people with expert knowledge before making a decision. Who would you ask about this example?

Keep these critical-thinking tools in mind as you work on the problems presented later in this module. These tools will help you strengthen your ability to analyze and solve problems that come up on the work site and in other areas of your life as well.

**Remember:** Do not accept information at face value. Dig a little deeper. Make decisions based on facts, not emotions. Consult experts or people you trust.

## Problem solving

The ability to solve problems is an important skill in any workplace. It's especially important in construction, where the workday is often not predictable or routine. In this section, you will learn a five-step process for solving problems. You can use this process to solve both workplace and personal problems. Let's take a look at the steps and then see how they can be applied to a job-related problem:

**Step 1** Define the problem.

This step is not as easy as it sounds. See the box titled "Defining the Problem—A Problem Itself."

**Step 2** Think about different ways to solve the problem.

There is often more than one solution to a problem, so you must think through each possible solution.

**Step 3** Pick the solution that seems best and figure out an action plan.

It's best to get input from the people most affected by the problem and its solution.

**Step 4** Test the solution to determine whether it actually works.

A lot of ideas sound good but may not work out in practice. If a solution does not work, don't immediately reject it. A simple change may be all that's needed.

**Step 5** Evaluate the process.

Review the steps taken to find and implement a solution. Could you have done anything better? If you are satisfied with the outcome, you can add this successful solution to your knowledge base.

## Applying the Problem-Solving Process

Now you will see how to apply the problem-solving process to a workplace problem. Read the following situation and review the steps used to correct it.

**Situation:** You are part of a team of workers assigned to work on a new shopping mall. The project will take about 18 months to complete. The only available parking is half a mile from the job site. The crew has to carry heavy toolboxes and safety equipment from their cars and trucks to the work area and then back again at the end of their shift.

| **Sample Solution Using the Five-Step Problem-Solving Process** | |
|---|---|
| **Step 1** Define the problem. | Workers are wasting time and energy hauling all their equipment to and from the work site. |
| **Step 2** Think about ways to solve the problem. | Several solutions are available:<br>Install lockers for tools and equipment closer to the work site.<br>Have workers drive up to the work site to drop off their tools and equipment before parking.<br>Bring in another construction trailer where workers can store their tools and equipment for the duration of the project.<br>Provide a round-trip shuttle service to ferry workers and their tools.<br>*Note:* Each solution will have pros and cons, so it's important to get input from the workers who are affected by the problem. For example, workers will probably object to any plan (like the drop-off plan) that leaves their tools open to theft. |
| **Step 3** Pick the solution that seems best and figure out an action plan. | The workers decide that the shuttle service makes the most sense. It should solve the time and energy problem, and workers can keep their tools with them.<br>To put the plan into effect, the project supervisor arranges for a large van and driver to provide the shuttle service. |
| **Step 4** Test the solution to determine whether it actually works. | The solution works, but there is a problem. All of the workers are scheduled to start and leave at the same time, so there is not enough room in the van for all the workers and their equipment. To solve this problem, the supervisor schedules trips spaced 15 minutes apart. The supervisor also adjusts the workers' schedules to correspond with the trips. That way all the workers won't try to get on the shuttle at the same time. |
| **Step 5** Evaluate the process. | This process gave both management and workers a chance to express an opinion and discuss the various solutions. Everyone feels pleased with the process and the solution. |

### Defining the Problem—A Problem Itself

In the example, we defined the problem for you. At work, you and your co-workers will have to define the problem, and everyone will probably have something different to say. For example, the workers dealing with the situation in this module might make the following comments:

- It's management's problem. They should figure out a way to get parking closer.
- It's not a problem. Everyone on this job whines too much. A little walking won't kill you.
- It's not my problem. I am just here to do framing.
- They should just pay us overtime for having to walk and carry our tools.

As you can see, none of these comments really defines the problem. Do you think that you could come up with a solution based *only* on these comments?

## Additional tips for problem solving

**1. Know who is authorized to carry out solutions.** Most companies appreciate employees who can solve problems creatively. However, you must solve problems within company rules and regulations. In the problem-solving example, although the workers came up with a solution for the problem, only the project supervisor is authorized to carry out the solution by arranging for a van and driver.

**2. Change negative thinking to positive thinking.** When a group of people get together to solve a problem, they tend to spend a lot of time complaining, which wastes everyone's time and energy. To head off this situation, get your team members to agree to hold all complaints until they can come up with at least two or three positive solutions.

**3. Learn to brainstorm.** A lot of good ideas never come to light because people are afraid they will sound silly. In a brainstorming session, you want to hear as many ideas as possible. They won't all be workable, but hearing different ideas will actually help you think of ideas you can use.

**4. Don't settle for the cheapest, easiest, or fastest solution.** It's important to save money, energy, and time, but these factors are not always the most important ones. Consider the following situations:

- You need new tires for your truck. Do you buy the bargain-basement tires or do you spend a little more money to get reliable tires backed by a warranty?
- You are up on a scaffold and want to close some cans of paint, but your mallet is down on the floor. Do you use the handle of your screwdriver to pound the cans shut or do you climb down to get the mallet?

**5. Don't complicate a simple problem.** Sometimes people make more of a problem than is necessary. For some types of problems, the best solution is often the simplest. Consider this example: You try to season your dinner, but too much salt comes out of the salt shaker, and you can barely get the coarse-ground pepper out of the pepper shaker. You could complain to someone. However, you notice that the lid of each shaker has different sized holes, so you carefully pour out the salt and pepper onto separate pieces of paper. You then pour the salt into the shaker with the small holes and the coarse ground pepper into the shaker with the large holes. Problem solved! But there's actually a much easier solution. Do you know what it is?

## Barriers to problem solving

Whether you are tackling a problem on your own or working with a group, you must be alert to barriers that prevent success. Watch out for the following pitfalls:

**1. Close-mindedness.** To find the best solution, you need to be open to new ideas. Sometimes the best solution is one you never even considered. Remember that other people have good ideas, too, so you should be willing to listen to them.

**2. Personality conflicts.** Sometimes someone you don't like offers the best solution. That shouldn't stop you from accepting and trying good ideas. Keep in mind that you can approve of the idea even if you don't really like the person who came up with it.

**3. Fear of change.** Many people are reluctant to change the traditional way of doing things. Most technological advances make work easier and more productive, so always be willing to learn new technologies and work with new equipment. In fact, as a construction professional, it's your duty to keep up with advances in your field.

### *On-the-Job Quiz*

Here's a quick quiz that asks you to apply what you've learned in this module.

1. When you think critically, you ____.
   a. pay close attention to information and evaluate it
   b. create a list of things that are being done incorrectly and criticize them
   c. criticize the work of others after thinking about it carefully and evaluating it
   d. think up simple, easy, fast, and cost-effective ways to deal with problems
2. Good critical thinkers make quick decisions.
   a. True
   b. False

3. At a sales presentation for a new backhoe, the sales representative shows a video, hands out glossy brochures, and says that the backhoe works twice as fast and will allow you to get twice as much work done as any other backhoe on the market. If you use your critical-thinking skills you would _____.
   a. evaluate the information based on the information included in the video and the brochure
   b. evaluate the information based on the company's reputation and your knowledge of backhoes
   c. decide to buy the backhoe because this company advertises a lot and has been making backhoes for a while
   d. decide that everything the sales representative said is true, because it's illegal to lie in a business situation
4. You see an ad for a drink mix that promises you increased muscle tone and strength in about three months. You are suspicious, but the ad looks convincing, nothing else you have tried works, and you want to look better quickly. To get the best information you should ask _____.
   a. your co-workers what they think
   b. a trainer at a local gym
   c. your supervisor for an opinion
   d. your doctor for advice
5. In the problem-solving process, defining a problem is not easy.
   a. True
   b. False
6. When solving a problem, it is necessary to get input from those who will be affected by the problem and its solution.
   a. True
   b. False
7. When a solution does not work after you test it, it is best to toss out the idea and start the problem-solving process over.
   a. True
   b. False

**8.** You are a supervisor who has just learned that a lumber delivery promised for Monday won't be delivered until Wednesday. The best way to solve this problem is to _____.

a. tell the supplier to delay someone else's delivery or be prepared to face a lawsuit for delaying your job
b. assign some members of your work crew to go pick up the lumber
c. have a meeting with your crew, ask them to brainstorm ideas to solve this problem, and offer a prize for the best idea
d. decide that nothing can be done and give the crew a couple of days off to save on the budget

**9.** Your company uses Brand X cement because it's a good product and is reasonably priced. Some workers have tried Brand Y but found it hard to work with. The Brand Y Company has now developed a new and improved cement that costs less than Brand X. Your supervisor is thinking about changing over to Brand Y. When your supervisor asks you for your opinion, what is your best response?

a. "I'm not sure, boss. Whatever you decide will be OK with me."
b. "We tried that stuff in the past and it wasn't any good. Let's just stick with what we know."
c. "The sales rep seems honest enough and said this stuff is great. Anyway, it costs less than Brand X. Let's go for it!"
d. "Let's test it first on a small project. If it works well for us, we should probably change brands."

**10.** Your co-worker T.J. has a track record for coming up with great ideas. But T.J. also has a know-it-all attitude that you and your co-workers find hard to take. Your boss, who thinks T.J. is wonderful, has asked you to put together a team to solve a drainage problem and to be sure to include T.J. You should _____.

a. explain to your boss that the workers can't stand T.J.'s attitude
b. suggest that your boss just ask T.J. to solve the problem
c. do as your boss asks, but freeze T.J. out of the discussions
d. do as your boss asks and focus on getting good ideas from everyone

# Individual Activities

## Activity 1: Thinking Critically

Your goal in this activity is to put your critical-thinking skills to use. Read each example, and then answer the questions that follow.

### *Example 1: Critical Reading*

It is your first day on the job and your supervisor tells you to read the company's safety guidelines for motorized vehicles. The guidelines follow:

#### *Safety Guidelines for Motorized Vehicles*

All workers must adhere to the following rules when operating motorized vehicles.

1. When working indoors, ensure that the work area is ventilated to prevent carbon dioxide poisoning.
2. Wear your seat belt. Ensure that any passengers are also wearing seat belts.
3. Closely obey all speed limits. Increase speed in crowded areas.
4. Check to make sure the back-up signal works. If it doesn't work, then use the motorized vehicle.
5. Make sure all rear-view mirrors and windows are clean and free of debris.
6. You should talk on a cell phone while operating the motorized vehicle.
7. When working in a crowded or tight area, use a signaler.
8. Do not sit in any motorized vehicle that is being loaded by excavating equipment.
9. Shut off the engine during refueling.
10. Set the brakes and turn off the engine when you're done using the vehicle.

**Example 1: Analysis**

1. List the errors in this example.

______________________________________________

______________________________________________

______________________________________________

2. Add any additional instructions or information you feel should be included to ensure the safe operation of motorized vehicles.

______________________________________________

______________________________________________

______________________________________________

3. Now that you've found these errors, you should

______________________________________________

______________________________________________

______________________________________________

## *Example 2: Critical Reading*

Following is a letter from a former worker to a boss. For this example, assume that you are the boss to whom the letter is addressed.

Dear Boss:

I worked for you for two years, and I'm glad I don't have to anymore. Getting fired was the best thing that ever happened to me.

So now that I don't have to put up with you and your stupid rules anymore, I want you to know a few things. First, nobody likes working for you. Even the people you think like you really hate your guts. Second, I bet you don't know that your favorite worker, T.C., talked about you behind your back the whole time I was there. I was so glad to get away from that goody-goody—always showing up for work early and working late. Always coming up with those stupid bright ideas. What a kiss up!

I'm at a much better job now. I can show up for work a little late and nobody gets on my case. If I come back a little late from lunch no one says anything to me. Not like someone else I know. And, I am making more money than before. So—thanks for getting rid of me. I'm really grateful!

**Example 2: Questions**

1. What parts of the letter do you believe? Why? What parts don't you believe? Why?

2. Do you feel that you lost a good worker? Why or why not?

3. The worker who wrote this letter probably enjoyed doing it. Do you think that it's a good idea to write a letter like this? Why or why not?

## Activity 2: Separating Fact from Opinion

To think critically, you must be able to tell the difference between facts and opinions. A fact is a statement that can be proven true or false. An opinion cannot be proven true or false; it is based on someone's personal point of view or interpretation of facts. Different people can have different opinions about the same fact. When someone expresses an opinion, you then need to evaluate that opinion and determine whether you agree with it or not. Consider the following statements. Notice that the opinion statements combine fact and opinion:

**Fact:** Many people in the United States are killed each year in incidents involving handguns.

**Opinion:** Guns are dangerous. We would all be safer if it were harder to buy guns.

**Opinion:** The world is dangerous. We would all be safer if it were easier to buy guns.

In this activity, you will practice identifying facts and opinions. Read each of the following examples. In the spaces provided, write "F" after sentences that are facts and "O" after sentences that are opinions. Use the critical-thinking tools you learned about in this module to carefully read and evaluate each statement.

### *Example 1: Wearing Hard Hats: Right or Wrong?*

Most construction companies make their workers wear hard hats on the work site. _____. That is because the Occupational Safety and Health Administration (OSHA) says that wearing hard hats reduces workplace injuries. _____. However, I think that construction workers should not have to wear hard hats if it makes them uncomfortable. _____. I have talked to some of my co-workers and they agree with me. _____. I hate wearing a hard hat. _____. I once worked for a whole hour without my hard hat on, and except for the boss yelling, nothing happened to me. _____. That just goes to show you that wearing a hard hat is not necessary. _____. And most people would agree with me, I'm sure. _____. Work is hard enough without having the government telling us what to do. _____. That's why I say that making us workers wear hard hats when none of us want to is wrong. _____.

### *Example 2: Paint or Wallpaper?*

My clients want me to hang wallpaper in the kitchen. _____. But I think that hanging wallpaper is a pain and painting is much easier. _____. Anyway, paint would look better on the wall than wallpaper. _____ . I have been painting and papering for 10 years. _____. My experience has been that, in kitchens, wallpaper generally does not hold up as well as paint. _____. I will paper if the clients insist, but they won't be happy two years from now. _____. Depending on the wallpaper they pick, the job will probably cost more if we paper. _____.

## Activity 3: Evaluating Information

You receive the following letter. Use your critical-thinking tools to carefully read and evaluate this letter.

Congratulations! You are one of the lucky few who have been specially selected to receive **this incredible offer.** We know how important **reliable construction equipment** is to you and your business. And we know that keeping the lid on **your construction budget** is also important. That's why we are making this **special offer** to you. Because of the downturn in the economy, we have a limited number of brand new Best Backhoes available for purchase **for only $3,995.*** These backhoes are the **finest backhoes available** in the trade today. Just look at these great features:

- Tubular steel construction for added strength and longer life
- Wide support base for stable, safe operation
- Rubber pads for stable operation on hard surfaces included *at no extra charge*
- Locking pins for safety pivot points included *at no extra charge*
- Adjustable seat offering six-point adjustment (three more than the industry standard!)
- Flexible bucket operation from 9" to 36" and rotation from 165 degrees to 172 degrees

One look will convince you that the Best Backhoe is indeed the best backhoe you've ever seen. **But don't delay. Only 12 backhoes** will be sold at this budget-saving price **this weekend only.** Call 1-800-123-1234 for directions to our special sales site. Only you and a select few other customers will have this **once in a lifetime opportunity.** Don't miss out on this great opportunity. This offer will never be repeated again.

Sincerely,

M. L. Smith

President, Best Backhoe Company

*Price based on Model 1XIJRM8. Prices for other models may vary. Taxes and additional fees not included. Does not include shipping. Purchasers may be required to provide advance credit information. No warranties, express or implied, apply to special sale items. All sales final. No refunds. Best Backhoe Company is a member in good standing of the All States Construction Association.

Assuming that you are in the market for a backhoe, here are some questions to consider:

1. How many people besides you do you think received this letter?

2. The letter explains why this deal is being offered. Why do you think the deal is being offered?

3. Do you know anything about Best Backhoes, the Best Backhoe Company, or the All States Construction Association? How can you find information about them?

4. How much does a brand new backhoe actually cost? Is this price really a deal or is it too good to be true? How can you find out?

5. Are you getting a good deal because some features are included at no extra charge? How can you find out whether these items are standard on all backhoes?

6. Is an adjustable seat an important factor in choosing a backhoe? What is the industry standard for this feature?

7. What "advance credit information" do you think the company wants from you? Why do you think the company wants it?

8. What is the meaning of the sentence (in the smaller print), "No warranties, express or implied, apply to special sale items"? If you don't know, how can you find out?

9. Who would you show this letter to for advice?

10. Based on your critical review of the letter, what will you do?

## Group Activities

### Activity 4: Practicing Problem Solving

Following are three typical construction problems, along with problem-solving grids. Your goal is to find the best solution for these problems. Working in groups of three or four, complete the grid for each situation. Follow the problem-solving process you learned in this module. (*Note:* An additional grid is also provided. Your instructor may give you an additional problem to solve, or someone on your team may suggest a problem that has come up on the job.)

**Team Members**

| | |
|---|---|
| 1. ______________________ | 2. ______________________ |
| 3. ______________________ | 4. ______________________ |

**Problem 1:** It's 7:00 A.M., and you are installing bathroom fixtures in a new house at a large subdivision. When installing the toilet, you realize that some parts are missing. Also, some of the parts included with the tank kit appear to be wrong. Your co-worker has taken the truck and the cell phone to another site and won't be back until this afternoon. The nearest parts store is 10 miles away. You must finish this project today.

| Five-Step Problem-Solving Process | | |
|---|---|---|
| **Step 1** | Define the problem. | |
| **Step 2** | Think about ways to solve the problem. | |
| **Step 3** | Pick the solution that seems best and figure out an action plan. | |
| **Step 4** | Test the solution to determine whether it actually works. | |
| **Step 5** | Evaluate the process. | |

**Problem 2:** You are used to wearing a hard hat to work; you and your co-workers have been doing this for years. Now your company is requiring everyone to wear safety belts and safety harnesses, even when your team does not think them necessary. A lot of workers are simply ignoring the new safety rules, and many workers have been reprimanded. Some have even been fired.

| **Five-Step Problem-Solving Process** | |
|---|---|
| **Step 1** Define the problem. | |
| **Step 2** Think about ways to solve the problem. | |
| **Step 3** Pick the solution that seems best and figure out an action plan. | |
| **Step 4** Test the solution to determine whether it actually works. | |
| **Step 5** Evaluate the process. | |

**Problem 3:** Workers have to carry lumber from the back corner of the lot, where it is stored, to the working area. This wastes time and energy. There is no room to store the lumber close to the working area because job site office trailers take up the space.

| Five-Step Problem-Solving Process | |
|---|---|
| **Step 1** Define the problem. | |
| **Step 2** Think about ways to solve the problem. | |
| **Step 3** Pick the solution that seems best and figure out an action plan. | |
| **Step 4** Test the solution to determine whether it actually works. | |
| **Step 5** Evaluate the process. | |

**Your work site problem:**

______________________________________________

______________________________________________

______________________________________________

| Five-Step Problem-Solving Process | |
|---|---|
| **Step 1** Define the problem. | |
| **Step 2** Think about ways to solve the problem. | |
| **Step 3** Pick the solution that seems best and figure out an action plan. | |
| **Step 4** Test the solution to determine whether it actually works. | |
| **Step 5** Evaluate the process. | |

## Activity 5: Evaluating Alternatives

As you have learned, there is often more than one solution to a problem. How do you choose when you have several alternative solutions? One way is to rank the solutions from the most workable to the least workable.

To complete this activity, each team member must first work alone, reading each case study and ranking the solutions from 1 to 5 (see the following scale). When everyone is finished, team members should discuss their rankings. Everyone will probably rank the solutions a little differently. Based on your discussion, decide which solution you will choose as a team.

### *Ranking Scale*

**1** I think this solution will work the best.

**2** This solution is OK, but I don't feel it will work as well as my first choice.

**3** This solution is also OK, but I would want to try my first and second choice before trying this solution.

**4** This solution may work, but I don't feel comfortable about it.

**5** Even though this solution may work, I just don't like it. I think it might cause some other problems.

**Team Members**

1. ______________________ 2. ______________________

3. ______________________ 4. ______________________

## Case Study 1: Problem with a Co-Worker

You and a co-worker have been working together a long time, and you've become good friends. Over the past two weeks, your co-worker, who has always been reliable, seems to be slipping. You've noticed the following problems:

- Increased tardiness
- Bloodshot eyes
- Problems with balance when walking
- Making a lot of small mistakes

You have had to spend your time catching and fixing your co-worker's mistakes. Today your co-worker made a bigger mistake, and you were almost injured. You suspect your co-worker may be drinking before coming to work.

**Rank the alternative solutions (from 1 to 5):**

A. _____ Take a wait-and-see approach. Give this situation a few more weeks to see whether the problems go away, and continue to fix any mistakes your co-worker makes.

B. _____ Take your co-worker out for a drink and ask what's going on. Be supportive but firm. Say that you are worried about your safety and about your co-worker's well-being.

C. _____ Ask your supervisor to deal with this problem. You don't know how to bring up the subject, and you are afraid that you will wreck your friendship.

D. _____ Be sympathetic to your co-worker, but understand that you have to watch out for your own safety. Ask your boss to assign you to a new partner, but make up some excuse for your request so you don't have to tell on your friend.

E. _____ Write an anonymous note to your co-worker in which you list the problems you've seen. State your concerns about your co-worker's safety and the safety of others. Say that unless your co-worker straightens out, you will tell the boss about the problems.

## *Case Study 2: Working with a Difficult Co-Worker*

You've been assigned to a project that requires a team of four workers. Your team members include the following workers:

- T.K., a friend of yours
- D.T., who does not talk very much but does a good job
- J.R., who argues with everyone and is difficult to work with

The job is scheduled to last eight weeks, but after only two weeks, J.R.'s attitude is driving you crazy. You wish J.R. were not on your team, but you have six weeks to go on the project.

**Rank the alternative solutions (from 1 to 5):**

A. _____ Wait until after work one day to meet with J.R. Your plan is to have a calm, professional discussion about J.R.'s behavior and its effect on the project.

B. _____ First find out if other members of the team are having the same problem with J.R.'s attitude. If so, you can all talk to J.R. together.

C. _____ Just put up with J.R. for the duration of the project and ignore the stress this situation causes you and your team.

D. _____ Give the situation another few weeks to improve. If things don't get better, you will ask your boss to talk to J.R.

E. _____ Complain to J.R. in front of the other team members. That way all the team members can talk about their feelings out in the open.

## Activity 6: Identifying Experts

In this activity, you and two or three of your classmates will identify experts you should consult for more advice to help you make workplace decisions. For each situation, fill in the names of people, companies, or printed materials that you can turn to for help back at your own job. Note that there are no right answers for this activity, only best answers. An answer is best if it applies to your particular situation.

**Team Members**

1. ______________________ 2. ______________________

3. ______________________ 4. ______________________

**Situation 1:** Your drill press is making weird noises, and you can't figure out what's wrong.

______________________________________________

______________________________________________

**Situation 2:** Your boss has asked you to finish a task by a certain time. You start to do the job, but several problems come up, and you realize that you won't meet the deadline.

______________________________________________

______________________________________________

**Situation 3:** You notice that some of your co-workers ignore the company safety rules whenever the boss is not around. You are worried about your safety and theirs, but you don't want to be a tattletale.

______________________________________________

______________________________________________

**Situation 4:** You are training to be a carpenter and have been given the opportunity to work on a custom home. On the first day, you are having a problem figuring out angle cuts for molding. Your measurements are correct, but your angles are not always meeting the way you'd like.

______________________________________________

______________________________________________

**Situation 5.** You notice a mistake in the employee safety manual. Someone who follows the instructions shown could get hurt.

______________________________________________

______________________________________________

**Situation 6:** A serious accident happens at the work site. A co-worker calls you up to let you know that a bunch of reporters are standing near the job site entrance and are asking workers what happened.

______________________________________________

______________________________________________

**Situation 7:** You have heard that another construction company is going out of business and that supplies and equipment will be sold at rock-bottom prices. You have never heard of this company, but that does not mean that it never existed.

____________________________________________

____________________________________________

**Situation 8:** You want to buy a pick-up truck that you can use to carry your tools to the job site. You think that you'd like to buy a certain model with the dealer's option package, but you are not really sure.

____________________________________________

____________________________________________

**Situation 9:** You have been taking a prescription painkiller as a result of a workplace accident about a year ago. Lately you have started to feel like you can't get through the day without taking more medication. Yesterday, you doubled up on the dose and felt OK, but you are worried that you might be getting addicted.

____________________________________________

____________________________________________

**Situation 10:** You have a lot of skill in drafting working drawings by hand. You enjoy the work and take pride in what you do, but computer software is making your skills obsolete. You feel frustrated and worried about this change and wonder whether you can stay employed.

____________________________________________

____________________________________________

## Activity 7: Brain Busters: Solving Puzzles

You may never encounter some of the puzzles included in this activity in real life. However, solving puzzles is good exercise for your brain. Try solving each puzzle on your own. Then compare your solutions with those of your team members. Work as a group on any puzzles you could not solve on your own.

**Team Members**

1. ____________________ 2. ____________________

3. ____________________ 4. ____________________

**Puzzle 1:** You want to finish the basement in your four-year-old home. You have to figure out how to get sheets of drywall down to the basement. The stairs from the first floor of your house to the basement turn at a 90-degree angle, so there's a landing halfway down. The builder installed drywall on the full length of the stairwell and painted it when the house was built. The basement windows measure 30½" × 24". A standard sheet of ¾" drywall at your local home improvement center measures 4' × 8'. There are no other ways to get into your basement. You don't want to cut down your drywall sheets because that will increase the amount of mudding and taping you will have to do. You figure out how to get the drywall into the basement without cutting it down. How?

**Puzzle 2:** You are assigned to drive covered truckloads of fill dirt onto a construction site. To get the most out of the deliveries, the fill-site supervisor makes sure that all the trucks are fully loaded and then some. The supervisor also insists that all loads be covered with a heavy-duty tarp so that no fill blows off during the trip to the construction site. Between the fill yard and the construction site are a series of overpasses. You drive under five of them with no problem. However, at the sixth overpass, you get stuck. What can you do to get moving again?

**Puzzle 3:** Your boss decides to test your thinking power one day and asks you to cut a square piece of paper into eight equal pieces. However, you are only allowed to make three cuts. How will you do this?

**Puzzle 4:** The construction site for a large job employs workers in shifts 24/7. Because of security concerns, a 10-foot-high chain-link fence surrounds the site. A sudden heavy storm causes a flash flood in a nearby stream. When the storm ends, there is a deep, wide, muddy puddle between the parking lot and the gated front entrance to the construction site. The workers don't want to carry their heavy tools through the mess. One worker proposes building a temporary bridge but is told that that will not be allowed. Another worker proposes draining the puddle but is told that that won't be allowed either. Yet the workers manage to come up with a way to get from their cars to the site without getting wet or muddy. How did they do it?

______________________________________________

______________________________________________

______________________________________________

______________________________________________

**Puzzle 5:** You are given two empty containers: one 3-gallon container and one 5-gallon container. Neither container has any measurement markings on it. You are told make only one trip to a large vat filled with paint and to bring back only 7 gallons of paint. You must go directly to the vat, get the paint, and return directly to your workstation. You don't have any way to measure and mark the cans, yet you successfully bring back exactly 7 gallons of paint. How?

______________________________________________

______________________________________________

______________________________________________

______________________________________________

## Activity 8: Using Logic to Sort Out Possible Solutions

Earlier in this module, you learned how workers solved the problem of getting from a distant parking lot with tools and equipment to a job site. Before those workers chose a shuttle service to solve their problem, they had to consider four possible solutions. In this example, you will learn how they used logic to consider each option.

Here are the solutions the workers considered:

*Solution 1:* Install lockers for tools and equipment closer to the work site.

*Solution 2:* Have workers drive up to the work site to drop off their tools and equipment before parking.

*Solution 3:* Bring in another construction trailer where workers can store their tools and equipment for the duration of the project.

*Solution 4:* Provide a shuttle service from the parking lot to the work site.

Here is how the workers logically considered each possible solution:

**Step 1** Will the proposed solution cause other problems?

❑ Yes. Choose another solution and return to step 1.

❑ No. Go to step 2.

**Step 2** Can we come up with a workable plan to carry out this solution?

❑ Yes. Go to step 3.

❑ No. Choose another solution and return to step 1.

**Step 3** Does everyone agree that this solution meets our needs?

❑ Yes. Choose this solution.

❑ No. Choose another solution, and return to step 1.

**Team Members**

| | |
|---|---|
| 1. ____________________ | 2. ____________________ |
| 3. ____________________ | 4. ____________________ |

This activity will give you and three of your team members a chance to practice this process on a fairly simple problem. For this activity, assume that you and your team members have to select only one meal for the entire group to eat for lunch. Assume also that you have collected $30.00 to pay for the group's lunch. Here are your options:

*Option 1:* Steak sandwich and fries: $7.50 per person

*Option 2:* Large pizza with pepperoni and sausage: $15.95

*Option 3:* Pulled pork sandwich and coleslaw: $6.25 per person

*Option 4:* Beef and bean burrito platter with salad, guacamole, and sour cream: $5.45 per person

Now answer the following questions for each option:

**Step 1** Will choosing this option cause other problems? (For example, some workers may have an allergy to certain foods.)

❑ Yes. (List the problems.) Choose another solution and return to step 1.

❑ No. Go to step 2.

**Step 2** Will our budget cover this option?

❑ Yes. Go to step 3.

❑ No. Choose another option and return to step 1. Or modify the budget and proceed to step 3.

**Step 3** Does everyone agree that this is the best choice?

❑ Yes. Enjoy lunch.

❑ No. Choose another option and return to step 1.

Your team may decide that it does not like any of the options presented here. If so, and if time allows, come up with other options by asking each team member to contribute one. Then use the logical process to choose one of those options.

## Activity 9: Solving Problems within Workplace Rules and Regulations

Solving a problem is very satisfying. It is even more satisfying when you see your solutions put into practice. At work, however, it's important to remember that you often cannot act independently. You may have to ask permission from your boss before carrying out some solutions, no matter how good they are. In addition, every workplace has unwritten rules that you must learn about and follow as well. In this activity, you and two or three of your classmates will read about solutions to some problems and then decide whether the problem solver acted within workplace rules and regulations—both the written and the unwritten ones. After you read each example, consider these questions:

1. Who else is affected by your actions?
2. Will your actions help or harm others?
3. Will your actions get you, your co-workers, or your boss into trouble?
4. Will your actions create additional problems?
5. What would be a better solution?

**Team Members**

| | |
|---|---|
| 1.____________________ | 2.____________________ |
| 3.____________________ | 4.____________________ |

**Example 1:** A supplier calls to speak to your boss, who is inspecting work at another site. The supplier tells you that the delivery truck has broken down, so you won't be getting a delivery of polyvinyl chloride (PVC) pipe promised for that afternoon. You know the pipe must arrive today in order for the job to stay on schedule. All of the construction site vehicles are in use, so you take a taxi to a rental agency, rent a truck, drive over to the supplier's location, and pick up the pipe yourself. You return the truck to the rental agency and take a taxi back to work. You then submit receipts for the taxi rides and truck rental and ask for reimbursement.

Did you act within workplace rules? ❑ Yes ❑ No

**Example 2:** You have been working on a natural gas pipeline job for about six months. The boss asks you to check over a new compressor that has just been delivered. You notice that the unit housing is damaged. In addition, one of the mechanical seals is cracked and no maintenance manual was included in the delivery. You fire off a letter to the manufacturer complaining about the problems and threatening to take your company's business elsewhere.

Did you act within workplace rules? ❑ Yes ❑ No

**Example 3:** It's a hot day and everyone is irritated. The boss, who is meeting with the client, has told you to "handle things" and to call only in case of an emergency. A couple of co-workers have been trading insults and then suddenly start throwing punches. Other workers gather around. It looks like matters will soon get out of control. You spot a hose nearby, pick it up, and turn the water onto the fighters. When they turn angrily in your direction, you point the hose straight up so that you get soaked too, grin at everyone, and say, "This feels great! Anyone else feel like cooling off?"

Did you act within workplace rules? ❑ Yes ❑ No

**Example 4:** You and your co-worker are taking a math course as part of your training. You like math and enjoy the course, but your co-worker is struggling to get through. In addition, problems with math are causing your co-worker to make some mistakes at work. You decide to tutor your co-worker a couple of nights a week until you see improvement. In the meantime, you also decide to watch out for and correct your co-worker's mistakes at work.

Did you act within workplace rules? ❑ Yes ❑ No

**Example 5:** Morale is really low at your job. The work is hard and the schedule is tight. Workers are grumbling and tempers are short. You think everyone could benefit from a little comic relief, so you show up at work early one day dressed as a clown. About 10 minutes before the start of your shift, you ride a child's tricycle around the work site, honking a horn, and handing out balloons.

Did you act within workplace rules? ❑ Yes ❑ No

**Example 6:** You have just finished a course on reading blueprints. You like reading blueprints and did very well in the course. One day you notice that room-framing measurements on a blueprint are not correct. You check and recheck the measurements and then show them to a co-worker who, after also checking the measurements, agrees with you. A little voice in your head tells you to check with the boss, but after all, you are right and the blueprint is wrong, and you are sure the boss will commend you for your initiative. You and your co-worker frame the room based on your calculations.

Did you act within workplace rules? ❑ Yes ❑ No

**Example 7:** There are a couple of beat-up picnic tables just outside your work site that the workers use for their meals and breaks. The tables are placed under some large, shady trees. You notice that the tables and benches are often sticky with sap from the trees. You also notice that the trees drop little green pods, pine needles, and leaves on the tables. Your co-workers don't seem to mind and just brush this stuff off before they sit down. You think the tables would be cleaner if they were not right under the trees, so one day you come to work a little early and move them out from under the trees.

Did you act within workplace rules? ❑ Yes ❑ No

**Example 8:** Your boss is walking through the work site with a client and invites you to come along to observe. At one point, your boss has to step aside to take a cell phone call. The client points out that ductwork running along the back wall of a large closet is a waste of storage space. You have been told that the client is always right and to always please the client, so you promise that the ductwork will be moved to another spot.

Did you act within workplace rules? ❑ Yes ❑ No

**Example 9:** Your co-worker whines all the time. The work is too hard. The weather is too hot or too cold. The pay is too low. The boss is too demanding. You are fed up with your co-worker acting and sounding like a baby. You organize a baby shower and have all of your co-workers bring in inexpensive baby toys. You present these to your co-worker and say, "Here, you can play with these or you can grow up."

Did you act within workplace rules? ❑ Yes ❑ No

**Example 10:** You have figured out a way to change the way the crew sets up for framing that will save everyone time and might just save the company a few dollars. Your boss, however, feels that trainees should be seen and not heard. You figure out all the steps needed to make the change and write them down in an email to your boss. You also make a list of how the workers will benefit. You show your idea and list to your co-workers to get their input. Then you send the email and ask your boss for an opinion.

Did you act within workplace rules? ❑ Yes ❑ No

## Activity 10: Your Turn— Solve a Problem Where You Work

It is usually difficult to solve problems effectively at work because everyone, including you, is so busy working. Taking a course like this one gives you the chance to think about, and perhaps solve, a problem specific to your workplace. To complete this activity, write down a brief description of a current workplace problem. (*Note:* It is best to describe your problem in general terms and not to mention any names.) Then read your problem aloud to two or three of your classmates and answer the following questions:

**Team Members**

| | |
|---|---|
| 1. ______________________ | 2. ______________________ |
| 3. ______________________ | 4. ______________________ |

**Problem Description**

______________________________________________

______________________________________________

### *Discussion Questions*

1. Is this just a problem for me, or does it affect others where I work?
2. If I could solve this problem, who would benefit from the solution besides me?
3. What obstacles stand in the way of solving the problem?
4. How can I overcome these obstacles?
5. Have any of my teammates in class had a similar problem where they worked? If so, how did they handle the problem?

# Resolving Conflict

## SELF-ASSESSMENT
## HOW WELL DO YOU HANDLE CONFLICT?

Can you quickly resolve disagreements with co-workers, or are you more likely to let conflicts linger? Take this self-assessment quiz to find out. Truthfully note your level of agreement with each statement, and then add up your score.

| | Strongly Agree | Sometimes Agree | Don't Agree |
|---|---|---|---|
| 1. I feel that I have to prove to others that my opinions are right. | ❑ | ❑ | ❑ |
| 2. I have a hard time working with people whose work habits are different from mine. | ❑ | ❑ | ❑ |
| 3. I get impatient easily. | ❑ | ❑ | ❑ |
| 4. When discussing problems, I lose my temper easily. | ❑ | ❑ | ❑ |
| 5. I get annoyed when someone makes a mistake. | ❑ | ❑ | ❑ |
| 6. I shout back when someone shouts at me. | ❑ | ❑ | ❑ |
| 7. I get involved in other people's arguments and side with the person I think is right. | ❑ | ❑ | ❑ |
| 8. I think that most people annoy others on purpose. | ❑ | ❑ | ❑ |
| 9. I feel that the best way to deal with problems is to ignore them and hope they go away. | ❑ | ❑ | ❑ |
| 10. In an argument or discussion, I feel that the most important thing is to get my way. | ❑ | ❑ | ❑ |
| 11. I have trouble admitting I am wrong. | ❑ | ❑ | ❑ |
| 12. I have trouble apologizing when I have done something wrong. | ❑ | ❑ | ❑ |
| 13. I do things to annoy my co-workers. | ❑ | ❑ | ❑ |
| 14. I tell people when they are annoying me. | ❑ | ❑ | ❑ |
| 15. I think that compromising is the same as losing. | ❑ | ❑ | ❑ |

***Scoring:*** A response of "Strongly Agree" is worth 1 point, a response of "Sometimes Agree" is worth 2 points, and a response of "Don't Agree" is worth 3 points. Count the number of times you gave each response, and multiply that number by its point value. Then add up your total score.

| | | | |
|---|---|---|---|
| Strongly Agree | ______ | × 1 = | ______ |
| Sometimes Agree | ______ | × 2 = | ______ |
| Don't Agree | ______ | × 3 = | ______ |
| TOTAL | | | ______ |

***Assessment:***

40–45 points: You are good at handling and resolving conflicts. This module will teach you some additional conflict-management skills that you'll find useful in your construction career.

30–39 points: You are swayed by different moods. Sometimes you try to resolve conflicts with others but may not always deal with conflict effectively. This module will teach you how to better resolve conflicts with others.

15–29 points: You tend to contribute to conflict rather than resolve it. This module will help you become more skillful at recognizing conflict and dealing with it in a positive way.

# Introduction

You may have good relationships with your supervisors and co-workers. Sometimes, though, you will get into arguments that strain those relationships. A little healthy disagreement is not a bad thing. Often you can learn something valuable as a result of conflict. However, you must not let disagreements escalate into fights or long-term resentments.

To prevent disagreements from getting out of control, you must manage and resolve conflicts as they occur. In this module, we offer tips and techniques for preventing conflict or resolving it quickly and effectively. This module also includes some suggestions for dealing with difficult co-workers. As you read this module, remember to have empathy for others and to focus on teamwork.

# The causes of conflict

We've all experienced conflict in our lives. But what exactly causes conflict? The answer is simple. Conflict occurs when people disagree. Disagreements can arise from just about anything, from differences in opinion to differences in personality to differences in age.

As the first step to managing conflict on the job, you must be aware of the sources of conflict. When you know the sources, you can take steps to prevent conflict from happening.

## Conflict with Co-Workers

Conflict can exist among co-workers for many reasons. Following are some of the most common causes of conflict at work:

**1. Different work habits.** People have different ways of working. Some are neat, while others seem messy and disorganized. Neat people can't understand how messy people get anything done. Messy people think that neat people are too fussy. Some people work quickly, while others are slow and methodical. Fast workers think that slower workers are unproductive. Slow workers think that fast workers don't take the time to do things carefully and well.

*Example:* You like to organize your tools and think through tasks before you start working. Your co-worker likes to dive right in and get the job done. You are both equally productive.

*Poor approach:* Say, "You drive me nuts the way you rush around! You're going to make a bunch of mistakes if you don't slow down!"

*Better approach:* Think, "My co-worker's rushing around does not really affect me. We both get the job done; we just get there by different routes."

**2. Different attitudes toward the company or job.** Some people take great pride in working and love their jobs. Others hate to get out of bed in the morning and work just to pay the bills. Some people get along well with their supervisors, and others dislike their bosses.

*Example:* Your co-worker complains about everything from the taste of the morning coffee to the way the boss handles things.

*Poor approach:* You listen to this co-worker and think, "You know, T.J. has a point. The coffee is lousy and the boss is too picky. I am getting fed up with this job, too."

*Better approach:* You tune out your co-worker's all-complaints, all-the-time broadcast and think, "This is a good job. Anyone as unhappy as T.J. should probably quit."

**3. Differences in personality and appearance.** People express themselves in widely different ways. Some are quiet and reserved. Others are chatty and outgoing. In addition, style of clothing, hair, weight, and even jewelry can cause conflict among workers. Keep in mind that the world is big enough to hold all kinds of people. You may not like the way co-workers look, dress, or express their personalities, but you can appreciate the work they do. If someone teases you about your appearance or personality, ask yourself whether it is worth getting into an argument over. Most people will soon stop teasing you if you refuse to take the bait.

*Example:* Your co-worker makes fun of your new haircut.

*Poor approach:* Make fun of something about your co-worker's appearance in return and trade insults.

*Better approach:* Ignore the comments. Your co-worker is being childish. If you trade insults, you will be childish as well.

**4. Differences in age.** People born in different generations may see the world differently. Older workers may think that younger workers lack a good work ethic. Younger workers may think that older workers are stuffy and old-fashioned. Both may think that they have nothing to learn from the other.

*Example:* You are assigned to work with an older co-worker who does not like using computer-assisted tools.

*Poor approach:* Think, "Older people never want to learn anything new. I wish I could work with someone my own age."

*Better approach:* Think, "My co-worker's experience can help me improve my skills. In return, I'll help my co-worker learn to use technology."

**5. Problems outside the job.** Personal problems can cause stress that leads to conflict at work. Try to keep personal problems away from work, but know when to ask your supervisor or co-workers for help or understanding. Be ready to help a team member work through personal problems if appropriate.

*Example:* Recently, you've been hit with several serious family-related problems. In time, things will get better, but you are having trouble focusing on work just now.

*Poor approach:* Hide your fears and worries. Pick fights with co-workers and resent your boss for telling you to keep your mind on the job.

*Better approach:* Talk to your boss and co-workers. Tell them in general terms that you are having a rough time. Say that you appreciate their patience and understanding while you work through your problems. Seek counseling if necessary.

## Conflict with Supervisors

Most workers experience conflict with their supervisor at one time or another. Most of this conflict is caused by one of the following factors:

**1. Workload.** The supervisor's job is to keep workers as productive as possible. However, workers can become resentful if they feel they're being pushed too hard.

*Example:* Your boss announces that overtime will be required to meet a scheduled deadline.

*Poor approach:* Say, "I am sick and tired of this. It's not my fault the job is behind schedule! I'm just going to leave at my regular time."

*Better approach:* Think, "The boss can't control the weather. That and a bunch of absences have put this job behind schedule. As a pro on this team, I have to do my part to get the job back on track."

**2. Absenteeism and lateness.** Construction supervisors point to absenteeism and lateness as their two biggest problems on the job. Both problems can cause serious delays and conflict. Arrive at your job on time. Don't call in sick unless you are sick. Don't use the excuse "I couldn't get a ride to work." Find a way to get to work. Don't make your supervisor guess your whereabouts; always call before the start of your shift if you will be late or are sick.

*Example:* You miss your bus and have to wait for the next one, which is scheduled to arrive in 30 minutes.

*Poor approach:* Relax and read the paper until the bus comes.

*Better approach:* If you don't have a cell phone, find a pay phone and let the boss know that you will be late.

**3. Criticism.** Your supervisor must point out mistakes so that you can be as efficient as possible. It's easy to take this constructive criticism personally, but don't. Constructive criticism can be a valuable learning tool. However, if you believe that the criticism is not appropriate, you should discuss the situation with your supervisor calmly and clearly. We offer some tips for dealing with constructive criticism in Module 10.

*Example:* Your boss says that you are forgetting to do certain tasks and recommends that you write down your work assignments each day.

*Poor approach:* Say, "Why are you always on my case? Nag, nag, nag. Just leave me alone!"

*Better approach:* Think, "Well, I don't like writing stuff down, but maybe the boss is right. I'll give this a try to see if it helps me remember what to do."

## Simple ways to prevent conflict

Most experienced supervisors try to build teams of people who can work well together and get the job done. Despite the best intentions, however, conflict sometimes does arise.

Many times, you can avoid conflict by making a simple attitude adjustment. Here are some suggestions for derailing conflict before it flares up:

**1. Think.** Then walk away. Choose not to get annoyed. In any situation with the potential for conflict, your best choice is to think before you react. Before you get into an argument, ask yourself, "Is this worth fighting about? Will any of this matter a week from now?" Nine times out of ten, it won't. Once you realize that what you're going to argue about isn't important, it's much easier to walk away.

*Example:* Your co-worker yells at you because you borrowed a saw without asking and calls you a lazy, worthless pig.

*Poor approach:* Say, "Yeah? Well if anyone is a pig around here, it's you! Your saw is a mess! You're a bigger pig than anyone else!"

*Better approach:* Think, "OK. I should have asked to borrow the saw. That's what I'd want if someone used my saw." Apologize for taking the saw without asking.

**2. Don't take it personally.** You may sometimes think that other people do things or act in certain ways just to annoy you. Recognize that others developed their habits and personalities long before they met you. Try not to be self-centered; recognize that very few people try to annoy you on purpose.

*Example:* Your co-worker's nervous laugh gets on your nerves.

*Poor approach:* Say, "I can't take another minute. I swear, T.J. laughs like that just to drive me nuts!"

*Better approach:* Think, "Maybe T.J. can't help laughing like that. I notice it gets worse when T.J. is really stressed."

**3. Avoid getting involved in other people's arguments.** You may feel that you can help other people resolve their conflicts. Generally, however, this is not a good idea. It is usually best to mind your own business. If you do find yourself in the middle of someone else's argument, don't take sides.

**Magic Words: "I'm sorry."**

Apologizing to someone else shows that you are strong enough to resist the impulse to fight back. When you have done something wrong, like coming in late or making a mistake, you waste a lot of time defending yourself. Instead, admit your mistake and apologize. You will be surprised at how much power there is in saying "I'm sorry."

*Example:* Two co-workers get into a fight over who made a measuring mistake. One co-worker turns to you and says, "You saw it, right? T.J. screwed up, not me!"

*Poor approach:* Say, "Yeah, T.J. You are always messing up!" (Now the fight has grown. It's you and your co-worker against T.J.)

*Better approach:* Say, "The only thing I see is that there's a mistake we have to fix. So let's get that done." (By focusing on the task at hand, you have responded as a professional.)

## Resolving conflicts quickly and effectively

The methods we've presented so far are useful for preventing minor conflicts. However, it's unrealistic to expect that you can avoid all conflicts on the job.

Conflict affects everyone negatively, even those not directly involved. For the good of the project, as well as for everyone's mental health, serious conflicts must be addressed quickly. In this section, you will learn how to resolve conflicts with your co-workers and your boss.

### Resolving Conflicts with Co-Workers

In an earlier module, you learned how to use step-by-step processes to think critically and to solve problems. You can also use a step-by-step process to resolve conflicts. For this process to succeed, all workers must establish some ground rules for working through the problem.

- Put emotions, especially anger and defensiveness, to one side.
- Agree to be polite and respectful of one another.
- Keep an open mind.
- Listen to others without interruption.

Following are the steps in the conflict resolution process. You can use this process to solve both workplace and personal problems. Let's take a look at the steps and then see how to apply them to a job-related situation:

**Step 1** Bring the conflict into the open.

Everyone must admit that the conflict exists or the process won't work.

**Step 2** Discuss and analyze the reasons for the conflict.

Everyone involved should try to discover why the conflict exists.

**Step 3** Develop possible solutions.

Workers can use two tools to accomplish step 3: collaboration (working together to find a solution everyone can live with) and compromise (everyone giving up something so that everyone gains something).

**Step 4** Choose and carry out a solution.

Everyone involved must agree on a solution and make a commitment to do things that will make the solution work.

**Step 5** Evaluate the solution.

Revisit the problem to clear up unresolved issues.

**Situation:** You feel that your co-worker, L.T., who has been working for the company longer than you have, has a superior attitude, is hostile toward you, and is hostile toward younger workers in general. You are working on a two-person project and must rely on each other.

| **Sample Solution Using the Five-Step Conflict Resolution Process** | |
|---|---|
| **Step 1** Bring the conflict into the open. | Choose a time when you can speak privately to L.T., and think about what you will say. For example, "We've been working together for awhile, but we're just not getting along. Do you agree?" If L.T. agrees, the door is open to proceed to step 2. |
| **Step 2** Discuss and analyze the reasons for the conflict. | Asking "who, what, when, where, and why" types of questions is helpful in this step.<br>How and when did the conflict start?<br>What things are keeping the conflict going?<br>Why can't we seem to get along?<br>In this example, you and L.T. learn several things:<br>1. You think L.T. has been hostile and disrespectful toward you since day one.<br>2. About one month into the project, you complained about L.T. to a friend. L.T. overheard these comments and says that is when the trouble started.<br>3. The sayings on some of your T-shirts annoy L.T., who finds them offensive.<br>4. You find L.T.'s sarcasm hard to take. |

*(continued)*

| Sample Solution Using the Five-Step Conflict Resolution Process | |
|---|---|
| **Step 3** Develop possible solutions. | You and L.T. decide to try collaboration and compromise to resolve your issues.<br>*Collaboration:* You both agree that you got off on the wrong foot and need to put past misunderstandings behind you. You also come up with three ideas to make working together more pleasant.<br>1. Greet each other politely each day and treat one another with respect during the workday.<br>2. Take lunch breaks together once a week.<br>3. Go out after work to unwind.<br>*Compromise:* You apologize for your comments and agree to stop wearing the offensive T-shirts. L.T. apologizes for not treating you with respect and agrees to stop saying sarcastic things about younger workers. |
| **Step 4** Choose and carry out a solution. | In this case, you and L.T. recognize that you will probably never become close friends. So eating lunch together or going out after work doesn't seem like a workable option. However, you both agree that you can treat each other professionally and with respect on the job, so you choose the first idea.<br>You and L.T. may feel a little silly when you first carry out this idea. However, you have both done something that is extremely difficult—you have found a way to get along peacefully in spite of your differences. |
| **Step 5** Evaluate the solution. | After your solution has been in place awhile, you and L.T. can touch base again to see how your solution is working. This is the most difficult step. Most people would rather not go back over a problem once it is solved, but touching base can help head off other problems. |

## A Few Tips on Collaboration and Compromise

Collaboration and compromise are skills that take time and practice to develop. When using these techniques, keep the following in mind:

- Show respect for others at all times.
- Listen at least as much as you talk.
- Search for common ground and work toward it.
- Be prepared to give up a little of what you want.
- Admit when you're wrong, and apologize for your mistakes.
- Accept that other people think differently than you do and have needs that differ from yours.
- Focus on problems and behavior, not on personalities and appearances.
- Talk about only one problem at a time. Otherwise, you're setting yourself up for failure.

- Don't insult others with name-calling or profane language.
- Don't threaten others with words or actions.
- Avoid saying "you never" or "you always." These phrases produce negative reactions.
- Keep any promises you make.

## Resolving Conflicts with Supervisors

When you resolve a conflict with a co-worker, you are dealing with someone who is your equal in the workplace. Unlike your supervisor, your co-workers don't have authority over your work assignments. They did not hire you and they cannot fire you. In most cases, they are also not held directly accountable for your work. When resolving conflicts with your boss, you need to take a somewhat different approach. Here are some tips:

**1. Gather your thoughts.** Think about the conflict and what has caused it. Some people find that writing down their thoughts helps to put things in perspective. After thinking or writing about the conflict, you may decide that there really is no conflict at all, or you may come up with a simple solution on your own. Or you may decide that the best solution is already in place.

**2. Respect your supervisor's work schedule.** In Module 2, you learned how to choose good times to communicate with your boss. That skill is especially important when you are trying to resolve a conflict. Don't just march up to your boss and launch into your problem. Instead, choose a time when your boss is less busy. For some conflicts, it may be best to ask your boss to set aside some time to meet with you. Here are some additional tips:

- Let your boss choose the time. If it is at the end of the workday, be willing to stay after hours.
- Ask to speak to your boss in private so that you won't be interrupted.
- If your boss gives you 15 minutes to state your case, be sure to stick to that. Don't ramble off onto other topics.

**3. Stay calm.** Speak slowly and carefully, and focus on the facts. Don't say anything you can't prove. Don't throw accusations at your boss, raise your voice, or make threats. Remember that your body language conveys as much about your emotions as your words do.

**4. Make your case clearly, and offer suggestions for resolving conflicts.** Focus on the conflict between you and your supervisor and the problems it is causing for you. Don't bring the problems of other workers into the discussion. When offering suggestions for resolving the conflict, focus on things that will benefit the project or the team, not just the things that will benefit you.

5. **Respect your supervisor's decisions.** Once your boss makes a decision, it's final. Sometimes supervisors feel backed into a corner when their employees confront them, and they may react hastily. Very often, they will sleep on the issue and try to make amends the next day. Give your boss time to make amends and accept them gracefully.

*Example:* You are angry about having to work overtime. You talk to some of your co-workers and learn that they think the boss is too picky about quality control. Just this morning, your boss reprimanded you for coming in late. You are feeling pressured and annoyed. In addition, putting in the overtime today means that you will miss a planned family event.

*Poor approach:* March up to the boss and say, "Why am I always the one who has to work overtime? You always pick on me. If you weren't such a control freak, things would get done on time. The rest of the crew hates the way you pick over everything."

*Better approach:* Think things over calmly. You know that coming in late causes problems, so the boss was right to reprimand you. In fact, your coming in late is probably why you have to work overtime. As for your co-workers, if they have a problem with the boss, they can talk to the boss themselves.

*Best approach:* You understand that you must put in overtime to make up for being late but don't want to miss your family event. You ask your boss for a few minutes to discuss the problem. You apologize for coming in late and ask the boss whether you can work off the time the next day, either by coming in early or staying late.

## Dealing with annoying behavior

Co-workers can behave in many ways that are annoying. At one time or another, we've all been annoyed by people who do one or more of the following:

| | | |
|---|---|---|
| Criticize others | Arrive late | Lie |
| Don't make eye contact | Leave early | Take themselves too seriously |
| Gossip | Think they're perfect | Don't take anything seriously |
| Talk too much | Are opinionated, racist, or sexist | Complain constantly |
| Talk too little | Brag | Are conceited |
| Use profanity | Are nosy | Do poor-quality work |
| Are accident prone | Shift blame | Don't take pride in their work or appearance |
| Make excuses | Exaggerate | Play music too loudly |
| Bring other people down | Take all the credit | Think they work harder than others |
| Resist change | Withhold information | Are overly sensitive |

Rather than letting annoying behaviors escalate into full-scale conflicts, it's best to defuse them. In this section, you will learn some general tips for dealing with annoying behavior and some suggestions for coping with certain types of difficult co-workers.

# General tips: Coping with annoying behavior

People usually don't try to be annoying on purpose. They're often unaware of the effects of their behavior. In most cases, it is the behavior that is annoying, not the person. Keep this in mind as you read the following suggestions for letting others know that their behavior is annoying.

**1. Be tactful and consider the other person's feelings.** Don't bring up an annoying behavior when other people are around. It's better to have a private conversation. Avoid saying things that could insult the person or result in hurt feelings.

*Example:* Your co-worker's sloppy eating habits are disgusting to you and other co-workers.

*Poor approach:* During lunch say loudly, "You're disgusting! You eat like a pig! Shut your mouth when you eat!"

*Better approach:* In private say, "It's kind of a turnoff when people talk with their mouths full. Did you know that you do that?"

**2. Use words that won't make others defensive.** Using the word *you* when talking to others about a problem can put them on the defensive. When people are on the defensive, it is harder to talk to them. When possible, try to use *I* or *we*. Using *we* emphasizes the importance of the team and teamwork.

*Example:* You feel that your co-worker is slacking off.

*Poor approach:* Say, "You are so lazy! You always leave all the work for me!"

*Better approach:* Say, "We all need to pull our share of the weight around here."

Note that in the workplace you can, in many cases, replace *I* or *we* with *the company, safety rules, manufacturer's guidelines, OSHA,* or *the code.* (OSHA stands for Occupational Safety and Health Administration.) Here are some examples:

*Poor approach:* "You idiot! Don't you know you're supposed to wear your hard hat?"

*Better approach:* "Company rules say that everyone has to wear a hard hat on the job site."

*Poor approach:* "You messed up on that shower head installation. You put it in at the wrong height."

*Better approach:* "The local code says the shower head has to be at least 60 inches above the faucet."

*Poor approach:* "You are a fool for going up there without a safety harness."

*Better approach:* "OSHA requires us to wear safety harnesses when we are working this high up."

**3. Use humor when appropriate.** Often, you can let someone know about annoying behavior by taking a humorous or light-hearted approach, but be careful. Humor works well only when you laugh with others and not at them.

*Example:* Your co-worker's constant talking is annoying to you and your crew members.

*Poor approach:* You and your co-workers groan loudly and clutch your ears every time your co-worker gets too chatty.

*Better approach:* You come into work one day wearing a T-shirt with the expression, "Silence Is Golden." Every time the chatty worker gets too talkative, your co-workers silently point to the T-shirt and smile.

**4. Help the other person save face.** In most cases, people are surprised and embarrassed to learn that their behavior annoys others. Whenever possible, give others the chance to change their behavior without calling a huge amount of attention to it. Let people off the hook gracefully, and they will appreciate it.

*Example:* You notice that a co-worker has suddenly developed an offensive body odor.

*Poor approach:* In public say loudly, "Whew! Did you forget to take a bath today or what?"

*Better approach:* In private say, "I don't want to embarrass you, but I couldn't help noticing a bad odor around you today. Were you aware of that?"

**5. Ask your boss for help, but only as a last resort.** As a professional, you should be able to deal sensibly with behavior that you find annoying in others. Most often, annoying behavior is a minor matter that you can work out with your co-workers. In some cases, however, you may feel that the behavior is too serious to handle on your own. In these cases you should ask your supervisor for help.

*Example:* Your co-worker is harassing you. You keep finding offensive notes at your work area. In addition, your co-worker often pushes or grabs you in a threatening way and does things that embarrass and upset you. You have confronted your co-worker and demanded to be treated with respect, but the behavior just gets worse.

*Poor approach:* Ignore the co-worker's harassing behavior in the hope that it will eventually stop.

*Better approach:* Talk to your boss about your co-worker's threatening behavior. Provide your boss with details of the things your co-worker has done and with copies of the offensive notes you have received.

## Coping with Difficult Co-Workers

Sometimes annoying behaviors seem to be part of everything some people do. How can you cope with these personality types? Read *Table 9–1* for a brief description of difficult people and some techniques for coping with them.

*Note:* You should use these techniques only with co-workers, not with your supervisor.

**Table 9-1. Types of Difficult People**

| Difficult Personality Type | Description | Coping Technique |
|---|---|---|
| Age resenters (older) | Think that younger workers are lazy and undisciplined. Resent younger people and feel threatened by them. | Respect their experience. Be willing to learn from them. Ask for advice when appropriate. Offer assistance when appropriate. |
| Age resenters (younger) | Think that older workers are stuck in the past and never want to try anything new. Resent older workers and feel threatened by them. | Respect their willingness to learn. Give them time to perfect their skills. Ask for advice when appropriate. Offer assistance when appropriate. |
| Blamers | Refuse to take responsibility for mistakes. Blame others when things go wrong. | Point out that blaming accomplishes nothing. Emphasize teamwork and personal responsibility. |
| Braggarts and know-it-alls | Boast about their talents, their intelligence, and their possessions. Think they know all the answers. Often withhold information to make themselves appear smarter. | Agree with them. This surprising reaction usually leaves them very little to say. |
| Brown-nosers | Flatter and butter up the boss constantly. Agree with everything the boss says or does. | Empathize. Maybe these people badly need a promotion to pay their bills. |
| Complainers | Gripe constantly. Prefer whining to finding a solution. | Point out that complaining accomplishes nothing. Ask them to focus on finding positive solutions. |
| Delegators | Pass off to others work that they should be doing. | Resist letting them dump their work responsibilities on you. Point out that all workers must do their share of the work. |
| Detailers | Can take a long time to finish tasks. Can be overly concerned about small details. | Respect the attention to detail, but point out that fine-tuning everything is not everyone's working style. |
| Dictators | Bully, harass, and intimidate others. Have no regard for others' feelings. Make demands and give nothing in return. | Be firm, strong, and unemotional. Refuse to let dictators bully you. |
| Gossips | Spread rumors. Rarely have anything nice to say. Attempt to pit workers against one another. | Avoid telling them things. Avoid listening to the things they say. |

*(continued)*

| Difficult Personality Type | Description | Coping Technique |
|---|---|---|
| Hotheads | Blow up quickly, even over small matters. | Talk to them only when necessary. Focus on work. Avoid saying and doing things you know will make them react. |
| Mood-swingers | Are unpredictable. Happy one day, depressed the next. | Avoid saying or doing things that would cause an emotional reaction. Focus on work. |
| Naysayers | Bring others down with their negative attitude. See the bad side of everything. | Maintain your positive focus. Resist being pulled down by negative thoughts. |
| Repulsive people | Have poor personal hygiene, bad social habits, or use profane language. | Privately and tactfully state that workers find these habits unpleasant. Offer help if appropriate. |
| Silent people | Rarely speak. Often don't appear to be paying attention. Are poor communicators. | Encourage them to communicate. Ask whether they have understood directions. Ask them to summarize directions given. |
| Snobs | Expect special treatment and feel they are better than everyone else. | Point out that all workers have to pull their own weight and that no one gets special treatment. |
| Tattletales | Tell the boss everything other workers do and say. | Focus on your job, and don't do or say anything they can take back to the boss. |

Following are some examples of how you might cope with difficult people on the work site. Notice that you are not trying to control or change these people. Instead, you are using your conflict resolution skills to keep a small annoyance from turning into a conflict.

*Example 1:* Your co-worker often says, "As long as you're going to get some coffee for yourself, how about getting some for me?" You would not mind, but your co-worker never returns the favor. In fact, your co-worker is now asking you to pick up an extra sandwich or a snack. You like your co-worker, but resent the attitude.

*Poor approach:* "Get it yourself, you lazy good-for-nothing. I'm sick of waiting on you!"

*Better approach:* "I don't mind getting you things as long as I'm going anyway, but be fair. How about returning the favor?"

*Example 2:* Your co-worker likes to refine details on every task. Although you don't feel the nitpicking is necessary, your co-worker's working style does not bother you. Things would be fine except that your co-worker criticizes you for a lack of attention to detail.

*Poor approach:* "Why do you have to always pick over every little thing? You're driving me crazy with all this fiddling."

*Better approach:* "You are really good with the detail stuff and I am more of a 'big picture' sort of person. Between us, we've got everything covered. I think we make a great team!"

*Example 3:* Your co-worker complains about everything and everybody. This negative attitude is starting to affect you.

*Poor approach:* "Ugh. You are such a downer. Why don't you just shut up? Get a life!"

*Better approach:* "Hey! Cheer up. It's almost the end of the week. I'm going to see that new movie. What fun things do you have planned?"

## On-the-Job Quiz

Here's a quick quiz that asks you to apply what you've learned in this module.

1. You decide to shave off all your hair and wear an earring in one ear. One of your co-workers teases you about this and makes a lot of sarcastic remarks. By lunchtime you are pretty fed up with the wisecracks, but you want to keep a good working relationship with your co-worker, so you _____.
   a. find something about your co-worker's appearance you can make fun of in return
   b. wait until lunchtime, then tell your co-worker that you don't appreciate the comments and to stop making them
   c. ignore the comments, figuring this just isn't worth arguing about, and that the comments will soon stop
   d. clench your fists and tell your co-worker to stop the remarks or else
2. Your boss calls you aside and talks to you about some serious mistakes you made the day before. You have to take apart what you did and do it over again. Your boss patiently and calmly explains what you must do and says that you will have to work some overtime to fix the mistakes. Later you tell a friend why you had to work late. If you empathize with your boss, which of the following would you say?
   a. "The boss was nice about it, but why wasn't I told about those mistakes yesterday? I am really steamed."
   b. "I'm glad the boss didn't talk to me in front of everybody. I should have spotted those mistakes myself, but I'll know better next time."
   c. "The boss was really decent with me, but I wish I wasn't pulled off to the side. I bet everyone thinks I did some horrible thing."
   d. "I pointed out to the boss that if I couldn't do it right the first time, I probably won't get it right the second time. I said that I thought someone else should fix the mistakes."

**3.** You are working on a task when two co-workers nearby begin to argue. They both want you to take sides and help settle the argument. You should _____.

a. tell them the argument is none of your business and they will have to work things out without your help
b. ask both workers to calmly explain what is going on and then side with the worker who is clearly right as a way of ending the argument
c. run and get the boss to break up the argument
d. tell them to shut up, stop acting like children, and just do their jobs

**4.** You and J.J. work together on a two-person job that requires both of you to take lunch at the same time. J.J. wants to break for lunch at 11:00 A.M. You would rather break at 12:30. To settle this conflict so that both of you get a little of what you want, you and J.J. would _____.

a. collaborate
b. delegate
c. compromise
d. empathize

**5.** You believe that one of your co-workers has made mistakes that will take you all day to fix. You lose your temper and chew out your co-worker. Later, you realize that you are also partly to blame for the mistakes. What is your best course of action?

a. Let things blow over, and promise yourself that you won't lose your temper again.
b. Admit your mistakes and apologize for losing your temper.
c. Apologize for losing your temper, but never admit your mistakes.
d. Admit that you were partly to blame, and buy your co-worker lunch.

**6.** Your boss has pointed out a number of mistakes you made this week. This morning, the boss jokingly called you a numbskull and told you to spend more time thinking before tackling your assigned tasks. You feel like the boss is picking on you unfairly and want to complain. What is your best course of action?

a. Wait until the next time the boss points out another mistake and then accuse your boss of micromanaging. List all the times your boss has complained about your work and say, "Get off my back."

b. Think about what you want to say. Decide that your boss must point out your mistakes but should not insult you. Tell your boss that you want to improve but don't appreciate being called names.

c. Decide to do nothing. After all, the boss is always right, and you are better off not saying anything at all.

d. Do nothing until you are really fed up. Then march up to the boss and complain. Point out that other workers seem to get away with making mistakes. Point out all the things that you think the boss does incorrectly.

**7.** Your co-worker has the annoying habit of laughing nervously after everything you say, whether it's funny or not. You want your co-worker to recognize the problem, so you say, _____

a. "Why do you laugh at everything I say? You think I'm funny or something?"

b. "Did you realize that when you laugh you sound sort of like a hyena or a wild pig or something?"

c. "I'm glad you are a happy person, but the way you laugh drives me nuts."

d. "It's hard for me to concentrate when there's so much laughing. Could you laugh a little less, please?"

**8.** You are an experienced worker who likes to work at a steady, even pace. You like to put tools away when you're done with them. When you are working, you prefer to be focused and quiet. You've been assigned a new trainee who chatters while working and leaves tools all over the place. The trainee works quickly and neatly but a little too fast for you to keep track of what's being done. What is your best course of action?

a. Say that you are in charge, you have the most experience, and the trainee must adopt your work habits.

b. Tell the trainee to stop talking so much because it breaks your concentration and really annoys you.

c. Change your working style so that it is more like that of your trainee. You might learn something new.

d. Compliment your trainee's good qualities and explain that you like to work more methodically and quietly.

9. Your boss tells your co-worker L.T. to cut and bend sheet metal for ductwork. L.T., who is a well-known delegator, does not like doing this task and asks you to please do it instead. What is your best course of action?
   a. Do as L.T. asks because the request was made politely.
   b. Lie and say that you don't know how to do that task.
   c. Say that you have your own work to do and point out that all workers must pull their own weight.
   d. Agree to do the task, but then don't do it, so L.T. will get in trouble with the boss and learn a lesson.

10. T.J. is one of the more experienced workers on the job and knows everything about everyone. T.J. passes along gossip whether the information is true or not. The best way to deal with T.J. is to _____.
   a. be careful what you say to T.J., and change the subject when T.J. wants to gossip
   b. explain to T.J. why gossiping in the workplace is not a good idea, and give a few examples of past gossip that has caused problems
   c. set a trap by giving T.J. phony information about yourself and others
   d. tell your boss about the damage T.J. is causing by spreading gossip

# Individual Activities

## Activity 1: Using Words That Won't Put Others on the Defensive

In this module, you learned that using the word *you* in conflict situations could make the other person defensive. Instead of saying *you,* it is better to say *I, we, the company rules, manufacturer's guidelines, OSHA,* or *the code.* Talking this way may feel a little awkward at first. This activity will give you a chance to practice. Read the following examples and change them so that your listener is not put on the defensive.

1. *Poor approach:* "It takes you two days longer than everyone else to do the same job."

   *Better approach:*________________________________________

   ____________________________________________________

2. *Poor approach:* "You're always criticizing me and finding fault with what I do."

   *Better approach:*________________________________________

   ____________________________________________________

3. *Poor approach:* "Are you crazy? Can't you see that cord's frayed? You trainees have to be told how to do everything."

   *Better approach:*________________________________________

   ____________________________________________________

4. *Poor approach:* "You installed that water heater all wrong. Can't you see you forgot the bracing?"

   *Better approach:*________________________________________

   ____________________________________________________

5. *Poor approach:* "You are really sloppy on the job. Your work area is a pigsty."

   *Better approach:*________________________________________

   ____________________________________________________

## Activity 2: Seeing the Positive Side of Conflict

Conflict is a part of everyday life, and we can't always avoid it. While we tend to think of conflict as a negative thing, it can have positive effects.

Think about some conflicts you've had with others recently. Did anything good happen as a result of those conflicts? Did you learn anything? Was a problem solved? Did it give you a chance to understand someone else's point of view? Write down positive outcomes of conflicts you have experienced.

1. ______________________________
2. ______________________________
3. ______________________________
4. ______________________________
5. ______________________________

## Activity 3: Are You a Difficult Type?

It can be hard to admit faults. This activity asks for your complete honesty and a certain amount of courage! To complete this activity, follow these steps:

1. Review *Table 9–1, Types of Difficult People.* Do you think you fit into any of these categories? If so, which?
2. Now survey five people you work with (or five classmates). Ask them to review the list and to tell you honestly which category or categories you fit into. List those categories here. Does your perception of yourself match other people's perceptions of you?
3. Based on the suggestions in this module, as well as suggestions from your co-workers or classmates, create an action plan for becoming a less difficult person. Outline the steps you will take here.

**My Action Plan for Becoming Less Difficult**

1. ______________________________
2. ______________________________
3. ______________________________
4. ______________________________
5. ______________________________

# Group Activities

## Activity 4: Resolving Conflict

Your goal in this activity is to resolve a conflict using the five-step conflict resolution process you learned in this module. After you've read and thought about the situation, work with two or three of your classmates to complete the conflict resolution grid. However, before you start completing the grid, set up some ground rules. Recall the ground rules you read about in this module, such as treating one another with respect and letting others speak without interruption.

**Team Members**

1. ______________________ 2. ______________________
3. ______________________ 4. ______________________

**Situation:** Two construction crews have been assigned to a new project. You are on one of the crews. To keep the job moving, the crews take staggered lunch breaks. Each day, both the drink and snack machines are completely empty by the time the second shift is ready to take its break. The workers in the second shift are upset about this situation, and now conflict and bad feelings have sprung up between the shifts. (Thanks to Mike Stilley, S&B Engineers and Constructors, Ltd., Houston, TX, for contributing the situation on which this activity is based.)

**Ground Rules**

1. ______________________________________________
2. ______________________________________________
3. ______________________________________________
4. ______________________________________________
5. ______________________________________________

To complete this activity, follow the conflict resolution steps:

| Five-Step Conflict Resolution Process | |
|---|---|
| **Step 1** Bring the conflict into the open. | |
| **Step 2** Discuss and analyze the reasons for the conflict. | |
| **Step 3** Develop possible solutions. Remember that all workers involved should collaborate and compromise. | |
| **Step 4** Choose and carry out a solution. | |
| **Step 5** Evaluate the solution. | |

## Discussion Questions

1. How can you bring this conflict into the open?
2. Is collaboration possible?
3. Is compromise possible?
4. What is the common ground? That is, what outcome will benefit all of you?
5. Once you've resolved the problem, how will you go about making sure that the conflict doesn't arise again?

## Activity 5: Recognizing the Potential for Conflict

Sometimes the best way to prevent conflict is to recognize the potential for it. When you're aware of situations that can result in conflict, you can take steps to improve the situation before conflict arises. To complete this activity, read the case study, then work in groups of three or four to answer the questions that follow. (Thanks to Mike Stilley, S&B Engineers and Constructors, Ltd., Houston, TX, for contributing the situation on which this activity is based.)

**Team Members**

1.____________________ 2.____________________

3.____________________ 4.____________________

### *Case Study: The Multicultural Construction Team*

**Kate** is a 26-year-old black woman. She attended a state college for two years and took courses in surveying and soil analysis. She then worked for a construction company for four years. During this time she completed her education and training at the ABC School, taking the Core Curriculum and Operators courses. She is now the new supervisor at another construction company, and her crew is made up of the following five people:

**Martin** A black man, age 45. He has 20 years' experience in construction and has worked for the company for the past 15 years. He is a high school graduate. An excellent worker, he expected to be promoted when the last supervisor left. He was surprised when he found out that Kate would be the new supervisor.

**Sam** A white man, age 30. He worked at several sales jobs after graduating from high school before joining the company. He has been with the company for seven years. When he was a teenager, his mother took a trip to Mexico, where she was mugged.

**Mary** A white woman, age 28. After one year of college, she got married and had three children. For eight years she was a homemaker. She hoped to someday complete her education, but a divorce forced her to go to work. She has worked for the company for two years.

**Raul** A Mexican-American, age 40, with 20 years' construction experience. For several years he owned his own company, but times have been tough and he had to shut down his business.

**Trevor** A black man, age 19. This is his first full-time job, and he is eager to learn and advance. He has a bossy older sister.

## Discussion Questions

I. Identify at least five possible sources of conflict in Kate's team.

1. ______
2. ______
3. ______
4. ______
5. ______

II. For each possible source, suggest one or two ways to prevent that conflict.

1. ______
______
2. ______
______
3. ______
______
4. ______
______
5. ______
______

## Activity 6: Your Turn— Working with Difficult People: Follow-Up Activity

In this module, you learned some ideas for coping with difficult people, such as the blamer, the complainer, and the know-it-all, but we may have missed some difficult types you have at your workplace. In this activity, you will apply your new knowledge of conflict resolution. In the following grid, list and describe the difficult types of people at your own workplace. Do not refer to these difficult persons by name. Work with your teammates to come up with coping techniques.

**Team Members**

1. ______ 2. ______
3. ______ 4. ______

| Type of Person | Description | Techniques for Coping |
|---|---|---|
| | | |
| | | |
| | | |
| | | |
| | | |

## Activity 7: Defining Success in Conflict Resolution

Most of us define success as winning. That definition is fine for competitive sports, where there must be a clear winner and a clear loser. When you resolve conflicts at work, however, you must define success differently. Success at work means that all parties feel satisfied, so work can continue without a lot of drama and tension.

In this activity, you and two or three of your classmates will review some typical job conflicts and then state whether you think the outcome is successful. Remember that in the workplace, conflicts are best resolved with collaboration and compromise. When everyone wins a little, the entire team wins a lot.

**Team Members**

| | |
|---|---|
| 1.____________________ | 2.____________________ |
| 3.____________________ | 4.____________________ |

## Discussion Questions

Read and think about each situation. Then answer the following questions:

1. Was this conflict resolution successful? Why or why not?
2. What are the possible good outcomes of this resolution? What are the possible bad outcomes?
3. If the resolution was not successful, what could have been done to change the outcome?

**Situation 1:** Your co-worker is messier than you. You can't stand seeing stuff all over the place. You tend to nag your co-worker about the messiness. You talk things over, and your co-worker agrees to pick up the area at least twice a week. You agree to learn to live with a little more messiness than you are used to and to stop nagging.

Successful resolution? ❑ Yes ❑ No

**Situation 2:** You and three co-workers agree to start a carpool to save money. You have the biggest vehicle and volunteer to drive. In exchange, your co-workers agree to pay for gas and parking fees. After awhile, however, you get tired of being the chauffeur and complain. Your co-workers offer to alternate driving your vehicle or to drive their own vehicles, but you don't want to do either of those things. Your co-workers' cars are too small and you don't want anyone touching your car. Your attitude makes everyone mad at you, and you get mad at everyone else. The carpool breaks up.

Successful resolution? ❑ Yes ❑ No

**Situation 3:** You are a man and are put on a team that includes two women. You make several disrespectful remarks about women in construction. You think you are just being funny, but the women don't appreciate your humor and are very cold toward you. You decide to apologize for your remarks and to be politically correct when the women are around. Once they are out of earshot, however, you revert to your old ways.

Successful resolution? ❑ Yes ❑ No

**Situation 4:** You work on the second shift. When you and your crew come in, the snack area is always a mess, with dirty cups, spilled condiments, and empty snack containers scattered about. Often one of the coffee pots has a burned-on film, and supplies have been used up and not replaced. You and your crew talk to the crew on the first shift and ask them to leave a clean snack area and to replace supplies. That's when you learn that they have to deal with your crew's mess at the start of their shift. You all agree to come up with a plan that will ensure that someone on each crew cleans up the area at the end of the shift and replaces supplies.

Successful resolution? ❑ Yes ❑ No

**Situation 5:** Your co-worker is a workaholic who comes to work early and stays late. You, on the other hand, believe that coming in to work on time and leaving on time is fine. You put in a good day's work each day, but your co-worker is constantly on you because you don't share the same work ethic. Fed up with this, you confront your co-worker one morning and say, "It's great that you love work so much. But I am sick of your bragging about what a great worker you are, and so is everybody else. Back off or you will get what's coming to you!" Your co-worker leaves you alone after that.

Successful resolution? ❑ Yes ❑ No

## Activity 8: Your Turn—Talking to the Boss

In this activity, you and two or three of your classmates will be the scriptwriters. Study each boss/worker conflict situation. Based on what you learned in this module, write what you think you should say.

**Team Members**

| | |
|---|---|
| 1.____________________ | 2.____________________ |
| 3.____________________ | 4.____________________ |

As you write your remarks, consider these questions:

1. Can I just walk up to the boss with this situation, or should I ask the boss if this is a good time to talk?
2. What can I say to keep from sounding negative or defensive?
3. What can I say to keep from sounding threatening?
4. How can I show the boss that I want to contribute to the solution?
5. Should I be asking the boss about this at all?

| Situation | Sample Remarks |
|---|---|
| 1. You've been late twice this week. The boss says you have to work overtime to make up for the lost time, but you play on a softball team and don't want to miss two scheduled games. | |
| 2. You are upset because you feel that the boss has passed you over for promotion. | |
| 3. You are upset because the boss criticized your work and made you redo it. | |
| 4. You feel like you are doing more work than everyone else. | |
| 5. You want the company to pay for some computer courses you want to take. | |
| 6. You want the boss to change your work schedule so that you can take some classes. | |
| 7. You want the boss to help get a bullying co-worker off your back. | |
| 8. At a crew meeting, the boss makes a blanket statement about "some workers" being late. You feel that the boss took the wrong approach. You want to tell the boss that the on-time workers are upset. | |
| 9. The boss made a hasty decision that you know will cause problems. You must tell the boss about these problems. | |
| 10. Although your company lost a job to a competitor recently, you need to ask for a raise. | |

## Activity 9: You, the Boss, or Forget about It

In this module, you learned that when it comes to conflict resolution, there are certain things you must handle yourself, there are other things that the boss must handle, and there are some situations you just have to walk away from or forget about. On the job site, these choices won't always be easy or the same, but this activity will give you practice in thinking about a conflict before you charge in to fix it or run to the boss with the problem. Working with two or three of your classmates, compete the following grid. Read each situation and check one of the following:

- You, if you should deal with the conflict
- The boss, if the boss must deal with it
- Forget about it, if this is a situation you should walk away from or ignore

**Team Members**

1.____________________ 2.____________________

3.____________________ 4.____________________

After you complete the grid, talk about your choices. Did you agree on all of them?

| Situation | You | The Boss | Forget about It |
|---|---|---|---|
| 1. A co-worker keeps borrowing money from you and often forgets to pay you back. | ❑ | ❑ | ❑ |
| 2. A co-worker threatens to beat you up after work. | ❑ | ❑ | ❑ |
| 3. You see a co-worker stealing tools from the work site. | ❑ | ❑ | ❑ |
| 4. You have to take orders from someone who is younger than you. | ❑ | ❑ | ❑ |
| 5. Your co-worker is sexually harassing you. | ❑ | ❑ | ❑ |
| 6. Your co-worker tells offensive and obscene jokes and has a foul mouth. | ❑ | ❑ | ❑ |
| 7. Two of your co-workers are constantly bickering. | ❑ | ❑ | ❑ |
| 8. You are in a carpool, and one of the members is late at least twice a week. | ❑ | ❑ | ❑ |
| 9. Your co-worker is openly rude and hostile and is making your worklife miserable. | ❑ | ❑ | ❑ |
| 10. Your co-worker often collects money for various charitable causes. You don't want to contribute and think your co-worker should not collect money on company time. | ❑ | ❑ | ❑ |
| 11. You and your spouse are having a difficult time, and you feel annoyed and irritated at work. | ❑ | ❑ | ❑ |
| 12. Your co-worker is a whiz at technology and makes you feel stupid. | ❑ | ❑ | ❑ |
| 13. Your co-worker hates the job and complains about it every day. | ❑ | ❑ | ❑ |
| 14. Your co-worker says that you have body odor. (You do.) | ❑ | ❑ | ❑ |
| 15. Your co-worker says that you have body odor. (You don't.) | ❑ | ❑ | ❑ |
| 16. Your co-worker likes to hum softly while working. | ❑ | ❑ | ❑ |
| 17. Your co-worker got a raise and you did not. | ❑ | ❑ | ❑ |
| 18. Your co-worker is a mean-spirited gossip. | ❑ | ❑ | ❑ |
| 19. Your co-worker tries to control everything and everybody, including you. | ❑ | ❑ | ❑ |
| 20. Your co-worker is from another country and struggles with English. | ❑ | ❑ | ❑ |

## Activity 10: True or False? Test Your Perceptions

A lot of conflict arises because of perceptions, or beliefs, we have about people or situations. In this activity, you will first read the statements and decide if they are true or false on your own. Then compare your answers with your team members'.

**Team Members**

1.______________________ 2.______________________

3.______________________ 4.______________________

### *Discussion Questions*

1. Did all of you choose the same answers?
2. Talk about the answers you differed on.
3. Did this exercise change your mind about anything?

| True or False | Statement |
|---|---|
| | 1. People who are older than me know more than I do about every subject. |
| | 2. I know more about computers and technology than someone who is older than me. |
| | 3. People who dress differently from everybody else are just weird. |
| | 4. Men are not supposed to wear earrings. |
| | 5. Women are OK in construction but should not be working in rigging or on roofs. |
| | 6. Workaholics think they are superior to the rest of us. |
| | 7. Bosses just don't know what it is like to be a worker. |
| | 8. Construction workers usually "discuss" their problems with their fists. |
| | 9. Older workers are not supposed to get along with younger workers. |
| | 10. People from different backgrounds can't work together in construction, and that's that. |

# Giving and Receiving Criticism

## Self-Assessment
## How critical are you?

Are you picky? Do you tend to find fault with others? Take this self-assessment quiz to find out. Check whether you agree or disagree with the following statements. Be sure to answer each question honestly.

| | Agree | Disagree |
|---|---|---|
| 1. I tend to lose my patience when things aren't done the way I want them to be done. | ❑ | ❑ |
| 2. If someone is wearing clothes, jewelry, or makeup that I think looks strange, I usually tell that person what I think. | ❑ | ❑ |
| 3. When I was growing up, I was criticized a lot. | ❑ | ❑ |
| 4. I don't like it when other people do a part of my job because I know they can't do it as well as I can. | ❑ | ❑ |
| 5. In the past month, I've called someone dumb or stupid or thought to myself that a person was dumb or stupid. | ❑ | ❑ |
| 6. When people show me things they have done, I tend to notice the flaws. | ❑ | ❑ |
| 7. I believe that when someone is wrong, you should always let that person know it. | ❑ | ❑ |
| 8. I am always looking for ways to improve things. | ❑ | ❑ |
| 9. I don't usually give people compliments when they've done something well. | ❑ | ❑ |
| 10. If one of my teammates makes an error, I'll probably get angry. | ❑ | ❑ |

***Scoring:*** Count the number of statements you agreed with. Number of "Agree" boxes checked: __________

***Assessment:***

8–10 boxes checked: You tend to notice and point out other people's mistakes. This is not necessarily a bad thing. You just need to make sure that your criticism is constructive and conveyed in a positive way. This module will help you do that. It will also help you learn to accept criticism when you make mistakes.

6–7 boxes checked: You like to have things your way, although you sometimes will accept another's standards or way of doing things. This module will help you understand the critical side of your nature and learn how to give constructive criticism to others. You will also learn how to react when somebody criticizes you.

1–5 boxes checked: You tend to be an easygoing person. You're probably not very critical, but you may have difficulty accepting criticism of yourself. This module will help you give constructive criticism when appropriate and deal with criticism you receive.

## Introduction

As you progress in your career, you'll learn new techniques, new processes, and new procedures. You're human, so you'll make mistakes once in a while. This doesn't mean you're incompetent or untalented. It just means that you need guidance as you learn your trade and perfect your skills. When you do something incorrectly, someone will probably tell you about it. If you expect to be criticized sometimes, you won't be caught off guard when it happens.

Sometimes you will be the person who does the criticizing. For example, you may be assigned to train a newly hired worker who makes some beginner's mistakes. You need to know how to point out the mistakes in a constructive and positive way, and get the worker focused on improving.

Sometimes, you will criticize yourself. You can be much harder on yourself than others might be. Whether you are criticizing yourself or others, you should know some basic techniques for giving and receiving criticism. You will learn those techniques in this module.

## What is criticism?

When we hear the word *criticism,* we often think of something negative, but criticism is not always negative. Used in the right way, criticism can be a valuable learning tool. There are two types of criticism: destructive and constructive.

Destructive criticism is hurtful and insulting. It strips people of their self-esteem, makes them feel worthless, and creates bad feelings. It has no place on the job or in life.

Constructive criticism is tactful and supportive. The goal of constructive criticism is to help others improve. It is the only type of criticism that you should use on the job or in life.

## Benefiting from constructive criticism

Most supervisors offer constructive criticism on a regular basis. Their goal is to help workers improve and refine their skills. Correcting your mistakes can mean the difference between success and failure or even between life and death. To benefit from the constructive criticism you receive on the job, keep several things in mind:

**1. Anticipate criticism and be aware of the source.** It's easier to deal with criticism if you expect it. Think of it as an opportunity to learn and to improve your skills. You must listen closely to any criticism from your supervisor or from an experienced co-worker. Keep in mind that your immediate supervisor is held responsible for your work. If you receive instructions from anyone other than your supervisor, it is best to check with your supervisor before doing anything.

**2. Don't take criticism of your job performance personally.** Recognize that your supervisor is criticizing your mistakes, not you personally. Get in the habit of thinking, "This isn't about me, it's about the job I'm doing, and I can learn how to do that better."

**3. Look at your work from your supervisor's point of view.** Imagine that you have to evaluate a task you've just done. When you haven't done a good job, deep down inside, you know it.

**4. Don't get defensive.** When somebody criticizes you, your first reaction may be to defend yourself or fight back. Resist that temptation, listen calmly, and keep an open mind.

**5. Don't make excuses.** You may want to explain your mistake or shift the blame to somebody else. Don't. It's much better to take responsibility for your mistakes and move on.

**6. Ask for clarification and specifics.** Some criticism is vague. Don't be afraid to ask questions if you don't fully understand what you did incorrectly. Ask those questions respectfully. Remember that your goal is to improve your performance, not defend your mistakes. For example, you might say, "I want to do a good job. Can you give me an example of how I can improve?"

**7. State your plan for improvement and carry it out.** There's no better way to impress your boss than to take criticism seriously. Tell your boss what you'll do to correct your mistakes. For example, if your boss reprimands you for being late, you might say, "I'm getting a better alarm clock so that I won't oversleep again." You must respond to criticism with words and action. So be sure to get that new alarm clock.

**8. Understand your right to disagree when the criticism is not warranted.** After carefully evaluating the criticism you receive, you may feel that it's not justified. Sometimes you *are* right, and the other person is wrong. In that case, offer your side of the story respectfully and clearly, and give examples to support your point of view.

## Dealing with destructive criticism

People often give destructive criticism because that is how others have criticized them. Some people let their emotions get the better of them and say hurtful and disrespectful things. To deal with someone who gives you destructive criticism, your best bet is to do the following:

- Control your emotions.
- Take some time to calm down.
- Remind yourself that you can deal constructively with destructive criticism.
- Ask the person to give you constructive criticism instead.
- Tell the person how the destructive criticism made you feel.

*Example:* Your boss has had a frustrating day and yells, "Why can't you do anything right? I have to watch you every minute. You are so dumb!"

*Your response:* Take a deep breath and calm down. Think. There are many things you can do right. The boss doesn't really watch you every minute, and you know you are not dumb. You could say, "Sorry, boss. Could you take a minute and show me what I did wrong? I want to do a good job, and it's not fair when you say I'm dumb."

## Giving constructive criticism

Giving constructive criticism is a skill that takes time and patience to develop. Following are some tools you can use to help you manage how and when you criticize others.

**1. Decide what is worth criticizing.** People tend to shut down if they hear too much criticism. Determine whether you really should criticize something. For example, if a worker isn't wearing a hard hat, you should definitely speak up. However, if you don't like the way a co-worker installs cabinets, hold your tongue. Work techniques can differ without affecting quality. Avoid criticizing personal qualities, such as hairstyle or music preferences, that have nothing to do with getting the job done safely and well.

Note that hair, jewelry, or clothing can affect safety. Therefore, workers must change their appearance when it conflicts with safety rules.

**2. Choose the time and place wisely.** Never criticize people in front of their peers. It will embarrass them and make them resent you. Take them off to the side, and choose a time when they are feeling less stressed or pressured.

**3. Choose your words carefully.** Don't swear or call others names. Avoid sounding angry, frustrated, or sarcastic. Stick to the facts and stay clear of personal comments.

**4. Criticize the behavior, not the person.** To prevent hard feelings, make it clear that you're criticizing the behavior or mistake, not the person. Consider the following example:

*Example:* A co-worker leaves the job site each day without putting the tools away.

*Destructive criticism:* "How many times do I have to tell you to put the tools away before you leave? Can't you understand simple directions?"

*Constructive criticism:* "It's important to put the tools away at the end of the day. We insist on that around here, and when it's not done it causes problems for everyone."

**5. Decide how many things to criticize at one time.** Usually, it's best to focus on one issue at a time. Sometimes, however, you have to talk about a number of issues. If you must criticize several things at one time, you should let the person know up front. Avoid "piling." That is, don't bring up issues that have already been addressed and resolved. Focus on the present, and let bygones be bygones.

*Example:* You are training a nervous trainee to install kitchen cabinets.

*Destructive criticism:* "You are messing up a lot! Look at all the mistakes you made just today! First, you racked that cabinet. Then you installed those bases out of plumb, and I can't believe your finish work. Look at all those nail holes!"

*Constructive criticism:* "Slow down. You're trying to get too much done too fast. You've made three mistakes. Let me show you how to do these jobs the right way." (Then review each mistake, one at a time, and point out how to fix them.)

It is important to point out improper behavior or incorrect work techniques the first time they occur. Don't let them go, because that's how people form bad habits. Criticize the poor behavior or mistake as soon as you are aware of it. Be aware that some work standards may vary depending on the company. Reminding your co-worker of the company's standards is an excellent way to give constructive criticism.

**6. Offer suggestions.** In an earlier module, you learned to offer solutions, not just complaints. The same is true when you criticize another's work.

*Example:* You and a co-worker are cutting wood to various lengths. You notice that your co-worker, who measures one time and then quickly cuts the wood, is cutting the wood to the wrong lengths and mixing up installation pieces with waste pieces.

*Destructive criticism:* "What's the matter with you? Can't you even do a simple thing like cutting wood right? Look at all this waste!"

*Constructive criticism:* "Here's a good tip to help you. To make sure you've measured correctly, measure twice before you cut. Then put an X on the waste piece."

**7. When possible, offer praise along with the criticism.** People are much more receptive to criticism if they also hear about the things they are doing right. While it is not always possible to praise someone's work, it's helpful if you can find something good to say.

*Example:* Your co-worker is struggling to make angle cuts in molding, has made several mistakes, and keeps trying to get the angles right.

*Destructive criticism:* "Look at this mess! You are never going to learn to do this right!"

*Constructive criticism:* "I admire your determination, but I think you are too eager to start cutting. Take the time to measure accurately and think through the steps before you turn on the saw. Let me show you how."

**8. Follow up.** To make sure that problems are not repeated, check up on the situation later on. Following up provides a good opportunity to offer your ongoing support. Ask, "How's it going? Anything I can help with? Did my advice help?"

**9. Learn how to criticize your own work.** Evaluate your work based on your experience and your company's standards. Don't tell yourself that you are better or worse than everyone else. Instead, focus on improving your knowledge and skills each day.

## On-the-Job Quiz

Here's a quick quiz that asks you to apply what you've learned in this module.

1. You overhear the boss say to one of the crew, "That was so stupid! I can't believe you mixed that cement before we were ready for it. It's all going to go to waste! You just don't pay attention to your work." If you were asked for your opinion of this situation, what would you say?
   a. The boss is right and handled the criticism appropriately.
   b. Everyone makes mistakes, and the boss should have let this one go.
   c. This is constructive criticism. The boss has to make sure everyone understands how wasteful the mistake was.
   d. This is destructive criticism. The boss could have handled the situation in a more positive way.
2. You are fastening deck boards to joists and you strip the threads on several screws. Your boss says, "Listen, this is not a huge deal. I can show you how to fix that mistake. I'll also show you how to change your technique so that it doesn't happen again." If you were asked for your opinion of this situation, what would you say?
   a. This is constructive criticism. The boss handled the situation well.
   b. This is constructive criticism. However, the boss was wrong to let you off the hook so easily.
   c. This is destructive criticism. The boss made you feel stupid by saying that this was not a huge deal.
   d. This is destructive criticism, but you deserved it for making the mistake in the first place.
3. The site supervisor tells you to move some scaffolding out of the way, and you do it. A few minutes later, your immediate supervisor criticizes you for moving the scaffolding. What is your best course of action?
   a. Keep quiet and just let your boss blow off some steam.
   b. Say that your boss is out of line because you were just following the site supervisor's orders.
   c. Apologize for not checking with your boss, and explain that you didn't think to question the site supervisor's orders.
   d. Apologize and ask the site supervisor to explain to your boss what happened because the site supervisor caused the problem.

**4.** Your boss takes you aside and points out several errors you made in framing a room. The boss shows you how to fix the errors and mentions that you should concentrate more on your work and spend less time joking with co-workers. What is your best response to this situation?

a. Decide that your boss is critiquing your work and work habits, not you personally.

b. Decide that your boss likes you as a person despite the comments about your work and joking.

c. Feel that your boss has it in for you and should cut you some slack.

d. Feel that the comments about the framing mistakes are fair and the comment about joking with co-workers is unfair.

**5.** It's the end of the day, and you're getting ready to leave work. Suddenly, one of your co-workers comes up to you and says angrily "Hey! Where do you think you're going? You better stay and fix what you messed up, 'cause I'm not staying late to cover for you." You don't have any idea what your co-worker is talking about, so you _____.

a. ignore your co-worker, punch out, and leave

b. say that your co-worker is not your boss and cannot tell you what to do

c. challenge your co-worker to prove that it was you who messed up

d. ask your co-worker to stop yelling and explain the problem

**6.** A more experienced co-worker tells you that you will never be any good at your job and that you are too stupid to learn anything. What is your best course of action?

a. Say, "Oh yeah? Well, you are too stupid to teach anything!"

b. Calm down. Tell your co-worker that you are able to learn and being called stupid is not helpful.

c. Calm down. Think that this worker just has a bad attitude and ignore the comments.

d. In a calm and respectful tone of voice say, "Did you realize that you are being mean-spirited and close-minded?"

**7.** You're training a new worker, B.K., who seems smart and efficient but who is heavily tattooed. What is the best way to deal with your co-worker's tattoos?

a. Say nothing. The tattoos have nothing to do with the job or B.K.'s ability to do it.

b. Say that the tattoos make B.K. look like a criminal.

c. Tell B.K. to cover up the tattoos when the two of you have to work together.

d. Ask the boss to tell B.K. to cover up the tattoos.

**8.** You're training a few new workers, and one of them, C.C., keeps making mistakes. You must point out these mistakes. What is your best course of action?

a. Talk about the mistakes publicly so that the whole crew can learn from them or offer helpful advice.
b. Talk about the mistakes in private and offer advice for avoiding them in the future.
c. Say, "C.C., you are a really nice person, but you sure make a lot of mistakes."
d. Talk to the team in general about how they must all work to avoid mistakes.

**9.** You notice that J.J., a trainee, has made three mistakes: one major and two minor. You decide to talk to J.J. about these mistakes. What is your best strategy?

a. Talk to J.J. about the major mistake, and let the minor mistakes slide for now.
b. Talk about all the mistakes to help J.J. form good habits.
c. Mention the minor mistakes at the work site and talk about the major mistake later in private.
d. Take a wait-and-see approach. J.J. may improve, and you can avoid having to give criticism.

**10.** P.J., a more experienced co-worker, has been teaching you a difficult new glazing technique. Now you're ready to try it on your own. What should you tell yourself as you get ready to begin the job?

a. There's no way I'll ever be as good at this as P.J.
b. I've got this stuff down cold. I'm probably better than P.J. now.
c. I know how to do this task now. I'll work carefully and ask P.J. for advice if I run into problems.
d. I won't worry too much about making mistakes. After all, I am just learning, and I can ask P.J. to fix them for me.

# Individual Activities

## Activity 1: Responding to Criticism

To complete this activity, read each criticism and decide whether it is constructive or destructive. Then, based on what you learned in this module, respond to each criticism. Be sure to write what you, as a professional, should say, not what you, in the heat of the moment, might want to say.

| Criticism | Source of Criticism | Constructive or Destructive? | Your Response |
|---|---|---|---|
| 1. You're not a team player. | Boss | | |
| 2. After that mistake I made, I know everyone hates me. I'll never be part of this team. | You | | |
| 3. You're really slowing me down. You're too young, and you don't know what you're doing. | Co-worker | | |
| 4. Hold on! It's not safe to use that chisel. See? The end is all flattened out. | Co-worker | | |
| 5. You need to pay closer attention when you set up the saw for angle cuts. I'll show you a good way to do that. | Boss | | |
| 6. I know I can be a better carpenter. I'm going to ask the boss about that training course. | You | | |
| 7. Whoa! Your goggles look like they've been in a fight! Get some new ones so you can see what you're doing. | Co-worker | | |
| 8. Why can't you figure out what you really need? I'm sick of taking stuff back. Get your act together! | Supplier | | |
| 9. This is the third day in a row that you've been late. You're lazy and unreliable. | Boss | | |
| 10. Here. Have some breath mints. Guess you had something with garlic in it for lunch, huh? | Co-worker | | |

## Activity 2: Converting Destructive Criticism into Constructive Criticism

To keep from giving destructive criticism to others, you must think before you speak. To complete this activity, read the following situations and the destructive criticism. Write out how you would turn the destructive criticism into constructive criticism. The first one has been completed as an example.

| Situation | Destructive Criticism | Constructive Criticism |
|---|---|---|
| 1. You're teaching a trainee to mud and sand drywall joints. Your trainee is too heavy-handed with the sander. | Yikes! Can't you watch what you're doing? Just look at this mess. Out of my way—I'll fix it. | Ease up. You don't have to wear yourself out. Let the tool do the work. Like this, see? Give it another try and go easy. |
| 2. One member of your team calls in sick a lot, takes long lunches, and often leaves early. | You're not a good team player. The rest of us are better off without you. | |
| 3. A co-worker cuts a 2 × 4 at the wrong angle. You are out of 2 × 4s, and now you can't finish the job today. | You know, you really messed me up. Thanks a lot for nothing! | |
| 4. You can't seem to get the hang of a power drill. You've stripped some screws, and you've buried a drill bit in a beam. | I'm so stupid. Why can't I get this? I bet everybody thinks I'm an idiot. None of them seem to be having any problems. | |
| 5. Your co-worker keeps misplacing or losing tools and supplies you need to get a job done. | I think you'd lose your head if it weren't attached. You know, someone who loses things is a loser. | |

## Activity 3: Your Action Plan for Improvement

As you learned in this module, one good way to deal with constructive criticism is to state and carry out an action plan for improvement. Most experts agree that writing down a plan is an important first step to success. To complete this activity, recall something your boss has criticized you about recently. Think about the following questions:

1. What am I doing incorrectly?
2. How much time do I think I will need to improve?
3. Do I need any tools, equipment, or training to help me improve?

Once you have thought about these questions, fill in the Self-Improvement Grid. In the first column, write down a constructive criticism your boss has given you recently. In the second column, write out your action plan; how long it will take you to carry it out; and whether you will need tools, equipment, or training to accomplish that goal.

**Self-Improvement Grid**

| Problem Statement | Action Plan |
|---|---|
| My boss has told me that I<br>____________________<br>____________________<br>____________________<br>____________________<br>____________________ | To correct this behavior, I will<br>____________________<br>____________________<br>____________________<br>____________________<br>To succeed, I might need<br>____________________<br>____________________ |

## Activity 4: And Another Thing!

Sometimes when we start criticizing another person, it is hard to know when to stop. This is especially true when we're upset or angry. In this activity, you have permission to "pile it on"—privately, of course. Think of someone and write down all the things you want to criticize about that person. Don't hold back. This list is for your eyes only. When you have completed your list, go back over it, and ask yourself the following questions:

1. Have any of the items on the list been addressed and resolved already?
2. If I had to pick items that won't matter two weeks from now, I would pick numbers ________.
3. What things can I learn to live with? What things must I learn to live with?
4. Do I contribute to any of the situations on my list? If so, how can I change to make things better?
5. If I had to pick only one item to constructively criticize, I would choose number _____.

You will find this exercise to be a useful tool when you must give criticism to another person. This technique will help you to focus on only the most important matters and keep you from piling it on.

**My List**

1. ________________________________________
2. ________________________________________
3. ________________________________________
4. ________________________________________
5. ________________________________________
6. ________________________________________
7. ________________________________________
8. ________________________________________
9. ________________________________________
10. ________________________________________

## Group Activities

### Activity 5: Giving Fair Criticism

Read the following case studies. Then, in groups of three or four, discuss the questions that follow.

**Team Members**

1. ____________________ 2. ____________________

3. ____________________ 4. ____________________

#### *Case Study #1*

T.R., who works on your team, is a neat and reliable plumber and also does the following things:

- Is often about 10 minutes late at the start of the workweek
- Hums softly while working
- Takes a little longer than the other plumbers to dry fit pipes
- Likes to read at lunch and is sometimes late getting back to work
- Has a habit of hoarding supplies
- Has a habit of swearing at the pipes and fittings
- Uses nicknames that some of the team find offensive
- Wears a bandanna with drawings of parrots on it

#### *Discussion Questions*

1. Which of T.R.'s behaviors must the boss handle? Which of T.R.'s behaviors should the team handle?
2. Which of T.R.'s behaviors should the team not bring up?
3. Choose one of the behaviors you think the team should handle and discuss how you would constructively criticize T.R.'s behavior.

### Case Study #2

M.L. is nursing a broken heart and is having money troubles. Normally reliable, M.L. can't seem to concentrate on anything and keeps making mistakes that set everyone back. This absentmindedness is becoming a safety issue. In the last week, the crew has noted the following in M.L.'s behavior:

- Is drinking more coffee than usual
- Has started to wear a T-shirt with "Life Sucks" printed on it
- Keeps forgetting to wear safety gear
- Keeps asking for instructions to be repeated
- Often sits and gazes off into the distance
- Is not paying attention when acting as a safety watch
- Has been giving the wrong hand signals to the crane operator

### Discussion Questions

1. Which of M.L.'s behaviors must the boss handle? Which of M.L.'s behaviors should the team handle?
2. Which of M.L.'s behaviors should the team not bring up?
3. Choose one of the behaviors you think the team should address, and discuss how you would constructively criticize M.L.'s behavior.

## Activity 6: Role-Playing Exercise: Giving and Receiving Criticism

This activity requires four people: one boss and three workers. To complete this activity, assign the following roles:

Boss: ______________________

T.J.: ______________________

Worker 1: ______________________

Worker 2 : ______________________

Note that only the boss and T.J. have speaking parts, and those class members should read through the script before acting it out for the class. Workers 1 and 2 are working nearby and should pretend they are digging holes to plant shrubs.

***Script:***

**Boss:** "T.J., I'd like to talk to you about a couple of things."

**T.J.:** *(Speak loudly.)* "Why? What's wrong? I didn't do anything wrong!"

**Workers 1 and 2:** *(Stop digging and look over at T.J. and the boss.)*

**Boss:** "Nothing is wrong. I just wanted to talk to you about some of the landscaping work you've been doing. I've been getting a few complaints from the homeowner."

**T.J.:** *(Speak loudly.)* "Oh man, this is just what I need. You know, I'm not the only person who's doing the landscaping work. Other people are doing it too!"

**Workers 1 and 2:** *(Cross your arms and look concerned.)*

**Boss:** "I realize that, T.J., but I've noticed you doing some things incorrectly. When you remove a shrub, you have to make sure you dig around the root ball, then wrap it in burlap. You've been breaking the roots and not protecting them. The shrubs have been going into shock, and they're dying because of it."

**T.J.:** "Oh! I thought I was doing it right. I'm sorry. So should I use a smaller shovel or switch over to a trowel?"

**Workers 1 and 2:** *(Lose interest in the conversation and return to digging.)*

**Boss:** "Just pay attention to where the root ball is and dig carefully around it. Take your time and lift each shrub out carefully. When you transplant the shrubs, don't pack the earth down around the roots—give 'em a little breathing room. Mulch and water them well and you should be OK. Oh, and one other thing—"

**T.J.:** "Oh great, here it comes. I knew you were going to get me for something!"

**Boss:** *(Raise your voice.)* "T.J., lose the attitude, all right? You're starting to tick me off. I'm trying to help you, and you're giving me attitude. You think I care if you lose your job? We'd be better off without you."

**Workers 1 and 2:** *(Get interested again and stop digging to watch the boss chew out T.J.)*

**T.J.:** "I'm sorry, Boss. You know this job means a lot to me. It just makes me mad when I make mistakes."

**Boss:** *(Speak in a normal tone of voice.)* "It's OK. Everyone makes mistakes. Just listen and you won't have to worry about making them again. The other thing I was going to tell you is don't rip down that old ivy—it leaves marks all over the walls. Use ammonium sulfate paste to kill it instead."

**T.J.:** "Oh, I didn't know that. I thought it was just easier to pull the plants down. No problem. I'll make sure I use the paste in the future. You said ammonium sulfate, right?"

**Boss:** "Yup. You've got the makings of a good landscaper, T.J. Just stay focused and you'll do fine."

**Workers 1 and 2:** *(Sensing that the excitement is over, return to digging.)*

1. Give examples of constructive criticism given by the boss.
2. Give examples of destructive criticism given by the boss.
3. Give examples that show that T.J. took the criticism gracefully.
4. Give examples of statements that show T.J. was being defensive. What is a better way for T.J. to respond?
5. How do you think productivity was affected when the boss gave constructive criticism? Destructive criticism?

## Activity 7: Your Turn—Take This Module on the Road

As a result of studying this module, you've had lots of practice in dealing with destructive criticism and giving constructive criticism at work. Now take those skills with you and apply them to situations outside the job. Working with a group of three or four classmates, study the following situations. Eliminate the negatives and find a fair, more positive way to talk about each situation.

**Team Members**

| | |
|---|---|
| 1. ______________________ | 2. ______________________ |
| 3. ______________________ | 4. ______________________ |

**Situation 1:** After a great year, your favorite team fails to make it into the playoffs, and you are disappointed. When you talk about the team, you say that they are a bunch of idiots who can't see straight. At a post-season game, you and your friends boo the team.

**Situation 2:** Your spouse decides to decorate the bedroom without asking for your opinion because you have not seemed interested in the project. The finished room looks good, and you can live with it, but it is not exactly your taste. You wish your spouse had talked to you first, and you say, "That's just like you, always thinking about yourself. You are so selfish. It's unbelievable!"

**Situation 3:** You and some friends decide to eat out. The restaurant is busy, and when the dinners arrive, yours is missing. When it is finally delivered, it's the wrong order. In an effort to quickly replace your plate with the right order, your server knocks a glass of water into your lap. You stand up and curse the server and the restaurant. "I can't believe this," you say. "I am paying good money here, and look at the way they are treating me!"

## Activity 8: Passing the Criticism Buck

Most of us would rather avoid giving criticism. If fact, we have to get pretty upset before we criticize anyone at all. That's why we tend to hear more destructive criticism than constructive criticism. Work with three or four of your classmates on this activity. Choose one member of the team to be the scorekeeper and one member to be the timekeeper. Note that when these team members take a turn, they must hand over their duties to another team member. Keep in mind that your goal is to give constructive criticism.

**Team Members**

| | |
|---|---|
| 1.____________________ | 2.____________________ |
| 3.____________________ | 4.____________________ |

### *Materials Required*

- Criticism slips (supplied by your instructor)
- Rating and scorecard (included)
- Watch or stopwatch
- Pencil

Your instructor will give your team several slips of paper. Each slip contains a situation for which constructive criticism must be given. To carry out this activity, follow these steps:

**Step 1** Choose a criticism slip and read it. You must decide whether you want to use this information to give constructive criticism to your classmate or pass the slip on. Note that each of you must give at least one criticism before the activity ends.

**Step 2** Say whether you will pass (and get no points) or go (for two points). If you decide to go, you have 30 seconds to think up what to say. If you can't figure out what to say in 30 seconds, you forfeit your turn and get no points.

**Step 3** If you decide to go, turn to the teammate on your right or left and deliver the criticism.

The scorekeeper will keep track of points using the following chart. Although one of you may get more points than everyone else, everyone who learns how to give constructive criticism wins in this game.

**Rating Grid and Scorecard**

| Rating Grid | |
|---|---|
| **Rating Points** | **Description** |
| 1 | My team member did not do a very good job of giving constructive criticism. (Give suggestions for improvement.) |
| 2 | My team member did a pretty good job, but there is room for improvement. (Give suggestions for improvement.) |
| 3 | My team member did a good job. (Give examples of statements that you thought were helpful and constructive.) |

| Scorecard | | | |
|---|---|---|---|
| **Team Member Name** | **Points for Giving Constructive Criticism (2)** | **Rating Points (from above)** | **Total** |
| 1. | | | |
| 2. | | | |
| 3. | | | |
| 4. | | | |

## Activity 9: You, the Boss, or Forget about It

In Module 9, we gave you a chart to determine who should deal with workplace conflict—you or the boss. We also noted that some conflicts were just not worth getting excited about. Here, you will do a similar activity. Only this time, you will decide who should give the criticism (you or the boss) or not to give the criticism at all (forget about it). Discuss your answers with your team members. Did you all agree?

**Team Members**

1. ______________________ 2. ______________________

3. ______________________ 4. ______________________

| Situation | You | The Boss | Forget about It |
|---|---|---|---|
| 1. Your co-worker likes to sing in Spanish occasionally. | ❑ | ❑ | ❑ |
| 2. Your co-worker uses unsharpened cutting tools. | ❑ | ❑ | ❑ |
| 3. Your co-worker sneaks out 15 minutes early every Friday. | ❑ | ❑ | ❑ |
| 4. Your co-worker misreads blueprints. | ❑ | ❑ | ❑ |
| 5. Your co-worker's hair hangs loosely to the waist. | ❑ | ❑ | ❑ |
| 6. Your co-worker borrows your tools and does not clean them. | ❑ | ❑ | ❑ |
| 7. Your co-worker calls everyone "captain" and wears T-shirts with cartoon characters printed on them. | ❑ | ❑ | ❑ |
| 8. Your co-worker dozes during safety meetings. | ❑ | ❑ | ❑ |
| 9. Your co-worker tends to hang back whenever there is heavy lifting to be done. | ❑ | ❑ | ❑ |
| 10. Your co-worker gives you praise but always adds a sarcastic comment. | ❑ | ❑ | ❑ |

## Activity 10: Challenging Unfair Criticism

As you learned in this module, sometimes the person criticizing you is wrong. However, getting others to recognize that they may have made a mistake in criticizing you takes patience and skill. In this activity, you will work with three or four of your classmates to practice how to handle unfair criticism.

To complete this activity, choose one situation. Each team member must take a different situation. Take a few moments to figure out what you will say and how you will say it. As you prepare your remarks, keep the following in mind:

- Show respect at all times.
- State your case clearly and calmly.
- Don't make threats or become defensive.

As you state your case, your team members must listen carefully. They will rate your response using the rating grid included with this activity.

**Team Members**

1. ______________________ 2. ______________________

3. ______________________ 4. ______________________

| Response Rating Grid | | | |
|---|---|---|---|
| **Observations** | **Yes** | **No** | **Tips for Improvement** |
| 1. My team member was respectful. | ☐ | ☐ | |
| 2. My team member's comments were clear and to the point. | ☐ | ☐ | |
| 3. My team member was calm. | ☐ | ☐ | |
| 4. My team member was defensive. | ☐ | ☐ | |

**Situation 1:** Early this morning you got a call from T.J., who was supposed to pick up supplies on the way to work. T.J.'s truck broke down, so you volunteer to drop T.J. off at work and then go get the supplies yourself. As a result, you are late punching in and your boss reprimands you pretty harshly. You recognize that you should have told the boss about this situation earlier, but you also feel that because the boss does not have all the facts, the criticism is unfair.

**Situation 2:** You arrive at work early one morning to find a co-worker drunk and stumbling around the work site. You take your co-worker to a nearby clinic, and then report back to work. Unfortunately, your co-worker splashed some beer on you and you smell like you've been drinking. The boss takes one whiff, lectures you about your lack of personal responsibility, and says that you are fired.

**Situation 3:** Your boss reprimands you for measuring mistakes made in framing several rooms in a house. Yesterday, you questioned your boss about the measurements when you began the framing. The boss told you that the architect said the measurements were correct. You have to remind the boss about that.

**Situation 4:** Your co-worker suddenly becomes very cold toward you. You ask why and learn that your co-worker believes you are the source of nasty gossip now circulating around the site. Your co-worker criticizes you for being a gossip and spreading rumors. You have not gossiped and, in fact, were not even aware that gossip was circulating.

# Sexual Harassment

## Self-Assessment

### Do you behave appropriately toward the opposite sex?

Throughout this book, you have learned about the importance of treating everyone with respect. Unfortunately, we sometimes forget this rule when dealing with members of the opposite sex. To see how you may be letting some attitudes influence how you treat members of the opposite sex, take this self-assessment quiz. Be sure to answer all the questions honestly.

| Situation | Yes | No |
|---|---|---|
| 1. I tell obscene jokes to workers of the opposite sex. | ❑ | ❑ |
| 2. I keep asking a co-worker for a date after the co-worker has said no. | ❑ | ❑ |
| 3. I keep asking a co-worker to have sex with me after the co-worker has said no. | ❑ | ❑ |
| 4. I make comments about a co-worker's physical characteristics. | ❑ | ❑ |
| 5. I get angry at or threaten a co-worker who refuses to date me or have sex with me. | ❑ | ❑ |
| 6. I discuss my sex life around my co-workers. | ❑ | ❑ |
| 7. I call members of the opposite sex by disrespectful names. | ❑ | ❑ |
| 8. I pass around pornography, display pornographic pictures or cartoons at the work site, or use email to send pornographic materials. | ❑ | ❑ |
| 9. I stand too close to co-workers or touch them inappropriately. | ❑ | ❑ |
| 10. I threaten or harass co-workers because of their sex or sexual preferences. | ❑ | ❑ |
| 11. I suggest that a co-worker's sex makes him or her unfit for a task. | ❑ | ❑ |
| 12. I refuse to work with someone because of his or her sex or sexual preferences. | ❑ | ❑ |

Unlike the other self-assessment quizzes in this module, you cannot rate the appropriateness of your behavior based only on the number of "Yes" or "No" answers. That is because in the eyes of the law, and depending on the circumstances, any one of the above behaviors may be enough to create legal problems for you and your company. The more boxes you checked, the greater the chances that you will have a problem. In this module, you will learn guidelines for treating members of the opposite sex respectfully and professionally.

# Introduction

When you report to work each day, you want to be able to do your job without being harassed because of your sex. Unfortunately, sexual harassment is common. It takes place in every type of job and in every type of industry. Many people believe that sexual harassment involves only men harassing women, and, in fact, most of the lawsuits brought against companies do involve sexual harassment of women by men. However, costly lawsuits also have been brought against companies for both reverse harassment (women harassing men) and same-sex harassment.

Many workers are confused because some of the behaviors considered to be sexual harassment (like telling dirty jokes) do not seem that serious to them. However, sexual harassment is illegal. When a company's workers sexually harass others, the company can be sued. Those lawsuits are costly, ranging from thousands to millions of dollars in damages. Therefore, many companies have strict polices against sexual harassment and will fire workers who engage in it.

In this module, you will learn the legal definition of sexual harassment. You will also learn how to avoid harassing others in the workplace and how to deal with situations in which you are being harassed.

# Before we begin...

Although women currently make up a small percentage of workers in the construction industry, their numbers are expected to increase. Yet in spite of the success women are experiencing in the trades, sexual harassment against them persists. In 1999, the National Institute for Occupational Safety and Health commissioned a survey of approximately 500 female construction workers nationwide. Here are some of the problems a majority of the survey respondents reported:

- Being issued personal protective equipment that was sized for the "average" man
- Having to deal with nonexistent, inadequate, or unsanitary restroom facilities
- Having to work in a hostile work environment
- Being made uncomfortable by unwelcome suggestive looks, comments, joking, or gestures
- Being improperly touched or asked for sex
- Being afraid to report sexual harassment problems for fear of losing their jobs

As more women enter the field and as more workers receive sexual harassment training, such incidents should happen less often. As a professional, you have an important part to play in helping to eliminate sexual harassment where you work.

## What is sexual harassment?

According to the Equal Employment Opportunity Commission, sexual harassment can occur in a variety of circumstances. These circumstances include but are not limited to the following:

- The victim as well as the harasser may be a woman or a man. The victim does not have to be of the opposite sex.
- The harasser can be the victim's supervisor, an agent of the employer, a supervisor in another area, a co-worker, or a non-employee.
- The victim does not have to be the person harassed but could be anyone affected by the offensive conduct.
- Unlawful sexual harassment may occur without economic injury to or discharge of the victim.
- The harasser's conduct must be unwelcome.

Refer to the box titled "Definition of Sexual Harassment." The following sections highlight and explain the main points of this definition.

Let's take this definition apart to give you a better sense of what it means.

**1. Unwelcome sexual advances, requests for sexual favors.** *Sexual advance* means more than just asking for sex. It may also mean pestering a co-worker for a date when that co-worker has said no. Note that the definition uses the term *unwelcome.* If your co-worker is interested in dating you, then your request is not unwelcome.

**2. Other verbal and/or physical conduct of a sexual nature.** Sexual harassment can be either verbal or physical. Following are some examples:

- Standing too close to co-workers in a way that makes them uncomfortable
- Touching a co-worker inappropriately or touching a co-worker who does not want to be touched
- Making vulgar comments, gestures, or sounds
- Calling co-workers by sexually offensive names

### *Definition of Sexual Harassment*

The Equal Employment Opportunity Act of 1972 defines sexual harassment as (1) unwelcome sexual advances, requests for sexual favors, and (2) other verbal or physical conduct of a sexual nature. Submission to such conduct is made either explicitly or implicitly (3) a term or condition of an individual's employment; submission to or rejection of such conduct by an employee is used as the basis for employment decisions affecting such individual; or such conduct has the purpose or effect of unreasonably interfering with an individual's work performance or (4) of creating an intimidating, hostile, or offensive working environment.

**3. Made a term or condition of employment.** Demanding sex from someone in exchange for keeping a job or getting a promotion is sexual harassment. But the definition does not stop there. If you take negative actions against a worker or threaten that worker for refusing your advances, you are also engaging in sexual harassment.

**4. An intimidating, hostile, or offensive working environment.** Sexual harassment is not limited to requests for sexual favors. It can also be any gender-based offensive behavior that makes the workplace threatening or offensive. Some behaviors that create an intimidating working environment include the following:

- Telling obscene jokes
- Talking about sex
- Displaying pornographic calendars, cartoons, or pictures
- Using email to send pornographic pictures, stories, or jokes
- Using profanity
- Referring to co-workers by demeaning terms
- Staring at a co-worker's body or making inappropriate comments about physical attributes
- Stating or implying that workers are less competent because of their sex
- Making obscene gestures

In most cases, sexual harassment involves more than one isolated incident. Generally, it is a pattern of behavior repeated over a period of time. However, some cases have resulted in legal action after only one incident.

## How to avoid sexually harassing others

Many times, people who are accused of sexual harassment honestly don't understand the accusation. They may feel that they didn't mean any harm, and they're not sure what they did wrong. So being told that they've sexually harassed someone comes as a surprise.

The best way to avoid being charged with sexual harassment is to think carefully about what you do and say around members of the opposite sex. You may have to change your behavior or your conversational style. Following are some ideas to help you do that:

**1. Be a professional.** Remember the qualities of a professional worker. Professionals behave with dignity and treat others with respect. Unfortunately, construction workers are sometimes portrayed as loud, rude people who treat others, especially women, badly. Don't let your behavior add to this unfair stereotype. Be professional at all times, whether you are dealing with men or women.

**2. Don't comment on anyone's physical appearance.** You never know how another person is going to receive your comments. When you compliment a co-worker's hair, figure, or clothing, that person may feel flattered. Or that person may be annoyed and wonder what you are up to. When you make comments about a co-worker's physical appearance—good or bad—you are headed for trouble.

**3. Don't use terms of endearment.** You may not mean any harm when you call another co-worker "honey" or "sweetie," but you don't know how these terms will be received. Here are just a few of the possible reactions:

- This person has no respect for me. I have a name.
- This person is coming on to me and I don't like it.
- I feel threatened by this person's comments.
- I am not this person's child.

**4. Think before you speak.** Are the people you work with comfortable hearing dirty jokes? Do you think that everyone in the group really wants to hear about your sexual adventures? When in doubt, the best course of action is to keep quiet.

**5. No means no.** Don't assume that a co-worker you are trying to date is playing hard to get. If someone won't date you or refuses your advances, then you must stop or face being charged with sexual harassment.

**6. Remember the empathy rule.** How would you feel if you worked in a hostile environment where everyone prejudged you, treated you disrespectfully, or harassed you because of your sex?

**7. Read your company's sexual harassment policy.** Most companies have a policy regarding sexual harassment. Read your company's policy and make sure you understand it.

## What to do if you've been sexually harassed

You do not have to suffer in silence if you feel that you are a victim of sexual harassment. You have two options:

- Confront the person who is sexually harassing you. You can say something like, "I don't like sexually oriented jokes" or "Take your hands off me right now! I won't put up with you touching me." Some experts also recommend writing a letter to the harasser as a way of showing how serious you are.
- You can complain to your supervisor or the harasser's supervisor. This is usually the best plan if the first course of action doesn't work. When you make your complaint, provide the specifics of time, place, and what was said or done. If your boss is harassing you, take your complaint to your boss's supervisor.

## On-the-Job Quiz

Here's a quick quiz that asks you to apply what you've learned in this module.

1. You ask a co-worker for a date, and your co-worker smiles and agrees to go out with you. This is sexual harassment.
   a. True
   b. False
2. You ask a co-worker for a date, and the co-worker says no. You don't ask again. This is sexual harassment.
   a. True
   b. False
3. A co-worker finds you very attractive and wants to have sex with you. You are attracted to your co-worker and agree. How would you describe this situation?
   a. There was no sexual harassment.
   b. Your co-worker sexually harassed you by asking you for sex.
   c. Your co-worker is trying to trap you into a reverse harassment charge.
   d. You and your co-worker sexually harassed each other.
4. A co-worker regularly stands too close to you, leans over you, or touches you in a way that makes you feel uncomfortable. Although you have asked the co-worker to stop, the behavior continues. This is sexual harassment.
   a. True
   b. False
5. You keep asking a co-worker to go out after repeated refusals. Then you start treating that person badly for rejecting you. You freeze the co-worker out of team meetings and events and insist that the co-worker be given only the hardest or dirtiest tasks. This is sexual harassment.
   a. True
   b. False
6. Your work crew includes four people: three men and one woman. You all get along well and eat lunch together. One day one of the men brings in a pornographic poster and shows it only to the men. Is this a good idea?
   a. Yes. The woman will understand that this is a "guy thing" and won't be offended.
   b. No. The man should show the poster to the woman as well so she won't feel left out.
   c. No. It is not a good idea to bring offensive pictures or drawings to work.
   d. Yes. As long as the woman does not see the poster, there's no harm done.

7. You're working on a skyscraper in a downtown area. At lunchtime, you and your co-workers (all men) whistle at and make loud remarks about the women who walk by. Is your behavior appropriate?
   a. Yes. Women expect this behavior from construction workers and are OK with it.
   b. Yes. None of these women works with you, so you can't be charged with sexual harassment.
   c. No. Your behavior is inappropriate and unprofessional, and it reflects poorly on you and your co-workers.
   d. Yes and no. The whistling is OK. However, the loud remarks are not OK.

8. You have to train two new hires. Both are women. One is the daughter of a close friend. You've never met the other woman. The first day on the job, you call both women "honey." Is your behavior appropriate?
   a. Yes. It was appropriate because you did not mean any harm.
   b. Yes. Because one of the women is the daughter of a friend, the other woman won't mind being called "honey" as well.
   c. Yes and no. It's OK to call your friend's daughter "honey," but not the other woman.
   d. No. At work, it is best to avoid using terms of endearment.

9. You are a male electrician and see three women electricians going over some plans. What would be appropriate to say to them as a greeting?
   a. "Hello, gals!"
   b. "Hey! How's it going?"
   c. "Ah, look at those beautiful electricians!"
   d. "Looking good, ladies!"

10. You are feeling harassed by another co-worker's vulgar language and casual touching. To deal with this situation, you might do all of the following, *except* _____.
   a. tell your co-worker to stop the behavior immediately or you will complain to the boss
   b. report your co-worker to the boss
   c. tell your co-worker to stop, then follow up with a note to show that you are serious
   d. ignore the behavior and hope that it will end soon

# Individual Activities

## Activity 1: Expanding Your Understanding of Sexual Harassment

The following quiz will help you understand sexual harassment further. Don't look for the answers in the module, because they're not here. Guess at the answers as best you can. Some of them may surprise you.

1. According to various studies and surveys, anywhere between _____ of women report that they have been sexually harassed on the job.
   a. 85 and 90 percent
   b. 40 and 70 percent
   c. 10 and 20 percent
2. According to various studies and surveys, anywhere between _____ of men report that they have been sexually harassed on the job.
   a. 50 and 55 percent
   b. 30 and 40 percent
   c. 10 and 20 percent
3. In the period between 1995 and 2000, the rate of sexual harassment complaints filed with the Equal Employment Opportunity Commission (EEOC) _____.
   a. increased
   b. decreased
   c. stayed about the same
4. According to a study conducted by the Pentagon in 1995, _____ of women in the military reported being sexually harassed.
   a. 28 percent
   b. 58 percent
   c. 78 percent
5. Which of the following situations is most common?
   a. A woman sexually harasses a co-worker.
   b. A male supervisor sexually harasses a female employee.
   c. A male employee sexually harasses a female supervisor.
6. Women are most likely to be sexually harassed when they work in _____.
   a. jobs that have traditionally been held by women
   b. schools and universities
   c. jobs that have traditionally been held by men
7. During the period between 1995 and 2000, approximately _____ sexual harassment suits per year were filed with the EEOC.
   a. 35,000
   b. 25,000
   c. 15,000

8. There is a fundamental difference between the sexes with regard to sexual advances. Seventy-five percent of men say that they're flattered when a woman makes sexual advances toward them, but _____ percent of women say sexual advances offend them.
   a. 75
   b. 50
   c. 25

9. According to the EEOC, in 2002 men filed _____ of all sexual harassment claims.
   a. 25 percent
   b. 15 percent
   c. 10 percent

10. In _____, Congress passed Title VII of the Civil Rights Act, which prohibits discrimination at work on the basis of race, color, religion, national origin, and sex.
   a. 1954
   b. 1964
   c. 1984

## Activity 2: Understanding When Sexual Harassment Occurs

Several situations are listed below. Your task is to determine whether or not sexual harassment occurred in each case.

| Is This Sexual Harassment? | Yes | No |
|---|---|---|
| 1. Linda reports to John, her supervisor. For the past several days, Linda has punched in late. John calls her off to the side and tells her sternly that she must report for work on time or face the consequences. | | |
| Did John sexually harass Linda? | ☐ | ☐ |
| 2. At a company-hosted party, Mike, who has had too much to drink, keeps following Lucy around. Mike likes Lucy and has tried to date her, but she always says no and tries to avoid him. Mike embraces Lucy and tells her to stop playing hard to get. Lucy pushes Mike away and leaves the party. | | |
| Did Mike sexually harass Lucy? | ☐ | ☐ |
| 3. Co-workers Fran and Steve are attracted to each other. They start to date and, when no one is around, Steve calls Fran "sweetheart." | | |
| Did Steve sexually harass Fran? | ☐ | ☐ |
| 4. Co-workers Brenda and Richard dated for a while and then broke up. Richard wants to get back together, but Brenda does not. Richard starts leaving anonymous threatening notes, hides Brenda's tools, has intentionally spilled his soda on Brenda twice, and has been heard muttering abusive words when she walks by. | | |
| Did Richard sexually harass Brenda? | ☐ | ☐ |

*(continued)*

5. Ellen is interested in Ken. She always smiles at him and asks how he is doing. Today Ken told Ellen how nice she looked and asked her if she'd like to have lunch with him. Ellen agrees to have lunch with Ken and says she is glad he asked.

   Did Ken sexually harass Ellen? ❑ ❑

6. Several male workers post pictures of naked women in the break room. So some of the women put up pictures of naked men.

   Was anyone sexually harassed? ❑ ❑

7. At your company, workers use email to communicate information about tasks and schedules. One worker is using the system to send pornographic jokes, photos, and drawings.

   Was anyone sexually harassed? ❑ ❑

8. Your co-workers, who are the same sex as you, are making your workday miserable. They taunt you, play a lot of mean-spirited practical jokes, and push or touch you in ways you find threatening.

   Are you being sexually harassed? ❑ ❑

9. One of your company's suppliers is pestering you for a date. Whenever the supplier is on site you feel uncomfortable because you know you will be subjected to unwanted advances.

   Are you being sexually harassed? ❑ ❑

10. Your co-worker is being sexually harassed by another co-worker. You are not directly involved, but the daily confrontations between these two are affecting your ability to do your job. In addition, you find the harasser's conduct offensive even though it is not directed toward you.

    Are you being sexually harassed? ❑ ❑

## Group Activities

### Activity 3: Empathizing with Victims of Sexual Harassment

Throughout this book we've emphasized the importance of empathy, of being able to put yourself into someone else's place and understand that person's feelings.

Usually, people don't talk about sexual harassment and when they do, they tend to treat the issue lightly. Your goal in this activity is to understand how people feel when they are the victims of sexual harassment. Ask someone you know if he or she would be willing to answer the questions in this sexual harassment questionnaire. Then, working in groups of three or four, compare what you learned.

**Team Members**

| | |
|---|---|
| 1.____________________ | 2.____________________ |
| 3.____________________ | 4.____________________ |

### *Discussion Questions*

1. Is this the first time we ever thought about how people feel when they are sexually harassed?
2. What do all of the reports have in common? How do they differ?
3. What can we learn from these reports?
4. Are there any behaviors that we should change?

### Sexual Harassment Questionnaire

1. Have you ever been the victim of sexual harassment? If so, where did the sexual harassment occur?
2. What was said or done to make you feel harassed?
3. How did the harassment make you feel?
4. Did you respond to the harasser? If so, what did you do or say?
5. Did you file a complaint against the harasser? How did having to make a complaint against the harasser make you feel?
6. If you filed a complaint, what happened?
7. Do you think that sexual harassment is common?
8. Which gender would you say is harassed most often?
9. Have many of your friends been harassed?
10. What advice would you give to your co-workers to help them avoid becoming harassers?

## Activity 4: Role-Playing Exercise—The Consequences of Sexual Harassment

To complete this activity, two class members should be asked to volunteer to play the following roles:

Ted: ______________________________

Shelly: ____________________________

The rest of the class should observe the behavior and be ready to address the discussion questions. Ted and Shelly are co-workers. They are both electricians who work as part of a team with three other workers. Ted has been after Shelly for a date, and she keeps turning him down. Lately Ted has become more aggressive. Yesterday, he hid some of Shelly's tools. Then he pretended to forget a message the boss asked him to give Shelly. As a result, the team is behind on several tasks. Today, Ted approaches Shelly again.

### *Script*

**Ted:** "Hey, Shelly, how's it going?"

**Shelly:** "Fine, Ted." *(Begin to walk away.)*

**Ted:** *(Step in front of Shelly.)* "Wait! What's the rush, babe?"

**Shelly:** *(Step to one side.)* "I'm busy. When you forgot to give me the boss's message you put us all behind. Are you trying to make me look bad or something?"

**Ted:** *(Step back in front of Shelly.)* "Oh wow. No! I am so sorry about that. Can't I make it up to you by telling you how fine you look today? I really am sorry!"

**Shelly:** *(Smile a little.)* "Uh. Well. OK. I guess anyone can make a mistake."

**Ted:** "So, how about going out with me tonight, babe?"

**Shelly:** *(Cross your arms and look exasperated.)* "Ted, I already told you I have a boyfriend!"

**Ted:** "So what? You're not married to the guy!"

**Shelly:** "Look, I said no! Why can't you just stop asking?"

**Ted:** "Come on, Shelly. I know you want to go out with me. Stop acting like you don't."

**Shelly:** "Look Ted. I keep telling you no and I mean it. I am not acting. Now leave me alone!" *(Walk away.)*

**Ted:** *(Frown and call after Shelly.)* "Yeah, yeah. Women always say no when they really mean yes! I know you want me!"

## Discussion Questions

1. Did sexual harassment occur in this situation?
2. What advice would you give to Ted?
3. Did Shelly handle herself properly? What advice would you give Shelly?
4. Did you think this script was realistic? Do men sometimes keep asking for a date even when a woman says no? Why do you think this happens?
5. What do you think about the tricks Ted is playing on Shelly? How do you think they affect Shelly's safety and productivity? How do you think they might affect the team's safety and productivity?

## Activity 5: Your Turn— Talk about Sexual Harassment at Work

Think about examples of sexual harassment you may have observed at work. Then, working with three or four of your classmates, talk about any sexual harassment behavior you have observed and answer the discussion questions.

**Team Members**

| | |
|---|---|
| 1.______________________________ | 2.______________________________ |
| 3.______________________________ | 4.______________________________ |

### *Discussion Questions*

1. Would I describe someone at my workplace (male or female) as a harasser? What things does this person do that make me think that?
2. What is my personal opinion of the harasser's behavior? Do I approve or disapprove?
3. How would I feel if the harasser victimized someone I know and care about? How would I feel if the harasser victimized me?
4. Do I know anyone who has been sexually harassed? How did that person handle the harassment?

## Activity 6: Your Turn— Change Behaviors at Work

Think about the harassing behavior you and your teammates discussed in Activity 5. You may think that harassers just come with the territory and that everybody has to put up with them. But that is not true. Harassers make the workday more difficult for everyone, not just the people they harass. In this activity, work with three or four of your classmates to come up with an action plan to deal with harassing behavior. Use the conflict resolution skills you learned in Module 9. A conflict resolution grid is provided to help you complete this activity.

**Team Members**

1. ____________________ 2. ____________________

3. ____________________ 4. ____________________

| Five-Step Conflict Resolution Process | |
|---|---|
| **Step 1** Bring the conflict into the open. | |
| **Step 2** Discuss and analyze the reasons for the conflict. | |
| **Step 3** Develop possible solutions. Remember that all workers involved should collaborate and compromise. | |
| **Step 4** Choose and carry out a solution. | |
| **Step 5** Evaluate the solution. | |

## Activity 7: The Law Says...

Several expensive lawsuits, some in the millions of dollars, have been brought against companies where sexual harassment has taken place. In many cases, people have been fired because they have sexually harassed others. However, many people still don't think sexual harassment is a problem. In this activity, you and three or four of your classmates will read and discuss some statements that people commonly make about sexual harassment. Decide whether each statement is accurate or not. Refer to the definition of sexual harassment included at the beginning of this module as you work through this activity.

**Team Members**

1. ______________________ 2. ______________________

3. ______________________ 4. ______________________

1. If you don't have authority over another person, you can't be accused of sexual harassment.
2. A man cannot accuse another man of sexual harassment, and a woman cannot accuse another woman of sexual harassment.
3. You can make a sexual harassment complaint if other workers sexually harass one of your co-workers and you are affected by the behavior.
4. If you make a sexual harassment complaint and your boss gives you a raise, you have no grounds for a lawsuit.
5. You can harass people who wear revealing clothes because they are just asking for it.

# Drug and Alcohol Abuse on the Job

## Awareness Questionnaire

### How much do you know about the effects of alcohol abuse?

Alcohol consumption is fairly common. It is so common, in fact, that many people don't stop to think about the negative effects of alcohol abuse. The following questionnaire is designed to make you more aware of the problems caused by alcohol abuse. You may be surprised at some of the answers.

1. People most likely to drive under the influence of alcohol are between the ages of _____.
   a. 16 and 20
   b. 21 and 34
   c. 35 and 55
2. On average, _____ will be involved in an alcohol-related crash at some point in their lives.
   a. 1 out of every 25 people
   b. 2 out of every 15 people
   c. 3 out of every 10 people
3. On average, drivers impaired by alcohol cause _____ of driving fatalities.
   a. 40 percent
   b. 29 percent
   c. 19 percent
4. Alcohol-related crashes are estimated to cost the U.S. economy _____ each year.
   a. $100 million
   b. $500 million
   c. $40 billion
5. The use of _____ is the number one substance abuse problem among young people.
   a. methamphetamines
   b. crack cocaine
   c. alcohol

## How much do you know about the effects of drug abuse?

Abuse of drugs—both illegal and legal—is also a serious problem. As with alcohol, abuse of drugs is tied to fatalities and long-term health problems. We all bear the cost of those problems, both financially and emotionally. To become more aware of these problems, take this quick quiz:

1. Cocaine is a highly addictive stimulant that directly affects your brain.
   a. True
   b. False
2. You can convince addicts to stop using drugs by talking to them about their addiction and showing them the harmful effects.
   a. True
   b. False
3. Approximately _____ of property crimes and muggings are drug related.
   a. 90 percent
   b. 50 percent
   c. 30 percent
4. On average, a person who is addicted to drugs needs about _____ each day to support the habit.
   a. $400
   b. $200
   c. $100
5. Substance abuse can begin in children as early as elementary school.
   a. True
   b. False

Review the correct answers with your instructor. Were you surprised at some of the answers? Did you learn something new about drugs and alcohol? Later in this module, you will see a list of sources you can contact for more information about alcohol and drugs.

## Introduction

Substance abusers (people who take illegal drugs or who abuse alcohol or legal drugs) cause serious problems for their families, their employers, and themselves. Many companies have adopted a zero-tolerance policy regarding drug and alcohol abuse. In this module you will learn about the effects of substance abuse. You will also learn how to recognize and deal with it.

## The effects of substance abuse

Drinking socially and in moderation is a common and accepted part of life. Moderate alcohol consumption generally does not affect a person's life negatively. However, it is not legal or socially acceptable to drink to excess, take illegal drugs, or abuse legal drugs. These behaviors can result in arrest and incarceration, addiction, long-term health problems, family and work-related problems, or death.

People who belong to such support groups as Alcoholics Anonymous or Narcotics Anonymous can testify to the horrifying effects of substance abuse and addiction. As you begin or continue your career in construction, remember the following:

1. **Substance abuse can prevent you from getting the job you want.** Safety is extremely important in construction work. Therefore, many employers screen applicants for drugs and alcohol. If your tests show that you take illegal drugs or abuse alcohol, you won't get the job.

2. **Substance abuse can get you fired on the spot.** Because most construction companies have a zero-tolerance policy for substance abuse, if you are drunk or high on the job, you will be fired immediately. Most companies don't want their workers drinking any amount of alcohol during the workday—even one beer at lunch. In addition, many companies do random drug testing among their employees at unexpected times. If you test positive, you will be fired.

3. **Substance abuse endangers your safety and that of your co-workers.** Construction work is often dangerous, involving the use of high-speed tools and equipment, potentially harmful solvents, and work in deep trenches or far above the ground. You must be alert at all times. Substance abuse has a negative effect on both your mental skills and your motor skills (your ability to use tools and equipment). Would you want to be building an offshore drilling platform with a co-worker who was drunk? How safe would you feel if a drug-addicted co-worker was operating a crane nearby?

4. **Substance abuse damages your well-being and quality of life.** Substance abusers do not perform at their best. They often have trouble paying their bills, dealing with emotional problems, and managing their lives. Drugs and alcohol keep them from thinking straight, and they tend to lie, make excuses for their behavior, or blame others for their problems.

**5. Substance abuse jeopardizes your relationships.** Substance abuse negatively affects your ability to get along with your friends, family, and co-workers. Consider how substance abuse affects your personal relationships:

- Your family cannot depend on you to work a steady job or to provide emotional and financial support.
- Your friends cannot depend on you to keep promises or pay back loans.
- Your co-workers cannot depend on you to do your share of the work, and they cannot trust you to work safely.

### An Important Note—Prescription Drugs

When people talk about substance abusers, they usually mean alcoholics or people who take illegal drugs. However, many people also abuse prescription drugs, sometimes on purpose and sometimes without realizing it. Because prescription drugs are legal and prescribed by a doctor, many people don't think of them as harmful, but people can become addicted to certain types of prescription drugs. Abuse of prescription drugs can produce the same harmful results as illegal drugs or alcohol. When using prescription drugs, keep the following things in mind:

**1. Take prescription drugs only as directed.** Your doctor and pharmacist will give you information about the drug and how and when it should be used. They will also tell you about side effects and tell you what activities you must avoid while taking the drug.

**2. Understand the side effects.** Some drugs can make you drowsy or less able to concentrate. You must tell your supervisor if you are taking a prescription drug that could affect your motor or mental skills. You must not drive or operate power tools or heavy equipment when taking certain types of prescription drugs.

**3. Don't extend or share your prescription.** When your prescription period is up, you must return to your doctor for an examination. Don't lie to your doctor to get more medication. Don't talk friends into getting your prescriptions filled for you. Never share your prescription medication with anyone else. When taken without a doctor's authorization and oversight, prescription drugs can be deadly.

**4. Know when to ask for help.** If you find that you cannot get through the day without a prescription drug, see your doctor immediately. People can become addicted to prescription drugs, especially painkillers, sometimes without realizing what is happening. Suddenly stopping a prescription drug could also be harmful. Your doctor can help you reduce your dependence on the drug safely.

## Recognizing and coping with substance abuse

At some point in your career, you may find yourself working with someone who may have a substance abuse problem. Sometimes, the signs are clear. For example, a co-worker may show up smelling of alcohol, stagger, or have slurred speech. At other times, the signs are not as noticeable.

Usually, your supervisor will notice the problem before you do. However, as a professional member of the work team, you must play your part in making sure that an impaired worker does not endanger others. In other modules, you learned that being a tattletale is not a good idea. However, here is one exception to the rule: You must report the behavior of an impaired worker to your boss immediately. Your boss can then step in to ensure that nobody gets hurt.

## The Signs of Substance Abuse

The following chart includes many of the signs of substance abuse. It is not your responsibility to figure out why a co-worker is having a problem or even what, exactly, the problem is. You simply need to be aware of behaviors that indicate a co-worker may have a problem. Note, also, that not everyone reacts the same way. In general, the more often you see the signs shown on the chart, the more likely it is that your co-worker needs help.

**The Warning Signs of Substance Abuse**

| Stage | Symptoms | Effect on Job Performance |
|---|---|---|
| Early | • Arrives late to work often<br>• Leaves work early often<br>• Seems disconnected from what's going on | • Misses deadlines often<br>• Makes occasional mistakes<br>• Leaves co-workers to pick up slack |
| Middle | • Takes days off for unexplained reasons<br>• Loses interest in grooming; may have sudden weight loss<br>• Is moody or unpredictable<br>• Reacts oddly or violently to common work situations<br>• Borrows money frequently<br>• Disappears from the job site<br>• Is absent more than present<br>• Doesn't pay attention; lacks ability to concentrate | • Lies to cover up absences and mistakes<br>• Sustains many minor injuries<br>• Shows anger or hostility toward co-workers and supervisors |
| Late | • Is absent for prolonged periods<br>• Drinks or takes drugs at work<br>• Has serious financial or family problems | • May injure co-workers<br>• Has escalating problems with co-workers and supervisors<br>• Picks fights and has arguments at work |

Source: Adapted from *Essentials of Human Resource Management.* Gary Dessler. Upper Saddle River, NJ: Prentice Hall, 1999, p. 265.

# Do you have a substance abuse problem?

If you think you might have a substance abuse problem, you should have one goal in mind:

**GET PROFESSIONAL HELP BEFORE IT IS TOO LATE.**

It is easy to find help. You can contact any of the organizations listed in Activity 2, many of which may have an office in your town. Local offices for many of these organizations are listed in your telephone book. In addition, a hospital or clinic in your town may offer programs that can help you.

To determine whether you might have a substance abuse problem, complete the following self-assessment questionnaire. Answer all the questions honestly. If you answer yes to three or more questions, you may have a substance abuse problem. If you do have a problem, you should talk to a counselor immediately. You can find free or inexpensive help from school-based, government-sponsored, or workplace-sponsored resources. Your local hospital can also refer you to excellent sources for help.

**Substance Abuse Questionnaire**

| Think about your life over the past year and then answer these questions. | Yes | No |
|---|---|---|
| 1. I have tried to stop drinking or taking drugs and could not stop for long. | ❑ | ❑ |
| 2. I get upset with people telling me that they are concerned about my drinking or taking drugs. | ❑ | ❑ |
| 3. I feel guilty about my drinking or taking drugs. | ❑ | ❑ |
| 4. I feel that I need a drink or a drug in the morning to get myself going. | ❑ | ❑ |
| 5. I drink or take drugs when I am alone. | ❑ | ❑ |
| 6. I drink or take drugs every day. | ❑ | ❑ |
| 7. I often say, "I need a drink" or "I need that drug." | ❑ | ❑ |
| 8. I lie about or conceal my substance abuse problem. | ❑ | ❑ |
| 9. I drink alcohol or take drugs to escape my worries and problems. | ❑ | ❑ |
| 10. I have abused prescription drugs. | ❑ | ❑ |
| 11. I have had to increase the amount of alcohol I drink or drugs I take to get high. | ❑ | ❑ |
| 12. I have forgotten what I did while drinking or using drugs. | ❑ | ❑ |
| 13. I have been surprised by how much I have been drinking or using drugs. | ❑ | ❑ |
| 14. I spend a lot of time or money getting alcohol or drugs. | ❑ | ❑ |
| 15. I prefer drinking or taking drugs to spending time with my family and friends. | ❑ | ❑ |
| 16. I got into a fight while drunk or on drugs. | ❑ | ❑ |
| 17. I missed work or made a mistake because I was drunk or on drugs. | ❑ | ❑ |
| 18. I have given up things I used to enjoy doing so I could drink or take drugs. | ❑ | ❑ |
| 19. I have called in sick or gone in late because I was hung over. | ❑ | ❑ |
| 20. I have driven a car or operated power tools or machinery while drunk or on drugs. | ❑ | ❑ |

*(continued)*

| | Yes | No |
|---|---|---|
| 21. I have been arrested as a result of being drunk or being high on drugs. | ❑ | ❑ |
| 22. I feel that I must drink or take drugs to have a good time. | ❑ | ❑ |
| 23. I keep drinking or using drugs even though I know about the problems this behavior can cause me. | ❑ | ❑ |
| 24. I have rejected planned social events in favor of drinking or taking drugs. | ❑ | ❑ |

Sources: Adapted from: *Keys to Success,* Second Edition. Carol Carter, Joyce Bishop, and Sarah Lyman Kravits. Upper Saddle River, N.J.: Prentice Hall, 1998, p. 340, and *Diagnostic and Statistical Manual of Mental Disorders,* Fourth Edition. "Criteria for Substance Dependence" and "Criteria for Substance Abuse," Washington, D.C.: American Psychiatric Association.

## On-the-Job Quiz

Here's a quick quiz that asks you to apply what you've learned in this module.

**1.** You are nervous about an interview for a construction job, so you have a few beers before the interview to calm down. What do you think is most likely to happen?
   a. The person interviewing you will understand that nerves made you drink and will probably hire you.
   b. You will not be hired.
   c. You will be told to sober up and come back to try again.
   d. No one will notice because you really did not have that much to drink.

**2.** At a job interview, the interviewer asks whether you take drugs. You smoke marijuana occasionally, but figure that doesn't count, so you say, "No." You then take a drug test. What do you think is most likely to happen?
   a. The test won't detect the marijuana because you don't smoke it all the time.
   b. The test will detect the marijuana, but the amount will be so small that it won't matter.
   c. The test will detect the marijuana, the interviewer will note that you lied, and you will not be hired.
   d. The interviewer will lecture you about lying, make you promise to give up marijuana, and give you a chance to prove yourself.

**3.** You drink all night on Sunday, have a few more drinks on Monday morning, and show up at work drunk. Your boss will probably _____.
   a. reprimand you
   b. fire you
   c. warn you
   d. tell you to come back when you are sober

4. You and a co-worker always get lunch off the job site at a bar, where you eat big sandwiches and fries and have a couple of beers each. Is drinking a couple of beers at lunchtime acceptable?
   a. Yes. A couple of beers won't affect job performance.
   b. Yes. The food absorbs the alcohol, and you won't be affected by it.
   c. No. You should not drink any amount of alcohol during the workday.
   d. No. Instead of beer, you should have had wine because you believe it has less alcohol than beer.

5. You and a co-worker are up on a scaffold to nail siding using pneumatic power nailers. You notice that your co-worker smells of beer. Once up on the scaffold, your co-worker looks around, sways a little, removes a bottle of beer from a hiding place, and takes a long swig. Should you be concerned?
   a. No. Your co-worker was able to climb the scaffold, so he or she should be able to operate the power nailer safely.
   b. Yes. Your co-worker might easily lose control over the power nailer or fall off the scaffold.
   c. No. Your co-worker is probably aware of how much alcohol he or she can safely handle.
   d. Yes. If anything happens, you will get the blame.

6. Following a period of emotional problems, you were given a prescription for Valium to help you stay calm. You are better now and the prescription has ended, but you like the way Valium makes you feel. A friend at the drugstore gets you refills. You share the Valium with this friend and others. Is your behavior acceptable?
   a. Yes. You had a prescription and still need the drug, even if your doctor does not agree.
   b. Yes. Valium is just a mild relaxer and is not an illegal drug like cocaine or heroin.
   c. Yes and no. You can keep using the Valium, but you shouldn't share it with your friends.
   d. No. You are breaking the law, abusing a prescription drug, and possibly endangering your life and the lives of your friends.

7. You are doing a two-person job that involves operating some heavy equipment. You strongly suspect your co-worker is drunk. What is your best course of action?
   a. Continue working and hope for the best.
   b. Do all of the harder or more dangerous tasks yourself and keep a watchful eye on your co-worker.
   c. Tell your boss that you suspect your co-worker is drunk and cannot do the job safely.
   d. Insist that your co-worker drink several cups of strong coffee to sober up.

**8.** You've been working with T.J. for six years. On Mondays, you usually talk about what you did over the weekend. Today, T.J. tells you about a reunion with old friends at which everyone got drunk. This is the first time T.J. has ever described drinking or getting drunk on the weekend. What is your most reasonable assumption?
   a. T.J. probably doesn't have an alcohol problem.
   b. T.J. might have gotten drunk as a result of depression.
   c. T.J. might be developing a serious alcohol problem, and you should be watchful.
   d. T.J. is probably an alcoholic, and you should suggest counseling or tell the boss.

**9.** K.C., one of your co-workers, used to show up well groomed and ready to work. Lately, however, K.C. often smells bad, wears wrinkled or dirty clothes, and has trouble concentrating on tasks and using tools properly. What is your best course of action?
   a. You figure that there is probably a lot on K.C.'s mind, and time will take care of things.
   b. You assume that whatever is bothering K.C. is none of your business, and you are not responsible for K.C.'s behavior.
   c. You assume that your boss has noticed the same things you have, but you should tell the boss about your concerns anyway.
   d. You tell K.C. to get cleaned up and straightened out.

**10.** You have started to drink more and more often. It relaxes you and puts you in a good mood. Lately, you don't seem to have enough money to pay your bills. What is your best course of action?
   a. Ask the boss for an advance on next week's pay.
   b. Borrow what you need from your co-workers.
   c. Get help for your drinking problem before it's too late.
   d. Ask everyone you owe money to for more time to pay.

# Individual Activities

## Activity 1: Facts about Alcohol

Here's an exercise to help you learn a little more about alcohol and its effects. Take your best guess at each question.

1. A 12-ounce bottle of beer or wine cooler contains as much alcohol as ____.
   a. 12 ounces of wine or 12 ounces of hard liquor
   b. one 5-ounce glass of wine or 1.5 ounces of 80-proof distilled spirits
   c. two 5-ounce glasses of wine or 5 ounces of 80-proof distilled spirits
2. In almost every state in the United States, you are legally drunk as soon as your blood alcohol level (the percentage of alcohol in your bloodstream) equals ____.
   a. 0.08 percent
   b. 0.25 percent
   c. 1.50 percent
3. Someone in America dies every ____ as a result of an alcohol-related crash.
   a. two hours
   b. hour
   c. 30 minutes
4. Alcohol abuse creates a reduced sensitivity to pain and an altered sense of time. For people who are drunk, time appears to pass more rapidly.
   a. True
   b. False
5. Alcohol generally improves sexual performance.
   a. True
   b. False

## Activity 2: Getting More Information about the Effects of Drug and Alcohol Abuse

Many organizations are devoted to helping people and families facing problems with alcohol or drugs. Contact any of the organizations listed here and ask them to send you a packet of information, or visit their web sites. Some of these organizations may have an office in your town, which you can find by looking in your local telephone book. Many of these organizations provide toolkits, fact sheets, and activities that can help you prevent or deal with the problems of substance abuse. Share this information with the class or with co-workers.

**Alanon/Alateen**
Family Group Headquarters, Inc.
1600 Corporate Landing Parkway
Virginia Beach, VA 23454-5617
888-4AL-ANON
http://www.al-anon.org

**Alcoholics Anonymous**
World Services, Inc.
475 Riverside Drive
New York, NY 10115
212-870-3400
http://www.alcoholics-anonymous.org

**Cocaine Anonymous**
World Service Office
3740 Overland Avenue, Suite C
Los Angeles, CA 90034
800-347-8998
http://www.ca.org

**Marijuana Anonymous**
World Services
P.O. Box 2912
Van Nuys, CA 91404
800-766-6779
http://www.marijuana-anonymous.org

**Mothers Against Drunk Driving (MADD)**
511 E. John Carpenter Freeway
Suite 700
Irving, TX 75062
800-GET-MADD (438-6233)
http://www.madd.org

**Narcotics Anonymous**
World Service Office
P.O. Box 9999
Van Nuys, CA 91409
818-773-9999
http://www.na.org

**National Association for Children of Alcoholics**
11426 Rockville Pike, Suite 100
Rockville, MD 20852
301-468-0985
888-554-COAS
http://www.nacoa.net

**National Clearinghouse for Alcohol and Drug Information**
U.S. Department for Health and Human Services
P.O. Box 2345
Rockville, MD 20847-2345
301-468-2600
800-729-6686
http://www.health.org

**National Council on Alcoholism and Drug Dependence**
20 Exchange Place, Suite 2902
New York, NY 10005
800-NCA-CALL
http://www.ncadd.org

**National Highway Traffic Safety Administration**
400 7th Street, SW
Washington, DC 20590
202-366-9550
Auto Safety Hotline: 800-424-9393
http://www.nhtsa.dot.gov

**National Institute on Alcohol Abuse and Alcoholism**
6000 Executive Boulevard
Willco Building
Bethesda, MD 20892-7003
http://www.niaaa.nih.gov

## Activity 3: Monitoring Your Caffeine and Tobacco Consumption

Caffeine and tobacco are drugs. Like aspirin, they are legal drugs. If they are abused, however, they can have a negative effect on your body, your mind, and your job performance. Both are addictive.

Caffeine is a stimulant. In small doses, it postpones fatigue and improves performance of simple physical tasks that require endurance but not fine motor coordination. It is found in many beverages and foods, including coffee, tea, cola, and chocolate.

In general, moderate amounts of caffeine are not harmful. With larger amounts, though, you may sleep less and feel less rested when you wake up. Large amounts of caffeine can also cause nervousness and irritability. Sudden withdrawal from caffeine can result in headaches, irritability, and cravings.

Smoking or chewing tobacco is one of America's greatest health problems. Tobacco contains nicotine, which is addictive. While many people believe that cigarette smoking helps to calm them down, smoking releases a hormone that creates stress. In addition, smoking causes respiratory problems and weakens the immune system. Sudden withdrawal from nicotine can result in headaches, irritability, and cravings.

Many people die each year of diseases linked to tobacco. Smoking or chewing tobacco increases your risk of the following diseases or conditions:

- Heart disease
- Cancer
- Stroke
- Emphysema
- Gastric ulcers
- Chronic bronchitis

Your goal in this activity is to find out just how much caffeine and tobacco you take in over a week. First estimate the following:

- Number of cups, cans, or bottles of caffeinated drinks you drank last week
- Number of cigarettes, pipes, or cigars you smoked last week
- Number of times you chewed tobacco last week

Write down your estimates. Then keep a log of your actual daily consumption for one week and compare the two lists. After comparing the lists, ask yourself the following questions:

1. Am I drinking more caffeine than I estimated?
2. Am I smoking or chewing tobacco more than I estimated?
3. If I am ready to cut down on my caffeine or tobacco intake, where can I go for help?

## Group Activities

### Activity 4: Your Turn—Talk about How Drug and Alcohol Abuse Affect You or Your Workplace

You are the local expert when it comes to information about how drug and alcohol abuse affect your workplace. With three or four of your classmates, answer the discussion questions.

**Team Members**

1. ______________________ 2. ______________________
3. ______________________ 4. ______________________

#### *Discussion Questions*

1. Do you know of a workplace accident or injury that was caused by alcohol or drug abuse?
2. If so, what could have been done to prevent the accident or injury?
3. What problems do you think are caused by workers who take drugs or drink to excess?
4. Have you tried to help anyone with a drug or alcohol problem? What did you do? What worked? What didn't?

### Activity 5: Your Turn—Dealing with Drug and Alcohol Problems at Work

You and your classmates may think that there is little you can do about drug and alcohol problems, but you can do more than you think. Many of the organizations listed in Activity 2 were started by ordinary people who were fed up with the problems and misery caused by alcohol and drugs. Most of the programs involve people who volunteer to get together regularly and make a commitment to help each other and their communities.

This activity is designed to get you and your classmates thinking about ways you can use your influence as a professional at work. Discuss the following questions with three or four of your classmates.

**Team Members**

1. ______________________ 2. ______________________
3. ______________________ 4. ______________________

## Discussion Questions

1. Do you know of any workers at your company who would benefit from help with addictions?
2. Does your workplace offer programs to help workers with substance abuse problems? If so, how can you learn more about these programs? If not, do you think that your company would be interested in starting such programs?
3. How do you feel about trying to help solve substance abuse problems at work?
4. List three benefits of working on a site where none of the workers has a substance abuse problem.

## Activity 6: True or False? Some Myths about Alcohol

People tend to believe certain things about alcohol, even when they are not true. For example, many people believe that you cannot have a good time at a party unless you get completely drunk. In this activity, you and three or four of your classmates will read statements that people commonly make about alcohol consumption. You must decide whether these statements are true or false.

**Team Members**

1. ______________________ 2. ______________________

3. ______________________ 4. ______________________

**Statements People Commonly Make about Alcohol**

| | True | False |
|---|---|---|
| 1. Alcohol gives you an energy boost. If you feel faint or unwell, a shot of whiskey will perk you back up again. | ❑ | ❑ |
| 2. Too much alcohol can give you more than just a nasty hangover. It can kill you. | ❑ | ❑ |
| 3. If you start out drinking beer and then switch to rum, you will get drunker than if you just kept drinking beer. | ❑ | ❑ |
| 4. If you drink too much, you can just take a cold shower, eat lots of bread, or drink lots of coffee to sober up. | ❑ | ❑ |
| 5. Alcoholism is an incurable disease. | ❑ | ❑ |
| 6. Alcoholics and people who drink too much hurt only themselves. | ❑ | ❑ |
| 7. Alcohol affects everyone the same way. | ❑ | ❑ |
| 8. If you get a hangover, you can cure it by drinking some more alcohol or by eating sausage, raw eggs mixed with hot sauce, or burnt toast. | ❑ | ❑ |
| 9. If a friend is determined to drink a lot, there is nothing you can do. | ❑ | ❑ |
| 10. You should admire people who can hold their liquor. | ❑ | ❑ |

Source: Adapted from information developed by the American Academy of Pediatrics, Washington, D.C., and the National Institute on Alcohol Abuse and Alcoholism.

## CONTREN® LEARNING SERIES — USER UPDATES

The NCCER makes every effort to keep these textbooks up-to-date and free of technical errors. We appreciate your help in this process. If you have an idea for improving this textbook, or if you find an error, a typographical mistake, or an inaccuracy in NCCER's Contren® textbooks, please write us, using this form or a photocopy. Be sure to include the exact module number, page number, a detailed description, and the correction, if applicable. Your input will be brought to the attention of the Technical Review Committee. Thank you for your assistance.

*Instructors* – If you found that additional materials were necessary in order to teach this module effectively, please let us know so that we may include them in the Equipment/Materials list in the Instructor's Guide.


**Write:** Product Development
National Center for Construction Education and Research
P.O. Box 141104, Gainesville, FL 32614-1104

**Fax:** 352-334-0932

**E-mail:** curriculum@nccer.org


Craft ____________________ Module Name ____________________

Copyright Date __________ Module Number __________ Page Number(s) __________

Description

____________________

____________________

____________________

____________________

(Optional) Correction

____________________

____________________

____________________

(Optional) Your Name and Address

____________________

____________________

____________________